josh luberisse

SURVIVING THE
COLLAPSE

The Citizen Defender's Guide to Guerrilla Tactics
and Strategic Resilience in a Lawless Society

SURVIVING THE COLLAPSE

The Citizen Defender's Guide to Guerrilla Tactics and Strategic Resilience in a Lawless Society

Josh Luberisse

Fortis Novum Mundum

Copyright © 2024 Fortis Novum Mundum, LLC

All rights reserved

No part of this book may be reproduced, or stored in a retrieval system, or transmitted in any form or by any means, electronic, mechanical, photocopying, recording, or otherwise, without express written permission of the publisher.

While every precaution has been taken in the preparation of this book, neither the publisher nor the author assume any responsibility for errors or omissions, or for damages resulting from the use of the information contained herein.

THE AUTHOR(S) AND PUBLISHER(S) EXPRESSLY DISCLAIM ANY AND ALL LIABILITY FOR ACTIONS TAKEN BASED ON THE CONTENT OF THIS WORK. READERS ASSUME ALL RISKS FOR ANY SUCH ACTIONS.

This work is intended for researchers, historians, emergency preparedness professionals, and those interested in theoretical explorations of societal resilience. It is not intended for individuals seeking to engage in illegal activities or extremism. It is the reader's responsibility to ensure that they comply with all applicable laws and ethical guidelines in their work. Ignorance of the law or of ethical standards is not an excuse for misuse.

We strongly caution against the misuse of this information. THE SCENARIOS DISCUSSED ASSUME A COMPLETE BREAKDOWN OF LAW AND ORDER, WHICH IS EXTREMELY RARE. IN NEARLY ALL REAL-WORLD SITUATIONS, EXISTING LEGAL AND SOCIETAL STRUCTURES REMAIN IN PLACE AND SHOULD BE RESPECTED. The content of this work is not applicable to normal circumstances or even most emergency situations.

The authors, publishers, and contributors to this book will not be held liable for any damage or harm caused by the misuse of the information contained within. All readers are advised and expected to use this information responsibly, ethically, and legally.

By reading and using the information in this book, you acknowledge and agree to these conditions. If you cannot agree to these conditions, please refrain from using this book and its content.

Cover design by: Fortis Novum Mundum, LLC

CONTENTS

Title Page
Copyright
Table of Contents
Disclaimer
Preface

Introduction	1
Chapter 1: Assessing the Breakdown	16
Chapter 2: Strategic Foundations of Survival	30
Chapter 3: Guerrilla Tactics for the Citizen Defender	44
Chapter 4: Small Arms and Tactical Proficiency	72
Chapter 5: Defending Urban Environments	95
Chapter 6: Rural Survival and Defense	119
Chapter 7: Information Warfare and Communications	141
Chapter 8: Logistics in a Collapsed Society	166
Chapter 9: Organizing Citizen Defense Units	191
Chapter 10: Defensive Strategies Against Larger Forces	218
Chapter 11: Navigating Ethical Dilemmas in Guerrilla Warfare	247
Chapter 12: Post-Conflict Recovery and Stabilization	269
Conclusion: Thriving in the Midst of Collapse	292
References	305

Books In This Series	311
Books By This Author	327
About The Author	357

TABLE OF CONTENTS

Disclaimer

Preface

Introduction

The End of Stability

Premise of The Collapse

Understanding Low-Intensity Conflicts

The Need for a New Type of Defense

Chapter 1: Assessing the Breakdown

Recognizing the Signs of Societal Collapse

Political Instability, Civil Unrest, and Paramilitary Conflict

When the Rule of Law No Longer Applies

Chapter 2: Strategic Foundations of Survival

Adopting a Survivor's Mindset

Building Mental Resilience in the Face of Chaos

Staying One Step Ahead: Anticipating Threats

Chapter 3: Guerrilla Tactics for the Citizen Defender

The Core Principles of Guerrilla Warfare

Using Asymmetry to Your Advantage

Mobility, Stealth, and Hit-and-Run Strategies

Chapter 4: Small Arms and Tactical Proficiency

Understanding the Role of Small Arms in Asymmetric Warfare

Mastering Small Arms in Urban and Rural Combat

Weapon Selection, Maintenance, and Ammunition Conservation

Precision and Discipline in Firefights

Chapter 5: Defending Urban Environments

Urban Fortifications: Turning Your Space into a Defensible Position

Tactics for Navigating Streets and Buildings Under Siege

Ambushes, Choke Points, and Defensive Traps

Chapter 6: Rural Survival and Defense

Leveraging the Natural Environment for Defense

Camouflage, Tracking, and Evasion in Rural Settings

Establishing Hidden Bases and Supply Caches

Chapter 7: Information Warfare and Communications

Controlling the Narrative: Disinformation and Psychological Tactics

Creating Encrypted and Covert Communication Channels

Sabotaging the Enemy's Communications and Intelligence

Chapter 8: Logistics in a Collapsed Society

Securing and Managing Essential Resources

Food, Water, Medical Supplies, and Ammunition Storage

Bartering, Raiding, and Self-Sufficiency

Chapter 9: Organizing Citizen Defense Units

Forming and Leading Small Defensive Teams

Maintaining Morale and Cohesion Under Extreme Conditions

Rotations, Rest, and Managing Psychological Fatigue

Chapter 10: Defensive Strategies Against Larger Forces

Dealing with Paramilitary and Conventional Forces

Tactics for Outnumbered and Outgunned Citizen Defenders

How to Exploit Enemy Weaknesses and Overwhelm Superior Forces

Chapter 11: Navigating Ethical Dilemmas in Guerrilla Warfare

The Moral Costs of Survival

Balancing Civilian Protections with Tactical Necessity

Rebuilding Society After the Collapse

Chapter 12: Post-Conflict Recovery and Stabilization

Transitioning from Conflict to Reconstruction

Establishing Alliances and Local Governance

Role of the Citizen Defender in Rebuilding Order

Conclusion: Thriving in the Midst of Collapse
Hope Amid Destruction: Building a New Normal
References

DISCLAIMER

This work is purely theoretical and academic in nature. It is intended solely for educational and informational purposes, exploring hypothetical scenarios of civil unrest and societal breakdown. The content herein should not be construed as advocating, encouraging, or instructing any illegal activities, violence, or extremism.

This work is a theoretical exploration based on historical analysis and academic research. All strategies, tactics, and scenarios discussed are speculative and do not reflect current real-world situations or conflicts. Readers are strongly advised to comply with all applicable local, state, and federal laws. Nothing in this work should be interpreted as encouraging violation of any laws or regulations.

This work prioritizes non-violent conflict resolution, de-escalation techniques, and community-building strategies. Any discussion of defensive tactics is purely theoretical and should not be implemented in real-world situations. In actual emergencies or civil unrest, individuals should seek guidance from qualified law enforcement, emergency management professionals, or appropriate government authorities.

THE AUTHOR(S) AND PUBLISHER(S) EXPRESSLY DISCLAIM ANY AND ALL LIABILITY FOR ACTIONS TAKEN BASED ON THE CONTENT OF THIS WORK. READERS ASSUME ALL RISKS FOR ANY SUCH ACTIONS. This is not a how-to manual for guerrilla warfare or paramilitary activities. It is an academic exploration of historical and theoretical concepts related to civil defense and societal resilience.

This work is intended for researchers, historians, emergency preparedness professionals, and those interested in theoretical explorations of societal resilience. It is not intended for individuals seeking to engage in illegal activities or extremism.

THE SCENARIOS DISCUSSED ASSUME A COMPLETE BREAKDOWN OF LAW AND ORDER, WHICH IS EXTREMELY RARE. IN NEARLY ALL REAL-WORLD SITUATIONS, EXISTING LEGAL AND SOCIETAL STRUCTURES REMAIN IN PLACE AND SHOULD BE RESPECTED. The content of this work is not applicable to normal circumstances or even most emergency situations.

By engaging with this material, readers acknowledge their understanding of this disclaimer and agree to approach the content as a theoretical academic work, not as practical advice for real-world application.

PREFACE

In writing this book, the intention is not only to prepare for the unimaginable but also to navigate the darkest moments with clarity, purpose, and resolve. We live in a world where the stability we once took for granted can unravel, where systems designed to protect and govern can fail, and where the very fabric of society can be torn apart by forces beyond our control. Yet, in the midst of collapse, there is always a choice: to succumb to the chaos or to rise above it, to not just survive but to build something stronger in its place.

This book is a guide to thriving in a world that may no longer resemble the one we once knew. It is for the citizen defenders who, when the institutions around them falter, take up the mantle of leadership. It is for the communities that band together in the face of destruction, determined to rebuild what has been lost and to reimagine what can be gained. It is for those who understand that survival is not enough and that the aftermath of collapse offers the rare opportunity to create a new and better order, grounded in resilience, justice, and collective strength.

The collapse of society, whether through conflict, natural disaster, or the erosion of governance, is not an abstract concept. History has shown us time and again that nations and empires, no matter how strong, can fall. What matters is how we respond when the structures we depend on no longer function. The lessons offered here are drawn from the hard realities of history, the principles of warfare, and the enduring spirit of human resilience. They are meant to be applied in moments of extreme crisis, where every decision could mean the difference between survival and extinction, between order and chaos.

Yet this is not a book about fear. It is not a book about simply reacting to collapse, but about harnessing the power of foresight, preparation, and mental discipline to lead in the midst of upheaval. It offers not only practical strategies for defense, survival, and rebuilding, but also a vision of hope: that even in the most devastating circumstances, we can find a way forward. That we can not only protect what remains but also lay the groundwork for a future that is more equitable, resilient, and just than the society that collapsed.

To those reading this book who are already living through the turmoil of a fractured world, my hope is that these pages provide not just guidance, but a sense of empowerment. You are not helpless in the face of collapse. Whether you are defending your community, organizing for survival, or helping to rebuild in the aftermath, know that your actions matter. The decisions you make in these critical moments will shape the future—not just for you, but for those who come after. You are not just survivors; you are architects of the new normal.

For those who read this in preparation, before the worst has arrived, take this as a call to strengthen your mind, your community, and your resolve. The future is always uncertain, but preparation is the key to resilience. No one can predict when or how a collapse may occur, but we can prepare ourselves, mentally and physically, to face whatever comes. To be ready not just to endure the trials ahead, but to lead through them.

As you journey through the chapters of this book, you will encounter the practical strategies needed for survival in a lawless world. You will explore the principles of guerrilla warfare, tactics for defending urban and rural environments, and the art of maintaining security in the absence of order. But more than that, you will find a message of hope. That even in the midst of destruction, there is opportunity. That chaos can give birth to renewal. And that you, as a citizen defender, have the power to shape the future, even in the darkest of times.

This book is dedicated to the indomitable spirit of those who rise to the challenge when others fall. It is for the leaders, the defenders, the builders, and the visionaries who will carry society forward, even when it seems to be crumbling around them. It is for you.

INTRODUCTION

The End of Stability

The stability you once knew is gone. The social, political, and economic frameworks that maintained order have crumbled. Whether due to a sudden civil conflict, widespread political instability, or the collapse of governance, you now find yourself in a world where the rule of law no longer functions. This is not a temporary state of unrest—it is a breakdown of the systems that once kept violence at bay and ensured the functioning of society.

In this environment, traditional methods of self-defense and security are inadequate. You cannot rely on the government or law enforcement agencies to provide safety. There is no one coming to restore order in the near future. The threats you face are not just from external forces but from the chaos bred within your own community. Ordinary citizens, once neighbors, may now pose a risk. Organized groups—paramilitary factions, gangs, or politically motivated militias—seek power and control over territory, resources, and lives.

You are now operating in a new reality where survival is contingent on adopting strategies that transcend ordinary self-defense. The situation demands a deeper understanding of guerrilla tactics, intelligence gathering, infiltration, and psychological warfare. These methods were once reserved for military operations in hostile foreign environments, but they are now essential for your survival in what has become a domestic conflict zone.

This guide is not about wishful thinking or reliance on external aid. It is about equipping you with the tools and strategies to defend yourself, your family, and your community in the absence of external authority. The principles outlined in this book are derived from proven military doctrines, adapted for use by citizen defenders in small-scale conflicts and societal breakdowns. You will learn how to leverage your environment, conserve resources, and build the mental resilience required to endure prolonged periods of instability.

In this state of collapse, the priorities are clear: survival, defense, and resistance. You must prepare to operate in a world where the usual rules no longer apply, and the conventional structures of power have fragmented. The strategies you employ will not follow the ordinary legal or social boundaries —they will be dictated by the reality of your environment and the need to protect what remains of your life and freedom.

Every action you take must be calculated and deliberate. There is no room for error or hesitation. The techniques in this guide have been designed for simplicity and effectiveness, enabling you to respond with precision in high-pressure situations. Whether you are securing a home, establishing supply lines, or defending against an incursion, the guidance here is meant to be followed without question. This is not a time for moral contemplation or doubt. It is a time for action, strategy, and survival.

The end of stability marks the beginning of a new way of thinking. You must shed the expectations of the old world and adapt to the harsh realities of life under duress. By mastering the principles in this guide, you can regain control, not just of your safety but of your ability to navigate this unpredictable and dangerous landscape. Prepare yourself for a life where the only constant is the struggle to survive.

Premise of The Collapse

Collapse is not an abstract concept or a distant possibility—it is the reality that confronts you now. The premise of collapse is the fundamental recognition that the structures of society, once taken for granted, have ceased to function. Government institutions, law enforcement, and essential services such as utilities and healthcare have either dissolved or are too overwhelmed to respond. What remains is a fractured society where violence, instability, and desperation prevail. This is the environment in which you must now learn to survive.

A collapse does not happen overnight. It is the result of cumulative failures—political unrest, economic breakdown, civil war, or natural disasters that have spiraled beyond control. It is marked by a critical erosion of public trust, where the established order no longer has the capacity to enforce laws, protect citizens, or manage resources. The very systems designed to provide stability and security are the first to fail, leaving a vacuum that is quickly filled by chaos, opportunism, and violence.

In this void, power is no longer centralized or governed by legal frameworks; it is contested by those who can impose their will, often through force. You may be facing factions of well-armed paramilitary groups, organized gangs, or even former government forces who have fragmented into rogue elements. The premise of collapse assumes that these forces are hostile, unpredictable, and opportunistic, exploiting the breakdown for personal or ideological gain.

For you, this means that survival is no longer a matter of evading petty crime or occasional threats—it is about defending yourself against sustained, organized aggression in a lawless environment. The collapse transforms every interaction, every decision, into a matter of life and death.

Resources such as food, water, fuel, and medicine become scarce commodities, and the competition for these necessities is often violent and unforgiving. What was once ordinary and accessible is now fought over with deadly consequences.

The premise of collapse also reshapes the way you think about safety. Your home, once a sanctuary, can become a target. Movement through familiar streets, once routine, now carries the risk of ambush or attack. The strategies you employ must adapt to this new reality—static defense and routine patterns will not suffice. Flexibility, mobility, and the ability to read your environment are crucial to staying ahead of emerging threats.

Furthermore, collapse disrupts the social fabric. Trust, once an integral part of community life, becomes a rare and fragile commodity. People who were once your allies or neighbors may now be competitors or threats, driven by desperation or loyalty to a different faction. The moral boundaries that governed interactions in a stable society are shattered. You must operate with the understanding that the world around you has fundamentally changed, and the people within it will behave in ways that reflect the brutal conditions they face.

This guide operates under the assumption that the collapse is ongoing and irreversible for the foreseeable future. The tactics and strategies discussed are not for temporary crises or brief disruptions. They are designed for prolonged conflict, where you will need to defend yourself and your resources against hostile actors who are equally determined to survive.

Collapse brings with it an undeniable shift in priorities. The rules of engagement have changed, and the concepts of safety, morality, and law are now dictated by those with the ability to enforce them. Your focus must remain on preserving your life, securing your resources, and fortifying your defenses. The premise of collapse demands that you shed any lingering illusions about returning to normalcy in the short term. This is a new, harsh reality, and your survival depends on your ability to adapt and execute the strategies outlined in this guide without hesitation or compromise.

Defining Collapse

Collapse occurs when the mechanisms that uphold societal stability fail to operate effectively. This failure can result from a multitude of factors acting individually or in combination, leading to a breakdown in governance, economic stability, public safety, and social cohesion. Unlike gradual decline, collapse is typically marked by sudden and severe disruptions that render existing structures incapable of maintaining order and meeting the population's basic needs.

Causes of Collapse

1. **Political Instability**: Erosion of governmental authority, widespread corruption, ineffective leadership, and internal conflicts can undermine the state's ability to govern. Political instability often leads to power vacuums, where competing factions vie for control, exacerbating chaos and disorder.

2. **Economic Decline**: Severe economic downturns, hyperinflation, unemployment, and resource scarcity can destabilize a society. Economic collapse diminishes the government's capacity to provide essential services, maintain infrastructure, and support public welfare, leading to increased civil unrest.

3. **Social Fragmentation**: Deep-seated social divisions based on ethnicity, religion, class, or ideology can lead to conflict and violence. When social cohesion disintegrates, communities become fragmented, making collective action and mutual support difficult.

4. **Environmental Catastrophes**: Natural disasters, climate

change, pandemics, and resource depletion can strain societal resources and infrastructure. Environmental crises can disrupt supply chains, displace populations, and create widespread humanitarian emergencies.

5. **Technological Failures**: Dependence on critical technologies makes societies vulnerable to cyber-attacks, infrastructure failures, and technological disruptions. The loss of communication networks, power grids, and transportation systems can paralyze essential functions.

6. **External Aggression**: Invasion, occupation, or sustained attacks by hostile entities can destabilize a society. External aggression can lead to the destruction of infrastructure, loss of life, and displacement of populations, further weakening societal resilience.

Indicators of Impending Collapse

Recognizing the signs of impending collapse allows individuals and communities to take proactive measures to mitigate risks. Key indicators include:

- **Government Dysfunction**: Frequent changes in leadership, legislative gridlock, and inability to enforce laws signal weakening governmental structures.

- **Economic Instability**: Rapid inflation, soaring debt, unemployment spikes, and declining GDP are signs of economic distress.

- **Rising Crime Rates**: Increases in theft, violence, and other criminal activities indicate deteriorating public safety and law enforcement capabilities.

- **Resource Shortages**: Scarcity of essential resources such as food, water, medicine, and energy points to supply chain disruptions and logistical challenges.

- **Social Unrest**: Protests, riots, and civil disturbances reflect growing dissatisfaction and loss of trust in institutions.

- **Infrastructure Decay**: Failure of critical infrastructure, including transportation, communication, and utilities, hampers societal functionality.
- **Health Crises**: Widespread disease outbreaks, lack of medical supplies, and overwhelmed healthcare systems highlight vulnerabilities in public health.

Scenarios Leading to Collapse

Collapse can manifest in various forms depending on the interplay of contributing factors. Common scenarios include:

1. **Gradual Degradation**: Slow erosion of institutions and economic stability due to persistent corruption, mismanagement, and policy failures. Over time, the cumulative effects weaken societal resilience until collapse becomes inevitable.

2. **Sudden Shock**: Abrupt events such as natural disasters, terrorist attacks, or abrupt economic crashes can trigger immediate and widespread destabilization, overwhelming the capacity of institutions to respond effectively.

3. **Compound Crises**: Simultaneous crises across multiple domains—political, economic, environmental, and social—can interact synergistically, amplifying their individual impacts and accelerating collapse.

4. **External Invasion**: Sustained military aggression or occupation by hostile forces can dismantle existing governance structures, disrupt economic activities, and displace populations, leading to societal breakdown.

Consequences of Collapse

The immediate and long-term effects of collapse are profound and multifaceted:

- **Loss of Public Order**: The absence of effective law enforcement leads to increased crime, violence, and chaos, making communities unsafe for civilians.
- **Economic Hardship**: Hyperinflation, unemployment, and scarcity of goods result in widespread poverty and deprivation.
- **Humanitarian Crises**: Displacement, lack of access to healthcare, and insufficient food and clean water create dire living conditions and high mortality rates.
- **Infrastructure Breakdown**: Failure of transportation, communication, and utilities disrupts daily life and hampers efforts to restore order.
- **Social Disintegration**: Erosion of trust and cooperation within communities leads to fragmentation and isolation, undermining collective survival efforts.
- **Psychological Impact**: Prolonged exposure to instability and danger can result in widespread psychological trauma and diminished morale.

Understanding Low-Intensity Conflicts

Low-intensity conflicts (LICs) differ fundamentally from full-scale warfare. These conflicts are often protracted, involving a combination of irregular military tactics, paramilitary operations, and guerrilla warfare. They exist in a gray zone between peace and total war, characterized by ongoing instability, intermittent violence, and widespread social, economic, and political disruption. Understanding low-intensity conflicts is key to navigating and surviving the challenges presented by such conflicts, particularly in a context where the rule of law has disintegrated.

CHARACTERISTICS OF LOW-INTENSITY CONFLICTS

Low-intensity conflicts are marked by several defining features:

1. **Asymmetry in Power**: Unlike conventional warfare, low-intensity conflicts often involve a significant power imbalance between combatants. This imbalance typically manifests in smaller, irregular forces—such as insurgents, militias, or guerrilla groups—fighting against larger, better-equipped state forces, or various factions vying for control in a collapsed society. These smaller groups rely on hit-and-run tactics, sabotage, ambushes, and psychological operations to offset their disadvantage in manpower and resources.

2. **Prolonged Duration**: LICs are often long-lasting, simmering for years or even decades. The slow nature of these conflicts creates an environment of sustained uncertainty and instability, where the lines between combatants and civilians are blurred. It is within this drawn-out turmoil that survival requires an adaptive, long-term mindset, focusing on maintaining resource supplies, operational security, and psychological resilience over extended periods.

3. **Civilian Involvement**: Civilians are frequently caught in the crossfire of low-intensity conflicts. Unlike conventional wars where battles may occur on distinct frontlines, LICs are often fought within cities, towns, and villages, with civilians directly impacted by the violence. As a result, civilian populations can become both the target and the support base for various factions, necessitating careful navigation of local allegiances and community dynamics.

4. **Irregular Warfare Tactics**: Low-intensity conflicts rely on tactics that diverge from conventional military doctrine. Guerrilla warfare, sabotage, insurgency, and clandestine operations are common. The goal of irregular forces in these

scenarios is often to wear down or destabilize larger forces over time rather than engage in direct confrontation. In such environments, defending oneself requires the adoption of similar unconventional methods—stealth, evasion, and ambushes.

5. **Psychological Warfare**: In LICs, psychological operations (PsyOps) are as crucial as physical confrontations. These conflicts are fought not only on the ground but also in the hearts and minds of both civilians and adversaries. Misinformation, fear, intimidation, and propaganda play significant roles in undermining enemy morale and gaining civilian support. Understanding these dynamics is vital for any citizen defender who seeks to remain resilient and effective in the midst of conflict.

6. **Decentralized Command**: Traditional military structures are often absent in low-intensity conflicts. Instead, smaller groups operate with decentralized command systems, where local leaders and individual cells act autonomously. This lack of a clear hierarchy makes it difficult for larger forces to fully eliminate resistance, as guerrilla units can disperse, regroup, and reform with relative ease. For those engaged in defensive operations, recognizing the strengths and weaknesses of decentralized command is critical to crafting effective resistance strategies.

7. **Hybrid Warfare**: LICs often blend elements of conventional warfare, irregular tactics, cyber operations, and information warfare into a single, hybrid approach. This multi-dimensional nature means that conflicts are waged not only with weapons and tactics but also through the control of information, infrastructure, and social systems. Defenders in these situations must be prepared to face threats across multiple domains, including physical, cyber, and psychological arenas.

EXAMPLES OF LOW-INTENSITY CONFLICTS

Historical examples of low-intensity conflicts provide valuable lessons in survival and strategy. These examples range from insurgencies in the Middle East to guerrilla movements in Latin America and Southeast Asia. In these conflicts, the combination of prolonged engagement, civilian involvement, and irregular warfare tactics played a pivotal role in shaping the strategies of both combatants and defenders.

1. **The Vietnam War (1955–1975)**: Though a conventional war in many respects, the guerrilla tactics employed by the Viet Cong represent classic LIC strategies. The use of ambushes, booby traps, underground tunnels, and psychological operations against superior U.S. forces exemplifies the effectiveness of asymmetric warfare in a protracted conflict.

2. **The Troubles in Northern Ireland (1969–1998)**: This conflict, involving the Irish Republican Army (IRA) and British forces, illustrates the dynamics of a low-intensity conflict within an urbanized, civilian-populated environment. The IRA utilized a decentralized structure, conducting bombings, assassinations, and sabotage operations. Civilian involvement —both as targets and supporters—was integral to the conflict.

3. **The Syrian Civil War (2011–present)**: This ongoing conflict has evolved into a protracted, multi-faceted low-intensity war involving a variety of insurgent groups, militias, and state forces. The decentralized nature of the conflict, the blurring of lines between combatants and civilians, and the integration of cyber and information warfare are hallmarks of LIC in modern times.

CHALLENGES OF LOW-INTENSITY CONFLICTS FOR CITIZEN DEFENDERS

For the average citizen caught in such a conflict, the challenges are unique and multifaceted. Traditional methods of protection—relying on law enforcement or civil defense— are no longer viable, requiring individuals to adopt a much more proactive and adaptive approach to survival.

1. **Blurring of Civilian and Combatant Roles**: In low-intensity conflicts, distinguishing between non-combatants and combatants becomes difficult. Defenders must be constantly vigilant, understanding that threats can emerge from unexpected quarters. This also complicates decisions about when to engage or retreat, as the risk of collateral damage and unintended consequences is high.

2. **Maintaining Supply Lines**: Sustaining access to food, water, medical supplies, and weapons becomes a constant struggle in LICs. Disruptions to critical infrastructure are common, and defenders must develop self-sufficient systems, rely on local alliances, and establish clandestine supply caches.

3. **Avoiding Detection**: Mobility and stealth are essential in low-intensity conflicts. Whether operating in an urban or rural environment, citizen defenders must know how to navigate their surroundings without being detected. This involves mastering techniques of camouflage, sound discipline, and movement under cover of darkness.

4. **Psychological Resilience**: The drawn-out nature of these conflicts takes a toll on mental health. The constant threat of violence, scarcity of resources, and the breakdown of social order can wear down morale. Maintaining psychological resilience through routine, training, and group cohesion becomes as important as tactical proficiency.

The fluid and evolving nature of low-intensity conflicts demands a flexible mindset and the ability to adapt quickly to changing circumstances. Unlike conventional wars, where objectives and battle lines are often clear, low-intensity conflicts are unpredictable. The capacity to improvise, innovate, and remain adaptable in the face of uncertainty is essential for any citizen defender.

This guide is designed to help you develop the mindset and skills required to navigate and survive these prolonged, volatile environments. By understanding the dynamics of low-intensity conflict, you can anticipate threats, formulate effective strategies, and enhance your chances of survival and success in a world where order has collapsed.

The Need for a New Type of Defense

In a world where the rule of law has collapsed and the traditional institutions responsible for maintaining order have failed, the need for a new type of defense becomes paramount. Conventional approaches to personal safety, security, and defense, which once relied heavily on police forces, governmental stability, and societal infrastructure, are no longer sufficient. Citizens find themselves in a situation where survival depends on adopting strategies that diverge sharply from the norms of a stable society. This new paradigm requires a shift in thinking, focusing on adaptability, resourcefulness, and unconventional tactics.

The collapse of traditional structures has rendered reliance on formal defense mechanisms impractical. In the absence of law enforcement and organized security, the burden of protection falls on the individual or small, localized groups. This environment is not characterized by the predictable forms of crime or unrest seen in stable societies; instead, it is marked by irregular and asymmetric threats. Civilians face dangers from organized paramilitary groups, opportunistic criminals, and even once-trusted neighbors. In this context, defending oneself and one's community requires a deep understanding of guerrilla warfare, stealth tactics, and decentralized forms of resistance.

Traditional self-defense methods, often focused on deterring isolated threats, fail to address the complexities of a full-scale societal breakdown. In a situation where the very fabric of society is fraying, individuals must be prepared to think strategically and act with precision. Defense is no longer just a matter of personal safety but involves protecting resources, securing vital infrastructure, and ensuring the continued functionality of essential systems. The new type of defense is not static; it requires mobility, the ability to blend into the environment, and the capacity to act preemptively against emerging threats.

Small arms proficiency becomes a crucial element of this defense strategy. However, unlike typical firearm training designed for home defense or sport, the skills required in a collapsed society focus on tactical efficiency and discipline. It is not about overwhelming force but precise, targeted actions. Knowing when to engage and when to retreat is just as important as knowing how to shoot. Ammunition is a finite resource, and noise discipline becomes a matter of survival, as loud engagements can attract unwanted attention. Additionally, maintaining and repairing weapons in the field becomes an essential skill, as access to professional services or new supplies becomes impossible.

This new defense model also emphasizes the importance of intelligence and reconnaissance. Information is a key asset in a destabilized environment. Defenders must cultivate the ability to gather, analyze, and act on intelligence from their surroundings. Understanding the movements of hostile groups, securing communication channels, and establishing covert networks for information exchange can be the difference between survival and destruction. In the absence of organized security forces, individuals must become their own intelligence operators, constantly evaluating risks and opportunities within their operational area.

Another critical aspect of this defense is the psychological component. Surviving in a post-collapse environment demands mental resilience and an unwavering focus on survival. The psychological toll of living in a constant state of alertness, where threats can materialize at any moment, is immense. Individuals must cultivate the ability to compartmentalize fear and stress while maintaining a clear sense of purpose. The new defense strategy is as much about maintaining mental and emotional discipline as it is about physical preparedness. Those who fail to develop this resilience will find it difficult to endure the prolonged instability that defines a collapsed society.

This form of defense also extends beyond direct confrontation. Guerrilla tactics often involve indirect methods of engagement—sabotage, misinformation, and the disruption of enemy resources. Individuals must learn to think asymmetrically, employing strategies that exploit the weaknesses of larger, more organized forces. This could mean targeting supply lines, disrupting communications, or using the environment itself as a weapon. The goal is not to achieve victory in the conventional sense but to outlast, outthink, and outmaneuver adversaries who may have superior resources but lack adaptability.

This new type of defense, therefore, is not just about combat or weaponry. It encompasses a broader understanding of survival, combining physical tactics with mental resilience, intelligence gathering, and unconventional strategies. In the absence of societal order, individuals must be prepared to take responsibility for their own safety, drawing on principles and tactics traditionally reserved for military operations. This defense is not just about surviving the collapse—it is about thriving in an environment where adaptability and strategic thinking become the most valuable assets.

CHAPTER 1: ASSESSING THE BREAKDOWN

The breakdown of society does not happen overnight. It is often a gradual unraveling, marked by subtle signs of instability before cascading into full-scale collapse. In a world where governmental institutions, law enforcement, and economic systems no longer function, understanding how to assess the breakdown becomes a critical skill for survival. The ability to recognize the early stages of societal disintegration allows you to prepare, adapt, and position yourself strategically in the midst of chaos. Assessing the breakdown is not about reacting to a single event, but about observing the accumulation of stressors that push a system past its breaking point.

In this chapter, we will explore how to evaluate your environment through a combination of observation, intelligence gathering, and situational awareness. Societal collapse manifests in various ways depending on the context, but it follows a general pattern: political instability, economic decline, social unrest, and infrastructural decay. When these factors align, the social order starts to weaken, leaving citizens vulnerable to threats from opportunistic forces, both organized and spontaneous. The key to surviving such a breakdown is recognizing the warning signs before the situation becomes irreversible.

Political instability is often the first indicator that societal order is beginning to fracture. Changes in leadership, corruption scandals, or widespread civil disobedience point to a weakening of governmental authority. In this stage, it may still be possible to navigate the system using existing institutions, but cracks in the structure will become increasingly evident. As governmental control diminishes, localized groups, paramilitary organizations, or factions with their own agendas may begin to fill the power vacuum, each attempting to assert dominance over sections of the population. This is the point where a breakdown in authority can lead to unpredictable threats.

Economic decline typically follows or runs parallel to political instability. With government services faltering and trust in economic institutions eroding, supply chains begin to break down. Inflation spirals out of control, and access to basic necessities—food, water, medicine—becomes more difficult. The rising cost of living and scarcity of essential goods push society toward desperation. The instability of currency, coupled with the inability of government structures to support economic recovery, leads to widespread unemployment, poverty, and lawlessness. Understanding these economic triggers is essential for preparing to secure resources when the collapse becomes more pronounced.

Social unrest intensifies during this phase. Protests, riots, and mass movements against perceived injustices become more frequent. At this stage, the unrest may still appear to be localized or manageable, but as the frequency and severity of these incidents increase, they can evolve into full-scale conflict. The breakdown of social cohesion, particularly in densely populated areas, can escalate into violence as rival factions, militias, or criminal groups vie for control. When assessing the breakdown, it is crucial to observe the behavior of crowds, monitor local news sources (if they are still operational), and remain vigilant for sudden shifts in the intensity of unrest. Social unrest is not only a reaction to economic and political failures but often a catalyst for the complete collapse of order.

Infrastructural decay marks the point where survival becomes a day-to-day struggle. Power outages, transportation halts, lack of running water, and communication failures signify that the infrastructure that once supported society is no longer functioning. Roads may become impassable, and emergency services, if they still exist, will be overwhelmed. The absence of reliable communication—whether due to government shutdowns, cyberattacks, or sheer infrastructural failure—further isolates individuals and communities. At this stage, self-sufficiency becomes essential, and the ability to gather intelligence about local conditions becomes critical to navigating your environment.

As you assess the breakdown, you must develop the ability to read your surroundings in real time. The signs of collapse are often layered, with multiple crises compounding each other. Your survival hinges on recognizing these layers and adapting to them before the majority of the population becomes aware of the full scale of the collapse. By understanding the phases of breakdown, you can avoid the rush of panic and position yourself to protect essential resources, form strategic alliances, and prepare for the inevitable conflict that arises when law and order are no longer present. This chapter will guide you through the process of assessing these stages, helping you anticipate the full collapse while remaining one step ahead of the threats it brings.

Recognizing the Signs of Societal Collapse

Recognizing the signs of societal collapse is a critical skill for anyone navigating an environment where the institutions that once maintained order are failing. The process of collapse is often incremental, marked by small but significant shifts that signal deeper, systemic failures. By staying attuned to these signs, you can better prepare for the breakdown of civil order and position yourself for survival. Recognizing these early indicators allows you to take action before the full weight of collapse hits, giving you a strategic advantage when resources are still available and movement is still possible.

One of the first signs to watch for is **political instability**. This often manifests in changes in leadership, widespread protests, or challenges to the legitimacy of governing bodies. Elections may be contested, and authority figures may struggle to maintain control over the population. In some cases, you will see increasing instances of state repression or crackdowns on dissent, which often serve as a prelude to broader unrest. Political instability may seem distant at first, affecting only certain regions or government sectors, but it is often a precursor to larger-scale disorder.

As the political structure begins to falter, **economic instability** typically follows. Hyperinflation, food shortages, and disruptions in supply chains are clear indicators that the economy is deteriorating. In this stage, access to basic goods and services becomes erratic, and prices rise rapidly. The government may introduce rationing systems or price controls, but these measures are often ineffective in the long term. Unemployment rises, and the value of currency plummets. This economic decay accelerates social tension, as people increasingly compete for dwindling resources. Keep an eye on the flow of goods, especially food, fuel, and medical supplies, as disruptions here can lead to panic and further breakdown.

Rising crime rates are another indicator of collapse. As government and law enforcement resources are stretched thin, the capacity to maintain public safety diminishes. You may notice an increase in opportunistic crimes such as theft and looting, followed by more organized criminal activity, including extortion and territorial control by gangs or militias. With fewer police on the streets and less capacity to prosecute crimes, communities will often take security into their own hands. Vigilante justice and local militias can become common, but they may also contribute to the overall instability by introducing new, often arbitrary forms of violence and control.

Another important sign to recognize is the **erosion of infrastructure**. In the early stages of societal collapse, public utilities such as water, electricity, and waste management will become less reliable. Power outages may become more frequent, internet access may become intermittent, and transportation systems may break down. As the breakdown progresses, essential services will be prioritized for certain groups, leaving others to fend for themselves. The decay of infrastructure signals that the government's ability to manage and maintain its resources is failing. This will have a cascading effect, as people are forced to adapt to new realities of living without basic services.

Social unrest is another major indicator of impending collapse. As dissatisfaction with the political and economic situation grows, protests and civil disturbances become more frequent. What begins as peaceful demonstrations can quickly devolve into riots, looting, and widespread violence. The social fabric of communities begins to fray, as trust in institutions and fellow citizens erodes. Mass gatherings and demonstrations can serve as flashpoints for more significant violence, especially when they are met with force by authorities. Recognizing these gatherings as early warning signs gives you the chance to distance yourself from areas likely to become conflict zones.

As society unravels, you may also notice a shift in **communication patterns**. Government and media channels may become more restricted, with censorship or blackouts being imposed in an attempt to control the narrative. At the same time, rumors, misinformation, and propaganda will spread rapidly, filling the vacuum left by credible sources of information. The ability to discern reliable intelligence from noise becomes critical, as false information can lead to dangerous decisions. Pay attention to disruptions in official communication channels, and be wary of sudden shifts in the messaging coming from those in power.

Militarization of civilian spaces is another unmistakable sign that societal collapse is underway. When armed forces or paramilitary groups begin to operate openly in cities and neighborhoods, it is a clear indication that the state is losing control of its monopoly on violence. Military or militia checkpoints, curfews, and the overt presence of armed factions suggest that the rule of law is breaking down, and localized conflicts are escalating. These groups may impose their own systems of control, replacing traditional authorities and further destabilizing the area.

Finally, **mass migration and displacement** often signal that the collapse has reached a critical point. As resources become scarce and violence escalates, people will begin to flee their homes in search of safety or better living conditions. These population movements can create additional pressures on already strained areas, leading to overcrowding, resource depletion, and further conflict. If you notice increasing numbers of displaced people moving through your area or gathering at border regions, it is a clear sign that conditions are deteriorating rapidly.

The ability to recognize these signs and assess their severity is essential for making informed decisions during a collapse.

By understanding how political, economic, and social systems unravel, you can anticipate the next stages of breakdown and take proactive measures to secure your safety and resources. Timing is critical in these scenarios; recognizing the early signs of collapse gives you the opportunity to act before the majority of the population realizes the full extent of the crisis. This awareness will be your greatest asset as you prepare to navigate the complex and dangerous environment of societal breakdown.

Political Instability, Civil Unrest, and Paramilitary Conflict

Political instability is often the first and most visible sign of societal collapse, setting off a chain reaction that leads to widespread civil unrest and, eventually, paramiiitary conflict. When a government begins to lose its grip on power—whether through corruption, inefficiency, or internal divisions—the foundations that maintain public order start to crack. The erosion of authority and legitimacy can lead to a volatile environment where traditional structures of governance are challenged or outright ignored. Once political institutions falter, the descent into civil unrest and paramilitary conflict becomes almost inevitable, with violence filling the vacuum left by the breakdown of the state.

In periods of political instability, leaders may lose the ability to govern effectively, either due to widespread public dissent or internal challenges from rival factions within the government. This instability often manifests in contested elections, legislative deadlock, or the open defiance of laws by both citizens and government officials. When the population no longer believes in the legitimacy of the existing political system, a shift occurs—from passive discontent to active resistance. Protests, strikes, and demonstrations become more frequent and increasingly confrontational, signaling that civil unrest is taking hold.

Civil unrest is not merely an expression of dissatisfaction; it is the embodiment of the breakdown in trust between the governed and their rulers. It starts with small, localized protests but can quickly escalate into larger, more coordinated actions. As grievances go unaddressed, frustration builds within the populace. Demonstrations may initially focus on specific issues, such as economic inequality, police brutality, or government corruption, but over time they often morph into broader movements demanding systemic change. These movements can attract diverse groups—students, labor unions, political activists, and ordinary citizens—who unite under a common cause to challenge the status quo.

The turning point from civil unrest to paramilitary conflict typically occurs when the state's response becomes more forceful, and opposition groups begin to organize themselves for armed resistance. Governments facing mass protests may attempt to reassert control through militarized police forces or the deployment of the military. Curfews, martial law, and other draconian measures are imposed in an effort to restore order. However, these actions often backfire, further inflaming tensions and creating a deeper sense of injustice among the population. In response, militant factions within the civilian population—whether driven by political ideology, ethnic identity, or regional loyalty—begin to organize paramilitary groups to fight back.

Paramilitary conflict is characterized by the emergence of armed factions that operate outside the formal military structure of the state. These groups may consist of former military personnel, civilians trained in guerrilla warfare, or criminal organizations taking advantage of the chaos. Unlike traditional armies, paramilitary groups tend to operate with a high degree of decentralization. They use asymmetrical warfare tactics, relying on sabotage, ambushes, and hit-and-run attacks to undermine government forces and seize control of territory. In some cases, these groups may align with external actors, receiving funding, weapons, or training from foreign governments or international organizations seeking to influence the outcome of the conflict.

The presence of paramilitary forces fundamentally changes the dynamics of a conflict. While civil unrest involves mostly unarmed or lightly armed civilians protesting against the state, paramilitary conflict introduces a new level of violence and organization. The lines between combatants and civilians blur, making it difficult to distinguish between those involved in the fighting and those simply trying to survive. This shift also signals that the state is losing its monopoly on the use of force, which is one of the hallmarks of a functional government. As paramilitary groups take control of certain areas, they often establish their own rules, justice systems, and economies, further eroding the authority of the central government.

In this environment, survival becomes increasingly precarious. Civilians are caught between government forces, insurgent paramilitary groups, and opportunistic criminal elements. Daily life is marked by uncertainty, as formerly safe areas become battlegrounds, and previously trustworthy institutions collapse. In many cases, local militias or neighborhood defense groups emerge as a means of providing security in the absence of functional law enforcement. However, these groups can be just as dangerous as the threats they aim to defend against, especially if they begin to operate outside any form of communal oversight.

The escalation from political instability to paramilitary conflict also creates a vicious cycle of violence and retaliation. As government forces crack down on dissent, paramilitary groups respond with attacks on infrastructure, supply lines, and government personnel. Each act of violence invites reprisal, deepening the conflict and making reconciliation increasingly difficult. In many cases, civil wars or long-standing internal conflicts grow out of these initial phases of political instability and civil unrest. Once paramilitary groups have taken root and established control over significant portions of a country, the pathway to peace becomes fraught with challenges.

For anyone living in such an environment, recognizing these stages of collapse is essential for survival. As political instability grows and civil unrest intensifies, the best course of action is often to remain alert, avoid large gatherings, and closely monitor developments. Once paramilitary conflict begins, mobility and discretion become key survival strategies. Staying out of the direct line of conflict, finding safe routes for evacuation, and maintaining a low profile are critical. In areas where paramilitary groups have taken control, blending in with the local population and understanding the new power dynamics can mean the difference between life and death.

Understanding the progression from political instability to civil unrest and finally to paramilitary conflict is not just an academic exercise; it is a vital component of survival in a collapsing society. By anticipating these developments and preparing for the specific threats they pose, you can increase your chances of navigating the chaos that comes with societal breakdown. This awareness, combined with practical defensive strategies, will enable you to endure the most dangerous phases of collapse, positioning you to survive and adapt in an environment where traditional forms of authority no longer exist.

When the Rule of Law No Longer Applies

When the rule of law no longer applies, the very foundation

of society disintegrates, leaving individuals to navigate a world governed by chaos, violence, and opportunism. In such a scenario, the established legal frameworks and protections that once governed human behavior and maintained public order are no longer functional. Courts, law enforcement, and governmental institutions become powerless or non-existent, rendering any formal recourse to justice meaningless. This marks a profound shift, one where survival and security depend on one's ability to adapt, organize, and defend oneself outside the traditional constraints of legal systems.

The collapse of the rule of law does not happen in a single moment; rather, it is a gradual process that begins with the erosion of trust in the government and its institutions. As political corruption, inefficiency, or internal conflict spread, the government's ability to enforce laws diminishes. At first, this may manifest as law enforcement agencies becoming understaffed, overwhelmed, or unable to respond to emergencies. Slowly, the ability to enforce basic laws—against theft, assault, or murder—breaks down, and as crime increases, the state's response grows weaker. What was once isolated lawlessness begins to spread, and before long, entire regions fall into a state of anarchy.

When the rule of law ceases to function, organized crime, militias, or insurgent groups often step in to fill the void, imposing their own arbitrary systems of justice and control. These groups can range from small, opportunistic gangs to large, well-organized paramilitary forces that assert their dominance over territories. In this environment, power is derived not from legal authority but from the capacity for violence and coercion. Laws are replaced by the will of the strongest, and personal safety becomes an individual responsibility.

For civilians, the absence of the rule of law radically alters how they must approach daily life. In a world without legal protection, the need for self-defense and tactical awareness becomes paramount. Individuals can no longer rely on calling the police for help or seeking judicial recourse for wrongs committed against them. Instead, personal and communal defense measures become the only reliable means of ensuring security. Communities may form local defense groups or militias to maintain some semblance of order, but these groups often operate outside the norms of fairness and legality, imposing their own rules through brute force.

The disappearance of the rule of law also forces a rethinking of morality and ethics in survival situations. Actions that would have been unthinkable in a civilized society—looting, trespassing, or even violence—become necessary for survival in a world where the state no longer functions. Resources become scarce, and competition for food, water, medicine, and shelter intensifies. In this context, the notion of property rights becomes tenuous at best. Desperate people may take what they need from others, and disputes are resolved not in courtrooms, but at gunpoint. Trust between individuals deteriorates, and paranoia grows, as no legal authority exists to mediate or prevent disputes from escalating into violence.

The lack of law enforcement also introduces a new level of unpredictability. Without a functioning system of justice, the balance of power constantly shifts. Armed groups may rise and fall, territories may change hands, and alliances can form and dissolve quickly. Navigating this landscape requires not only physical preparedness but also an acute awareness of these shifting power dynamics. Identifying who controls specific areas, understanding the motivations of different factions, and staying informed about potential threats are key to survival.

In this lawless environment, even basic freedoms and human rights become fragile. Without the protection of a legal system, civilians are subject to arbitrary detentions, kidnappings, and extortion by whoever holds power at any given moment. Freedom of speech, movement, and assembly are curtailed, as any dissent against local power brokers could result in brutal consequences. This suppression of freedoms leads to an environment where fear reigns, and individuals must make constant calculations about whether it is safer to speak out or remain silent, to stay or flee, to cooperate or resist.

For those unaccustomed to operating outside the framework of legal systems, this new reality can be disorienting and terrifying. The predictability that laws and norms once provided is replaced by constant uncertainty. Survival hinges on adaptability and the willingness to engage in behavior that may once have been unthinkable. The ability to form and maintain strategic alliances becomes crucial, as trust is no longer guaranteed by legal contracts or social norms, but by the mutual need for protection and survival.

Psychological resilience is equally important. The collapse of the rule of law creates an environment where fear, stress, and trauma are ever-present. The breakdown of social order, the constant threat of violence, and the loss of personal safety take a heavy toll on mental health. Maintaining a clear head and a sense of purpose amid such chaos is essential. Those who can remain calm under pressure, think strategically, and stay focused on their goals are more likely to endure the psychological strain of living in a lawless society.

When the rule of law no longer applies, the world becomes a place where only the most adaptable, resourceful, and prepared individuals thrive. The old rules—both legal and social—are gone, and in their place, a brutal form of survivalism takes over. It is a world where you cannot afford to be complacent, where every decision carries life-or-death consequences, and where security must be won by force, strategy, and resilience. This is the reality of living in a society that has collapsed, and the sooner one adapts to this new paradigm, the better the chances of surviving.

CHAPTER 2: STRATEGIC FOUNDATIONS OF SURVIVAL

Survival in the face of societal collapse is not a matter of chance or mere instinct. It requires a strategic mindset, a set of guiding principles that will shape your actions and decisions as you navigate the chaos. The old systems of governance, infrastructure, and security that once provided a framework for daily life are gone, and in their place lies uncertainty and danger. In this environment, a new set of rules must be adopted—rules grounded in strategy, foresight, and the willingness to adapt. The foundation of your survival will depend on your ability to think beyond immediate needs and consider the long-term challenges ahead.

At the heart of any survival strategy is the cultivation of a new mindset. This mindset rejects passivity and embraces the reality of the situation: no one is coming to save you. The sooner you internalize this fact, the better prepared you will be to face the challenges ahead. This is not a time for wishful thinking or reliance on old habits. It is a time for clear-headed decision-making, where every move is calculated to improve your chances of survival. In this world, hesitation is your enemy, and complacency will get you killed. Your actions must be deliberate, your focus unwavering.

Strategic survival begins with understanding the environment around you. The collapse of society creates a fluid and unpredictable landscape where threats can emerge from any direction. The political, social, and geographical terrain shifts constantly, and your ability to assess these changes will determine how well you can navigate them. This means gathering intelligence—both about your immediate surroundings and the broader context of the collapse. Who controls what territory? Where are the resources located? Which groups pose a threat, and which might be allies? Information is as valuable as food or ammunition in a collapsed society, and those who can gather and act on reliable intelligence will be the ones who stay ahead of the chaos.

Preparation is another cornerstone of strategic survival. The immediate aftermath of collapse will test the limits of your resources—food, water, medical supplies, and shelter will become precious commodities. Stockpiling essentials, identifying secure locations, and ensuring access to clean water are not reactive measures but preemptive actions that must be taken before the full brunt of the collapse hits. However, preparation goes beyond the physical. You must also be prepared mentally for the long haul. Survival is not a short-term endeavor. The collapse may last months, years, or longer, and the psychological resilience to endure prolonged hardship is just as important as the practical skills you develop.

A strategic approach to survival also involves building and maintaining alliances. In a world where the rule of law has disappeared, trust is rare and valuable. Identifying those you can depend on and forming mutually beneficial relationships can be a critical factor in survival. But these alliances must be built on clear, practical terms. In the absence of formal contracts or societal norms, relationships will be forged through shared necessity and mutual goals. However, as the dynamics of survival change, so too may your alliances. Being strategic means knowing when to align yourself with others—and when to distance yourself from them to avoid becoming a target.

Security, both personal and communal, is another pillar of strategic survival. In a collapsed society, threats to your safety will come not only from the collapse itself but from opportunists who seek to exploit the lawlessness. You must adopt a tactical mindset that goes beyond simple self-defense. Securing your environment, whether urban or rural, involves fortification, mobility, and an understanding of your terrain. Defensive strategies are not static; they must evolve as threats change. Being adaptable, moving when necessary, and using the terrain to your advantage are key to ensuring your long-term security.

Finally, strategy in survival involves long-term planning. While immediate needs may dominate your attention, you must always think ahead. How will you maintain access to resources when they become scarce? What contingencies do you have in place if your current location becomes unsafe? Can you ensure that you are not simply surviving day-to-day but positioning yourself to thrive in the new world that emerges from the ashes of the old one? Survival is not just about endurance—it is about positioning yourself to rebuild and reclaim some sense of normalcy, even in the midst of societal collapse.

This chapter will explore these strategic foundations in greater detail. It will provide a framework for approaching survival as a methodical, deliberate process, rooted in foresight and adaptability. By adopting this strategic mindset, you will be better equipped to face the unpredictable challenges of a world without order.

Adopting a Survivor's Mindset

Adopting a survivor's mindset is the first and most critical step in preparing for life during societal collapse. The mindset you bring to a crisis is often more important than the physical resources or skills you possess. Survival is not simply a matter of having the right tools or knowledge, though those are important. It is about how you think, how you approach challenges, and how you adapt to rapidly changing and often hostile environments. In a world where stability has been replaced by chaos, adopting a mindset focused on survival will help you stay focused, avoid panic, and make the tough decisions necessary to endure.

The first aspect of a survivor's mindset is **acceptance**. Acknowledge that the world you once knew is gone, and there is no guarantee it will return to the way it was. Holding on to expectations of normalcy or hoping for a quick resolution to the chaos will only cloud your judgment. Denial is dangerous in a survival situation. By accepting the new reality, you can begin to think clearly and take action without the distraction of wishful thinking. Acceptance doesn't mean giving up hope, but it does mean letting go of old assumptions and preparing mentally for a long, uncertain journey.

Another key element of a survivor's mindset is **mental toughness**. Survival will test not only your physical endurance but also your psychological resilience. Fear, stress, and fatigue will be constant companions, and how you manage these emotions will greatly influence your ability to survive. Mental toughness means staying calm under pressure, making rational decisions even when fear threatens to overwhelm you, and maintaining a clear focus on your survival goals. It's about learning to control your emotions instead of letting them control you. This doesn't mean ignoring fear; fear can be useful when it sharpens your instincts. But it does mean using that fear to fuel your focus and determination rather than letting it paralyze you.

Adaptability is another essential trait in the survivor's mindset. In a collapsed society, nothing is static. The environment, threats, and opportunities will change constantly, often without warning. Those who cling rigidly to a single plan or who refuse to adjust their thinking in response to new challenges will find themselves outpaced by the chaos. Adaptability means being flexible in your thinking, willing to change strategies as circumstances evolve. It's about seeing obstacles not as insurmountable barriers but as problems to be solved. The ability to quickly reassess a situation, identify new risks or opportunities, and pivot your approach is what will allow you to thrive in an unpredictable environment.

Another crucial component of the survivor's mindset is **resourcefulness**. In a world where supplies are limited and the normal systems of production and distribution have collapsed, you must learn to make do with what is available. Resourcefulness means seeing potential in what others might overlook—whether it's finding creative uses for discarded materials, repurposing everyday objects for survival, or bartering with others for critical supplies. It also means learning to improvise in the face of shortages. When resources are scarce, those who can think creatively and find alternative solutions will have a distinct advantage over those who are unable to adapt their strategies.

A survivor must also cultivate **self-reliance**. In a collapsed society, you can no longer depend on government institutions, law enforcement, or even traditional community structures to provide for your needs. While building alliances and networks is important, you must first and foremost develop the ability to take care of yourself. This doesn't mean isolation, but rather building the skills, knowledge, and mental fortitude to ensure that you can meet your basic needs—food, water, shelter, and security—independently if necessary. Self-reliance requires a mindset of personal responsibility, where you take control of your own survival instead of waiting for external help.

Situational awareness is another indispensable trait in the survivor's mindset. This means being constantly aware of your surroundings, attuned to changes in the environment, and alert to both opportunities and threats. Survival in a collapsed society is often about seeing what others do not—whether it's recognizing a potential danger before it escalates, noticing a resource that could be useful, or understanding the dynamics of power and control in your immediate environment. By staying observant and maintaining a heightened sense of awareness, you will be better positioned to avoid dangers and take advantage of emerging opportunities.

Finally, a critical aspect of the survivor's mindset is **determination**. Survival is not easy, and it often requires pushing through physical and mental barriers. There will be moments when giving up feels like the easiest option, when the exhaustion, fear, and uncertainty seem overwhelming. But survival requires a deep-seated determination to keep going no matter the odds. This kind of determination is fueled by having clear survival goals and a strong sense of purpose. Whether it's the desire to protect your family, rebuild your community, or simply live to see another day, that purpose will drive you forward when things seem impossible.

Adopting a survivor's mindset is not just about thinking differently—it is about transforming how you approach every aspect of life during a collapse. It means accepting the new reality, staying mentally tough, being adaptable and resourceful, relying on yourself, maintaining situational awareness, and drawing on a deep well of determination. With this mindset, you will be better equipped to face the challenges of a world in collapse and position yourself to not just survive, but to outlast the chaos.

Building Mental Resilience in the Face of Chaos

Building mental resilience in the face of chaos is one of the most important aspects of surviving in a collapsed society. Mental resilience is the ability to withstand stress, maintain focus, and recover from setbacks in situations of extreme uncertainty and danger. In a world where societal norms have broken down, fear, anxiety, and confusion can easily overtake even the most prepared individual. Developing mental resilience enables you to navigate the constant pressures of survival, think clearly under duress, and maintain the endurance required to face prolonged challenges.

The first step in building mental resilience is **accepting uncertainty**. Chaos and unpredictability will be constants in a collapsed society, and your ability to thrive in this environment depends on how well you can tolerate the unknown. In times of collapse, information will be scarce, and clear answers even scarcer. Events will unfold rapidly, often without explanation, and you may find yourself in situations where you have to act without knowing all the facts. Accepting that uncertainty is part of the new reality allows you to remain flexible, avoiding the paralysis that comes with expecting clarity in a world that no longer provides it. You must train yourself to make decisions in the absence of full information, trusting your instincts and experience to guide you.

Another critical component of mental resilience is **emotional control**. Fear, anger, and frustration will be frequent companions in a world of chaos, but allowing these emotions to dominate your thinking will cloud your judgment and lead to poor decision-making. Resilient individuals learn to manage their emotions, recognizing when fear is a useful tool and when it becomes a hindrance. Emotional control doesn't mean ignoring or suppressing feelings—it means acknowledging them, but not letting them dictate your actions. This is particularly important in high-stakes situations where clear thinking is crucial. By learning to compartmentalize fear and anger, you can maintain focus on your survival goals, using your emotions as a source of motivation rather than letting them become obstacles.

Routine and structure also play an essential role in fostering mental resilience. When the external world is chaotic, creating a sense of order in your daily life provides stability and helps you stay grounded. Even in the absence of societal systems, establishing a personal routine—whether through regular training, securing resources, or maintaining your living space—gives you a sense of control over your environment. This routine can act as a psychological anchor, helping you feel more in control when external events seem overwhelming. The more you are able to establish small routines, the easier it will be to cope with the constant unpredictability around you.

Staying connected with others is another key factor in maintaining mental resilience. While self-reliance is critical in a collapsed society, complete isolation can erode your psychological strength over time. Humans are social creatures, and even in extreme situations, maintaining contact with others—whether through alliances, support networks, or trusted companions—helps sustain mental well-being. Social bonds offer emotional support, reduce feelings of isolation, and provide a source of collective problem-solving. However, it's important to choose carefully whom to trust, as alliances in a lawless world are fragile and must be built on mutual benefit and reliability.

Problem-solving skills are another crucial aspect of resilience. Chaos creates an environment where challenges and obstacles emerge constantly, and resilient individuals excel at finding solutions in difficult situations. Developing problem-solving skills means approaching obstacles with a mindset of curiosity and determination rather than frustration. Whether you are faced with the scarcity of resources, a new threat, or an unexpected change in circumstances, your ability to think critically and find creative solutions will determine how well you can adapt and overcome. This approach also helps reduce feelings of helplessness, as it encourages action over despair.

A significant aspect of mental resilience is the ability to **focus on what you can control**. In a collapsed society, many factors will be beyond your influence, and dwelling on what you cannot change will drain your mental energy. Instead, focus on what you can do in the moment—whether it's securing resources, strengthening your defenses, or improving your own skills. By channeling your efforts into actions that have a tangible impact on your survival, you keep yourself engaged and mentally active, preventing the sense of powerlessness that comes from fixating on uncontrollable events.

Maintaining perspective is also essential. Chaos and collapse can make the world feel overwhelmingly dangerous and hostile, but maintaining a broader perspective helps to prevent burnout. Survival is a long-term goal, and resilient individuals keep in mind that no single setback defines their overall progress. Understanding that bad days will come, but that they are part of a larger journey, helps reduce the psychological toll of temporary failures or setbacks. Keeping your mind on the larger picture allows you to view challenges as part of the process, rather than insurmountable obstacles.

Finally, **physical fitness and mental resilience** are deeply interconnected. Physical health directly impacts your ability to cope with stress. A body that is strong and well-nourished is better equipped to handle the rigors of survival, and physical activity itself can reduce stress, improve mood, and sharpen mental focus. Maintaining physical fitness through regular exercise and ensuring proper nutrition is critical, even when resources are scarce. The discipline of taking care of your physical needs translates into greater mental toughness, as it reinforces your ability to meet challenges head-on.

In building mental resilience, you are not only preparing yourself to endure the immediate challenges of survival, but also ensuring that you have the endurance to face long-term uncertainty. In a world of chaos, mental toughness, emotional control, problem-solving, and adaptability are your most valuable tools. By cultivating these traits, you build the psychological armor necessary to withstand the pressures of collapse, allowing you to continue moving forward even when the world around you seems to be falling apart.

Staying One Step Ahead: Anticipating Threats

In a collapsed society, where the rule of law has evaporated and uncertainty reigns, the ability to stay one step ahead of emerging threats becomes an indispensable survival skill. Anticipating danger before it strikes not only keeps you out of harm's way, but also gives you the strategic advantage necessary to secure resources, plan effectively, and maintain control over your environment. This proactive mindset is what separates those who merely react to events from those who can navigate the chaos with purpose and foresight.

To stay one step ahead, the first critical element is **situational awareness**. Situational awareness goes beyond simply observing your surroundings—it involves actively scanning the environment for subtle changes that signal danger, opportunity, or shifting dynamics. The collapse of societal norms creates a fluid landscape where power struggles, resource shortages, and spontaneous violence can occur without warning. Maintaining constant vigilance is essential.

This means training yourself to notice the movement of people, changes in atmosphere, unusual behavior, and anything that deviates from the ordinary flow of events. It is not just about seeing but about interpreting what those changes mean in the broader context of survival.

Part of maintaining situational awareness is developing a keen sense for **patterns and anomalies**. Threats rarely appear out of nowhere—they build over time and often follow a pattern. Whether it's the increased presence of an armed group in your area, a sudden rise in the cost of essential supplies, or the gradual withdrawal of people from a certain part of the city, these patterns provide clues about what is coming next. Learning to detect anomalies—anything that seems out of place or doesn't fit the usual pattern—can give you early warning of developing threats. In a chaotic environment, what may seem like small changes can be the harbingers of significant shifts, and identifying them early can make the difference between being caught off guard and staying ahead of the curve.

Intelligence gathering is another vital component of staying one step ahead. Information is one of the most valuable commodities in a collapsed society. Whether it's knowing which routes are safe, understanding the intentions of local factions, or predicting where the next wave of violence will erupt, having reliable intelligence gives you the ability to make informed decisions. This intelligence can come from a variety of sources: listening to local chatter, observing the behavior of groups, forming discreet alliances, or intercepting communications. The more information you can gather, the more complete your understanding of your environment will be. But gathering intelligence also means filtering out misinformation and being careful about who you trust.

Another crucial factor in anticipating threats is **understanding power dynamics**. In a society without formal law and order, power becomes decentralized and often falls into the hands of local warlords, gangs, or self-proclaimed leaders. These power brokers control access to resources, enforce their own laws, and dictate the flow of violence. Understanding who holds power in a given area—and how that power shifts over time—allows you to predict where conflicts will arise and how the balance of power will affect your ability to survive. You need to be able to read these dynamics and position yourself accordingly, either by staying out of conflict zones, forming strategic alliances, or preparing for the possibility of hostile takeover.

Mobility and adaptability are also essential to staying one step ahead. In a world that is constantly changing, the ability to move quickly and adapt to new circumstances can often mean the difference between life and death. You must be ready to change locations, alter your plans, or abandon an approach that is no longer working. Mobility doesn't just mean physical movement—it also refers to your mental flexibility and willingness to pivot strategies when necessary. A static mindset in a fluid environment will leave you vulnerable to threats as they emerge. The most successful survivors are those who keep their options open, always have an escape route in mind, and remain flexible enough to adjust to new realities.

Predicting resource scarcity is another key component of staying ahead. In a collapsed society, resources like food, water, fuel, and medical supplies will quickly become scarce, and competition for these essentials will intensify. Being able to predict where and when these shortages will occur allows you to secure what you need before the situation becomes dire. This involves paying attention to supply lines, trade routes, and local distribution patterns. If a certain area is experiencing a rapid decline in available resources, or if black markets are emerging in place of traditional supply chains, these are signs that scarcity is spreading. Securing your supplies before panic sets in and stockpiles are depleted is a critical survival tactic.

An often overlooked but equally important aspect of anticipating threats is **observing human behavior**. In the absence of law and order, desperation and fear will drive people to act in unpredictable ways. Understanding the psychology of desperation allows you to predict how others might react in stressful situations. Individuals and groups under extreme pressure may resort to violence, theft, or betrayal, even if they have previously been peaceful or cooperative. Learning to read body language, emotional cues, and shifts in group behavior gives you insight into when someone is becoming a potential threat. This allows you to either defuse the situation early or take steps to protect yourself before the threat fully materializes.

Finally, **planning for contingencies** is critical. Staying one step ahead means not just reacting to immediate threats but preparing for future scenarios that may arise. You must always ask yourself: What if this situation worsens? What if my location is compromised? What if supplies run out faster than expected? By considering these potential scenarios, you can develop contingency plans for each one. These plans might include alternative routes to safer areas, backup supply caches, or new alliances with trusted individuals. Having multiple plans in place means that when a threat does materialize, you are not caught scrambling for solutions—you are already ready to act.

Staying one step ahead is about cultivating an acute sense of awareness, gathering intelligence, understanding shifting power structures, and being ready to move and adapt as conditions change. By anticipating threats rather than simply reacting to them, you position yourself strategically to survive in a world of chaos and danger. This mindset ensures that you are not merely surviving moment to moment, but actively shaping your own path through the unpredictability, always one step ahead of the collapse around you.

CHAPTER 3: GUERRILLA TACTICS FOR THE CITIZEN DEFENDER

Guerrilla tactics represent a fundamental shift in how you think about defense in a collapsed society. Unlike conventional methods of warfare, which rely on overwhelming firepower, structured hierarchies, and set battle lines, guerrilla warfare is rooted in adaptability, stealth, and exploiting the vulnerabilities of a stronger opponent. For the citizen defender—an individual who must protect themselves, their family, or their community without the backing of a formal military structure—understanding and mastering these tactics becomes a matter of survival. Guerrilla warfare has been the weapon of the underdog for centuries, used by smaller, less equipped forces to outmaneuver and outlast larger, more powerful adversaries. This chapter will introduce the core principles of guerrilla tactics and explain how they can be applied effectively in a domestic setting where the rule of law has collapsed, and survival is paramount.

At its core, guerrilla warfare is about **asymmetry**. In a societal collapse, you are likely to be outmatched by the strength, numbers, or resources of various hostile groups, whether they be organized militias, criminal gangs, or rogue paramilitary forces. Engaging in a direct confrontation with these groups is often a losing strategy. Instead, guerrilla tactics allow you to exploit your environment, strike at opportune moments, and remain elusive, avoiding prolonged engagements where the odds are against you. As a citizen defender, your goal is not to overpower your opponent in a single battle but to outthink them, erode their will, and make their efforts to control or eliminate you more costly than they are willing to bear.

Mobility and stealth are the foundation of guerrilla tactics. You must learn to move swiftly and silently, using the terrain—whether urban or rural—to your advantage. In urban environments, this means navigating streets, buildings, and alleyways in ways that minimize your exposure to enemies while maximizing your ability to strike from unexpected angles. In rural or forested environments, it involves using natural cover, moving through difficult terrain, and making yourself difficult to track. Staying light on your feet and constantly changing locations keeps you from becoming an easy target, while also keeping your adversaries on edge, never knowing where or when you might strike next. This constant state of movement requires discipline and awareness of your surroundings at all times.

Ambushes are a classic guerrilla tactic that allows you to engage stronger forces on your terms. An ambush turns the advantage of surprise into a powerful weapon, allowing you to strike with precision before your opponent has a chance to react. Setting up an ambush requires detailed planning, knowledge of the terrain, and patience. You must know your enemy's movements, predict their routes, and choose a location where they are most vulnerable—such as a narrow street, a bend in the road, or a chokepoint in a forest trail. The goal of an ambush is not necessarily to destroy the enemy entirely, but to inflict maximum damage in a short period of time before disappearing back into the landscape. Successful ambushes create fear and uncertainty among your opponents, forcing them to alter their tactics and become more defensive, which in turn gives you greater freedom of movement.

Another essential element of guerrilla tactics is the principle of **hit-and-run**. Unlike conventional engagements, where both sides remain locked in battle until a decisive outcome is reached, guerrilla warfare is fluid. You strike quickly and retreat before your enemy can effectively respond. This tactic not only reduces your exposure to counterattacks but also allows you to conserve resources, including ammunition, supplies, and manpower. The goal is not to win battles in the traditional sense but to wear down your adversary over time, draining their morale and resources while you remain agile and elusive. Hit-and-run tactics are especially useful in environments where you are outnumbered or outgunned, as they allow you to fight on your own terms and dictate the pace of the conflict.

Psychological warfare is another critical component of guerrilla tactics. In a collapsed society, where order has already disintegrated, fear and uncertainty are rampant. Guerrilla forces thrive on exacerbating this psychological stress. By remaining unpredictable, striking at unexpected times, and avoiding direct confrontation, you can create a sense of paranoia in your adversaries. They will waste resources guarding against attacks that may never come, and their morale will slowly erode as they realize they are fighting an enemy that cannot be easily tracked or defeated. Psychological warfare isn't just about terrifying your opponent, though—it's also about maintaining the perception of your strength and resilience, even when you may be running low on resources. Appearances are crucial in guerrilla warfare, and keeping your adversaries off balance through misinformation and psychological manipulation can give you a significant edge.

The use of **sabotage** is another effective guerrilla tactic.

Rather than engaging in direct combat, sabotage allows you to weaken your adversary's infrastructure, supply chains, and communication networks. This could involve disabling vehicles, cutting off access to resources, or disrupting their ability to move freely through an area. Sabotage targets the lifelines of larger forces, making it more difficult for them to maintain their operations. In a domestic setting, this could mean taking down communications towers, blocking roads, or destroying fuel supplies. By targeting these critical areas, you can force your opponent to divert resources toward protecting infrastructure rather than advancing their control over territory.

Intelligence gathering is a cornerstone of successful guerrilla operations. Unlike a conventional army, which may rely on overwhelming force to secure victory, guerrilla fighters must rely on knowledge—of their enemy, the environment, and potential resources. You need to gather information constantly, whether through direct observation, covert surveillance, or gathering intelligence from local populations. Understanding your enemy's movements, supply routes, vulnerabilities, and plans will allow you to strike when they least expect it. In a collapsed society, where formal lines of communication are often broken, being able to gather and interpret intelligence can give you a decisive advantage.

Finally, **resilience and endurance** are at the heart of guerrilla tactics for the citizen defender. This type of warfare is not about quick victories—it is about survival, persistence, and the long game. Guerrilla fighters must be prepared for drawn-out conflicts where resources are limited, and setbacks are inevitable. The key to success is maintaining your will to fight, even when the odds seem overwhelming. Guerrilla warfare is a battle of attrition, both physical and psychological. Those who are mentally prepared for the long haul—who can endure hardship, remain disciplined, and continue to adapt—will outlast their opponents.

In this chapter, you will learn how to apply these guerrilla tactics to your own survival strategy, adapting them to the unique challenges of a collapsed society where formal rules of engagement no longer apply. These tactics are not about winning in a conventional sense but about creating the conditions for survival in a hostile, unpredictable environment. By mastering the principles of mobility, stealth, ambush, psychological warfare, and intelligence, you can level the playing field against stronger forces and protect yourself and those who depend on you.

The Core Principles of Guerrilla Warfare

The core principles of guerrilla warfare are designed to exploit the weaknesses of a more powerful enemy while leveraging mobility, stealth, and adaptability. These principles have been refined over centuries of conflict and are laid out clearly in the *U.S. Army Guerrilla Warfare Handbook* and the *Guerrilla Warfare and Special Forces Operations* field manual. In a world where the rule of law has collapsed and survival depends on unconventional tactics, these principles form the foundation of an effective defensive strategy. For the citizen defender, understanding and applying these principles with precision will be key to navigating hostile environments and outlasting superior forces.

1. Asymmetry and Exploiting Weaknesses

Guerrilla warfare is fundamentally asymmetric. Unlike conventional military forces, guerrilla fighters do not seek direct confrontation with stronger enemies. Instead, they exploit weaknesses in their opponent's logistics, morale, and command structure. In the context of a societal collapse, where larger factions or militias may control key resources or territories, guerrilla forces capitalize on the enemy's reliance on fixed supply lines, predictable movements, and centralized leadership. Your goal as a citizen defender is to avoid open battles and instead focus on destabilizing your enemy's operations through targeted strikes, disruption, and psychological pressure.

The *U.S. Army Guerrilla Warfare Handbook* emphasizes the importance of understanding your enemy's vulnerabilities, whether it's in their communication networks, fuel supplies, or troop morale. Identifying these weaknesses allows you to mount attacks that have a disproportionate impact, forcing your adversary to expend resources and energy defending vulnerable points rather than pursuing you directly.

2. Mobility and Flexibility

The ability to move quickly and unpredictably is central to guerrilla warfare. Mobility prevents your forces from being pinned down or eliminated in a single confrontation. This principle is particularly important in urban or rural environments where the terrain can be used to your advantage. Guerrilla fighters must remain constantly on the move, blending into the environment and utilizing both natural and man-made cover to stay hidden from larger forces. In urban environments, this may mean using back streets, alleyways, and buildings to disappear after an attack. In rural or forested areas, it involves leveraging the terrain, using dense forests, hills, or rivers to escape and relocate undetected.

The *Guerrilla Warfare and Special Forces Operations* manual highlights the necessity of avoiding prolonged engagements. The longer you stay in one place, the more vulnerable you become. A successful guerrilla fighter must be able to strike quickly and vanish before the enemy can organize a counterattack. Maintaining operational flexibility allows you to exploit opportunities as they arise and avoid being trapped by more organized forces.

3. Stealth and Camouflage

Stealth is a critical component of guerrilla tactics. Remaining undetected while gathering intelligence, moving between locations, or staging an ambush is vital to success. Guerrilla forces operate in environments where they are often outnumbered, making it essential to avoid detection until the moment of attack. Camouflage, both in terms of physical appearance and blending into civilian populations, is a key part of this principle.

The *U.S. Army Guerrilla Warfare Handbook* emphasizes the importance of understanding the environment and using it to your advantage. Whether it's adopting the appearance of civilians in an urban setting or using natural camouflage in a rural one, the goal is to remain invisible until it is time to strike. The ability to move unseen allows you to gather intelligence, conduct reconnaissance, and prepare for operations without alerting the enemy.

4. Intelligence and Reconnaissance

Gathering accurate intelligence is one of the most important principles of guerrilla warfare. Successful guerrilla fighters are always informed about their enemy's movements, resources, and vulnerabilities. Intelligence allows you to strike at the right moment, avoiding unnecessary risks and maximizing the impact of your operations. Reconnaissance should be continuous, with every available resource dedicated to monitoring enemy activities, identifying weak points, and evaluating the terrain.

Both the *U.S. Army Guerrilla Warfare Handbook* and the *Guerrilla Warfare and Special Forces Operations* manual stress that intelligence must be gathered covertly, using a combination of human sources, observation posts, and, when available, intercepted communications. In a collapsed society, where formal intelligence networks may no longer exist, guerrilla fighters must develop their own systems for gathering and analyzing information. This can include cultivating local contacts, using civilians to gather information discreetly, or setting up observation points in high-traffic areas.

5. Ambush and Surprise

The element of surprise is a powerful force multiplier in guerrilla warfare. Guerrilla fighters never engage on the enemy's terms. Instead, they rely on carefully planned ambushes to inflict maximum damage in the shortest amount of time, before disappearing back into the terrain. Ambushes are usually set up in locations where the enemy is most vulnerable—such as narrow streets, forest trails, or supply routes—where it is difficult for them to maneuver or bring their superior firepower to bear.

The *Guerrilla Warfare and Special Forces Operations* manual provides detailed guidance on setting up effective ambushes. Successful ambushes are based on thorough reconnaissance, proper selection of the ambush site, and precise timing. The goal is not only to inflict casualties but to create confusion and lower the enemy's morale, forcing them to be constantly on guard. Ambushes should be followed by a rapid withdrawal to avoid becoming engaged in a prolonged fight, where guerrilla forces may be outgunned or surrounded.

6. Hit-and-Run Tactics

Guerrilla warfare thrives on hit-and-run tactics, where small, fast-moving units strike the enemy quickly and then retreat before a counterattack can be organized. These tactics allow you to engage the enemy without becoming bogged down in drawn-out battles that favor their superior numbers and firepower. The aim is to harass, frustrate, and gradually weaken the enemy over time, rather than seeking a decisive, large-scale victory.

The *U.S. Army Guerrilla Warfare Handbook* emphasizes that hit-and-run tactics are not about overwhelming force, but about precision and efficiency. A small, well-timed raid on an enemy convoy or outpost can have a significant impact if it disrupts supply lines, damages key infrastructure, or undermines the enemy's confidence. These attacks, while small in scale, accumulate over time, wearing down the enemy's resources and will to fight.

7. Sabotage and Disruption

Sabotage is a key weapon in the guerrilla arsenal. Rather than engaging the enemy directly, sabotage allows you to weaken their infrastructure, disrupt supply lines, and interfere with their ability to operate effectively. This can include damaging vehicles, destroying supply depots, cutting communication lines, or interfering with transportation networks. Sabotage creates logistical problems for the enemy, forcing them to divert resources toward protecting or repairing critical infrastructure.

The Guerrilla Warfare and Special Forces Operations manual outlines the importance of targeting the enemy's logistical support system. Sabotage operations should be carefully planned to have the maximum impact with minimal risk to the guerrilla forces involved. By striking at the enemy's logistics, you reduce their ability to sustain prolonged operations and weaken their overall fighting capacity.

8. Psychological Warfare

Guerrilla warfare is as much about psychology as it is about physical combat. By creating a sense of fear, uncertainty, and frustration in the enemy, guerrilla fighters can erode their morale and sap their will to fight. Psychological warfare includes spreading misinformation, staging attacks that create disproportionate fear, and exploiting the enemy's weaknesses to make them feel vulnerable.

Both the *U.S. Army Guerrilla Warfare Handbook* and the *Guerrilla Warfare and Special Forces Operations* manual stress the importance of maintaining the psychological upper hand. By remaining unpredictable, avoiding direct engagements, and conducting operations that maximize the enemy's fear of the unknown, you can make your opponent feel like they are constantly under threat, even when they are not. This psychological pressure forces them to divert energy and resources into defending themselves against perceived threats, which further weakens their overall position.

9. Decentralization and Flexibility

One of the hallmarks of successful guerrilla warfare is its decentralized structure. Guerrilla units are typically organized into small, independent cells, each capable of operating autonomously without direct oversight from a central command. This decentralization allows for flexibility, making it difficult for larger forces to decapitate the movement by targeting a single leader or headquarters. In a collapsed society, where formal communications may be limited or compromised, decentralization ensures that each unit can continue to function and adapt to the changing circumstances without waiting for orders from a higher authority.

The *Guerrilla Warfare and Special Forces Operations* manual emphasizes the importance of empowering local commanders and units to make decisions based on real-time intelligence and the situation on the ground. This flexibility enables guerrilla forces to respond rapidly to opportunities or threats, allowing them to outmaneuver a more rigid, hierarchical enemy force. As a citizen defender, understanding and adopting a decentralized structure within your defense group will allow you to remain operational even if communication lines are severed or key leaders are lost.

10. Secure Communication and Secrecy

In any conflict, secure communication is essential, but in guerrilla warfare, it is paramount. Given that guerrilla forces are often outmatched in terms of firepower and resources, maintaining operational security through secure and clandestine communications is vital to ensure that the enemy does not gain an advantage by intercepting plans or movements. Communication must be brief, discreet, and, where possible, encrypted or coded to prevent eavesdropping or interception.

Drawing from lessons in the *U.S. Army Guerrilla Warfare Handbook*, it is crucial for guerrilla forces to establish secure communication networks early. These may include low-tech methods such as couriers, signal flares, or coded messages delivered in person, as well as more advanced solutions like encrypted digital communication if the infrastructure allows. The key is to ensure that sensitive information about your plans, movements, or supply locations does not fall into enemy hands. Additionally, guerrilla fighters must understand the principle of compartmentalization—wherein different cells or units only know the information necessary for their specific operations, minimizing the risk of total compromise if one unit is captured or infiltrated.

11. Supply Chains and Resource Management

While guerrilla fighters are typically light and mobile, they are still dependent on access to critical resources such as food, water, ammunition, and medical supplies. Unlike a conventional army, which may have formal supply lines, guerrilla forces must develop improvised, decentralized supply networks. These supply lines need to be flexible, adaptable, and resilient to enemy disruption. The *Guerrilla*

Warfare and Special Forces Operations manual stresses the importance of establishing hidden caches of supplies throughout your operational area. These caches ensure that fighters have access to critical materials even when traditional supply routes are cut off.

For the citizen defender, maintaining a steady and secure supply chain involves not only stockpiling supplies but also forming alliances with local communities or individuals who can provide support in exchange for protection or other services. Securing resources without drawing attention to your activities is also essential. Resource management requires discipline, with careful consideration of how and when to expend limited supplies. Mismanagement of resources or the failure to resupply can quickly lead to the collapse of even the most well-organized guerrilla group.

12. Civilian Support and Legitimacy

Guerrilla warfare, particularly in the context of societal collapse, cannot succeed without the support of the local civilian population. Civilians provide vital intelligence, shelter, and supplies to guerrilla fighters, while also serving as a buffer against enemy forces. Maintaining the trust and cooperation of the local population is essential for sustaining long-term operations. This is achieved through a combination of protection, respect, and mutual benefit. The U.S. Army Guerrilla Warfare Handbook and other relevant primary sources stress the importance of maintaining legitimacy in the eyes of the population. Guerrilla forces must avoid harming civilians, stealing resources, or committing acts of violence that could alienate potential allies.

In a collapsed society, where civilians may be caught between warring factions or criminal groups, guerrilla forces that protect and defend the populace will be more likely to secure their support. Providing security to communities in exchange for information, supplies, or shelter creates a symbiotic relationship where both parties benefit. Additionally, guerrilla fighters must be aware of the need for psychological operations that frame them as defenders of the people, contrasting themselves with the brutality or corruption of other armed groups. Winning the hearts and minds of civilians is a key component of guerrilla success.

13. Urban and Rural Warfare Adaptation

While guerrilla tactics share common principles, the specific strategies employed will vary greatly depending on the environment. Urban environments, with their dense population centers, infrastructure, and limited open spaces, present different challenges and opportunities compared to rural or forested areas. In urban warfare, guerrilla fighters must adapt to the complexity of street fighting, using buildings, tunnels, and infrastructure as cover and relying heavily on ambushes, sabotage, and blending in with civilian populations to avoid detection.

The *Guerrilla Warfare and Special Forces Operations* manual emphasizes the importance of knowing your environment intimately—whether in the city or the countryside. In urban settings, guerrilla forces must exploit the dense infrastructure to hide in plain sight, utilizing rooftops, alleyways, and underground systems to avoid larger forces. In rural or forested environments, guerrilla fighters must be skilled in using natural terrain to their advantage, employing hit-and-run tactics, and moving through forests, mountains, or jungles without leaving a trace.

For the citizen defender, understanding how to adapt guerrilla tactics to different environments is critical for survival. In urban areas, knowing the layout of streets, key landmarks, and escape routes will allow you to strike quickly and retreat before the enemy can mount a response. In rural areas, your knowledge of the natural landscape will be your greatest asset, allowing you to evade capture and outmaneuver enemies who are unfamiliar with the terrain.

14. Evasion and Escape

One of the key tenets of guerrilla warfare is knowing when to fight and when to disappear. Evasion and escape are not signs of weakness; they are essential tactics that prevent you from being overwhelmed by a superior force. Guerrilla fighters must master the art of retreating before an enemy can mount a counterattack, moving swiftly and silently to avoid detection. This principle applies to both small engagements and larger strategic decisions. Knowing when to disengage allows you to preserve your forces for future operations rather than risking total annihilation in a single confrontation.

The *U.S. Army Guerrilla Warfare Handbook* outlines techniques for evading enemy detection, including the use of terrain, camouflage, and decoys. Guerrilla fighters must plan their retreats as carefully as their attacks, ensuring they have pre-designated escape routes and hidden locations where they can regroup. In a collapsed society, your ability to blend into the population or disappear into the wilderness will determine whether you can live to fight another day.

15. Endurance and Long-Term Resistance

Guerrilla warfare is not about quick victories; it is a war of attrition designed to outlast and wear down a more powerful opponent over time. This requires both physical and mental endurance. As a guerrilla fighter, you must be prepared for long, protracted conflict where the traditional markers of success—such as territory gained or battles won—are secondary to survival and persistence. The enemy may have superior numbers, weapons, or technology, but guerrilla warfare is about surviving and continuing the fight, no matter the odds.

The *Guerrilla Warfare and Special Forces Operations* manual stresses the importance of resilience in the face of setbacks. Guerrilla fighters must be prepared to endure periods of isolation, scarcity, and defeat without losing their will to resist. This long-term focus requires discipline, commitment, and the ability to adapt to changing circumstances. Guerrilla forces often win by outlasting their opponents, forcing them to expend resources and morale over months or years until the enemy is no longer willing or able to continue the fight.

For the citizen defender, this means adopting a mindset of patience and perseverance. Victory may not come in the form of a decisive battle, but in the ability to continue resisting, to survive against the odds, and to remain a thorn in the enemy's side long after they expect you to give up. By mastering the core principles of guerrilla warfare, you will not only improve your chances of survival in a collapsed society but also become a formidable defender of your home, family, and community.

These core principles form the backbone of guerrilla warfare, providing the citizen defender with a blueprint for survival and resistance in a collapsed society. By mastering these tactics, you can level the playing field against stronger, better-equipped adversaries and create the conditions for long-term survival.

Using Asymmetry to Your Advantage

Using asymmetry to your advantage is at the heart of guerrilla warfare and is perhaps the most important concept for the citizen defender. In a collapsed society, you are likely to face adversaries who have superior numbers, more advanced weaponry, and greater logistical support. However, those advantages can be neutralized when you adopt an asymmetric strategy, leveraging your environment, mobility, and unpredictability to shift the balance of power. Asymmetry is not just about physical disparities between forces—it's about thinking differently and exploiting the vulnerabilities of a stronger enemy by using unconventional methods.

In asymmetrical conflict, your objective is not to engage in head-to-head combat with an adversary that can outgun you. Instead, your goal is to undermine their strength by forcing them into situations where their advantages are either diminished or irrelevant. This requires a shift in perspective: instead of seeking decisive battles, you aim to disrupt, harass, and gradually erode the enemy's ability to project power. You must be constantly aware of the resources and capabilities your opponent relies on—whether it's supply lines, communications, or control over key territory—and find ways to exploit their dependence on these structures.

One of the most effective ways to use asymmetry is by employing **mobility and speed** to counteract the enemy's static positions or slower-moving forces. Larger, more conventional forces often rely on established supply routes and secure bases of operation, which makes them slower and more predictable. As a smaller, more agile defender, you can use this to your advantage by remaining mobile, avoiding fixed positions that can be targeted or overrun. The key to this tactic is staying light, operating in small, self-sufficient units, and constantly changing locations to keep the enemy guessing.

For example, a well-timed attack on a convoy or supply depot, followed by a rapid withdrawal, can have a disproportionate impact on an enemy force that relies on constant resupply. Even if the attack itself only causes minimal casualties or damage, it forces the enemy to divert resources to protect their supply lines, weakening their ability to operate in other areas. This tactic also creates psychological stress, as the enemy can never be certain when or where they will be struck next. The unpredictability of these hit-and-run tactics allows you to maintain the initiative, keeping the enemy off balance.

Another critical aspect of asymmetry is the **use of terrain**. Terrain plays a significant role in leveling the playing field, especially when you are facing a more powerful opponent. By exploiting natural or urban landscapes, you can nullify many of the enemy's advantages. In densely populated urban areas, buildings, narrow streets, and alleyways become natural chokepoints that can be used to set up ambushes or escape routes. In rural environments, forests, mountains, and rivers offer concealment and allow for rapid movement through terrain that heavier, conventional forces may find difficult to navigate.

The key is to **understand your environment intimately** and use it to your advantage. Knowledge of local geography, including hidden paths, defensible positions, and choke points, allows you to maneuver freely while restricting the enemy's movements. This ability to disappear into the landscape after an attack not only protects you from retaliation but also allows you to dictate when and where engagements occur. The terrain becomes both your shield and your weapon, frustrating the enemy's attempts to use their superior firepower or technology effectively.

Psychological warfare is another critical element of asymmetry. In guerrilla warfare, the goal is not just to inflict physical damage on your opponent but to weaken their resolve. By employing asymmetric tactics, you can exploit the psychological vulnerabilities of a larger force. Constant harassment, sabotage, and the ability to strike unexpectedly create a climate of fear and uncertainty. Over time, this erodes the enemy's morale, causing them to expend energy and resources defending against an unseen threat.

Psychological warfare also involves leveraging your own resilience and ability to endure hardship. As a guerrilla fighter, you are prepared for a protracted conflict, whereas the enemy may be expecting a quick resolution. By outlasting their patience and wearing down their will to fight, you can turn the tide in your favor. Even if the enemy has the upper hand militarily, the mental strain of constant attacks, coupled with the inability to decisively engage or defeat you, will lead to frustration and, eventually, mistakes.

Asymmetry also comes into play when you focus on **targeting vulnerabilities** rather than attempting to engage the enemy's strengths directly. In conventional warfare, the objective might be to defeat the enemy's main force or capture key territory. In guerrilla warfare, however, the focus is on weakening the enemy through indirect methods. This could involve attacking supply lines, disrupting communication networks, or conducting sabotage operations that damage infrastructure.

By focusing on these weak points, you force the enemy to expend significant resources on defense, stretching their forces thinner and making them more vulnerable elsewhere. For example, a small team of guerrilla fighters might destroy a critical bridge or disable a communication tower, causing logistical bottlenecks that affect the entire enemy operation. Such actions may not yield immediate, visible results in terms of territory gained, but they slowly erode the enemy's ability to sustain their operations over time.

Finally, **information warfare** is an essential tool in asymmetric conflict. Information can be more powerful than bullets when used correctly. Disinformation, deception, and manipulation of the enemy's perception are crucial to maintaining the element of surprise and keeping your opponent off balance. You can create false trails, use decoys, or spread rumors that mislead the enemy about your strength, numbers, or intentions. By controlling the flow of information, you can create confusion and force the enemy to make decisions based on faulty intelligence.

At the same time, it is vital to **control the narrative** in the eyes of local populations. Guerrilla warfare often relies on the support or at least the acquiescence of civilians. Maintaining a favorable or neutral stance from the population helps you gather intelligence, gain supplies, and operate freely. By presenting yourself as a protector or a force for good, you can undermine the enemy's legitimacy and increase the pressure on them from multiple angles.

Using asymmetry to your advantage means refusing to engage the enemy on their terms. Instead, you create a conflict where you are strongest—exploiting the enemy's weaknesses, avoiding their strengths, and constantly adapting to changing circumstances. Through mobility, intelligence, psychological pressure, and the effective use of terrain, you turn your disadvantages into assets, ultimately achieving success not through brute force but through strategy, patience, and adaptability.

In a collapsed society, citizen defenders face the unique challenge of protecting themselves, their families, and their communities in an environment where formal institutions have disintegrated, and conventional security forces no longer exist. In such a situation, using asymmetry to your advantage becomes even more critical, as the citizen defender often lacks access to advanced weaponry, organized support, or secure supply chains. Here, the strategies of guerrilla warfare must be adapted specifically to the realities faced by civilians who find themselves in the midst of paramilitary conflict, criminal violence, or territorial control by hostile factions.

The first step for the citizen defender is to **blend into the environment**, both physically and socially. Unlike formal military forces or armed groups, you are not seeking direct confrontation but rather survival and defense. This means becoming invisible when necessary, whether by dressing like the local population or by avoiding drawing attention to yourself or your activities. The ability to seamlessly transition between being a civilian and a defender is key to maintaining mobility and reducing your risk of becoming a target. In urban settings, this might involve wearing common, inconspicuous clothing and using public spaces or abandoned buildings as temporary cover. In rural environments, it could mean using the landscape to hide supply caches, building hidden shelters, or learning to travel without leaving a trace.

As a citizen defender, you are not part of a standing army, and **concealing your intentions and capabilities** from both enemies and potential rivals is vital. This requires strategic use of misinformation, deception, and disinformation. For example, in a neighborhood under threat from organized criminal gangs, you may need to feign compliance while secretly building alliances with other like-minded defenders or stockpiling resources. By carefully controlling what others know about your preparations, you reduce the likelihood of betrayal or preemptive strikes from hostile forces.

In a collapsed society, **information gathering** becomes an even more critical tool. Without access to formal intelligence networks or technological surveillance, you must rely on local knowledge, community networks, and direct observation. One way to maintain a steady flow of intelligence is by establishing a network of trusted individuals who can discreetly share information about movements of hostile groups, shortages of resources, or potential opportunities. For example, a local vendor might hear rumors about which faction is controlling a nearby checkpoint, or a neighbor could have noticed an unfamiliar vehicle patrolling the area. Every piece of information, no matter how small, helps you paint a larger picture of the evolving situation.

It's important to remember that **asymmetry works both**

ways, meaning that you must guard against infiltration, betrayal, or surveillance from hostile elements. Maintaining **operational security** is crucial to preventing sensitive information from falling into enemy hands. In a collapsed society, the lines between friend and foe can blur, and trust must be carefully built and maintained. Limiting the number of people who know about your defensive plans, supply locations, or movements reduces the risk of leaks. Furthermore, maintaining compartmentalized information within your group ensures that if one member is compromised, they cannot expose the entirety of your network.

Citizen defenders must also embrace **mobility as a defensive tool**. In a collapsed society, fixed positions, such as homes or communal defense points, can quickly become liabilities. Once your defensive position is known, it can be targeted by hostile forces seeking to raid your supplies or eliminate you as a threat. To avoid this, adopt a **mobile defense strategy** that allows you to quickly relocate when necessary. This could involve preparing multiple fallback locations, whether they are abandoned buildings, underground shelters, or safe houses set up with allies. By keeping your movements fluid and unpredictable, you make it more difficult for enemies to track or trap you.

For example, if criminal groups are known to operate in certain areas at predictable times, your mobility allows you to avoid their patrols while still securing necessary supplies or conducting reconnaissance. You can establish **temporary defensive perimeters** only when needed, such as during supply runs or when repelling direct attacks, then disband and relocate before your position is compromised. This reduces your risk of becoming cornered or outgunned by superior forces.

In terms of offensive tactics, **hit-and-run operations** can be adapted to the scale of a civilian defense. Instead of large-scale engagements, your goal is to harass and disrupt enemies without exposing yourself to unnecessary risk. This could involve small ambushes or sabotage operations designed to weaken the enemy without direct confrontation. For instance, targeting a group's supply lines by puncturing vehicle tires, damaging fuel reserves, or cutting off access to essential resources can force a hostile group to expend energy defending these critical assets instead of advancing their control. Simple acts of sabotage, like disabling communication equipment or blocking access roads with debris, can slow down a stronger force and buy time for defenders to regroup or escape.

Psychological warfare is particularly effective in the context of citizen defense. Even small groups of defenders can create an outsized impression of their strength through **rumor and deception**. Spreading misinformation about the size or capabilities of your group can make enemies overestimate the risks of engaging with you, prompting them to avoid direct conflict or waste resources on defensive measures against threats that do not exist. For example, if hostile factions believe that your neighborhood is heavily fortified or booby-trapped, they may choose to bypass it entirely, sparing your community from unnecessary violence.

At the same time, **maintaining the morale** of your own group is equally important. In a collapsed society, where despair and hopelessness can take root, the psychological resilience of defenders can be the difference between survival and defeat. Ensuring that your group understands the **long-term nature** of the conflict is crucial, as guerrilla warfare—especially in a civilian context—is a war of endurance. You may not win every engagement, but your survival depends on your ability to regroup, adapt, and outlast opponents who may be more concerned with short-term gains.

Citizen defenders must also be prepared for **resource scarcity** and the potential for supply lines to be cut off entirely. While guerrilla forces often rely on external support or sympathetic populations, in a collapsed society, you may find yourself isolated, with little outside help. **Resource management** becomes a critical aspect of your defense strategy. You should create hidden supply caches in multiple locations to ensure that food, water, medicine, and ammunition are accessible even if your primary stockpiles are compromised. These caches should be carefully hidden and protected, ensuring that they are not easily found by scavengers or hostile groups.

Finally, **alliances with local populations** play a pivotal role in the success of citizen defense. In many cases, the local civilian population will be caught between rival groups or criminal factions, unsure of who to trust. By offering protection, sharing resources, or providing security, you can cultivate support among civilians, who in turn may offer valuable intelligence, shelter, or assistance. Winning over the population is not only about providing for their material needs—it's about demonstrating that you are a stabilizing force in a chaotic environment. The trust and cooperation of the local population can provide you with safe harbor, early warnings about enemy movements, and a broader network for gathering intelligence.

As a citizen defender in a collapsed society, you are not fighting a conventional war. Your primary objective is survival, and the application of asymmetrical tactics allows you to achieve this goal while minimizing direct confrontation and maximizing the impact of your efforts. By staying mobile, using the terrain and urban landscapes to your advantage, maintaining operational security, and leveraging psychological warfare, you can defend against stronger enemies and continue to protect your community against the ongoing threats that define life in a lawless environment.

Mobility, Stealth, and Hit-and-Run Strategies

Mobility, stealth, and hit-and-run strategies form the backbone of guerrilla warfare for the citizen defender in a collapsed society. These tactics enable defenders to compensate for their relative lack of resources, manpower, and firepower by focusing on speed, surprise, and the element of unpredictability. In an environment where conventional defenses are overwhelmed or ineffective, mastering these strategies can keep you alive, allowing you to engage stronger enemies on your own terms and retreat before becoming vulnerable to counterattacks.

Mobility is essential for survival in a fluid, ever-changing environment. Unlike conventional forces, which may rely on fortified positions or secure bases, the citizen defender must remain light and ready to relocate at a moment's notice. In a collapsed society, where threats can emerge quickly from any direction, being tethered to a fixed location often becomes a liability. The ability to move quickly, whether to avoid an advancing force, gather supplies, or take advantage of a strategic opportunity, allows you to stay ahead of potential threats and maintain a tactical advantage.

One of the key principles of mobility is **not becoming attached to any one place for too long**. Whether you're operating in an urban or rural environment, your base of operations should never be static. If enemies know where to find you, they can surround, siege, or raid your position. By moving frequently and unpredictably, you deny the enemy the opportunity to prepare a concentrated attack. In urban environments, this might involve rotating between safe houses, shifting from one section of a neighborhood to another, or using abandoned buildings to keep your movements hidden. In rural environments, it could mean using natural features like forests, mountains, or rivers to relocate frequently, making it difficult for the enemy to pin down your exact location.

Stealth complements mobility by allowing you to remain undetected as you move. Operating quietly and out of sight is critical when navigating hostile areas. The less visible and audible you are, the less likely you are to encounter resistance or draw attention to your movements. Stealth requires discipline in everything from choosing the right time to move to how you communicate with your group. Night movements, for example, offer better concealment and are harder for enemies to track, but they require you to have the skills and equipment necessary for navigation in darkness.

In urban environments, stealth often means **blending in** with civilian populations. By maintaining a low profile and using the chaos of a collapsed society to your advantage, you can avoid drawing attention to yourself. You may need to dress in ordinary clothing, avoid carrying obvious weapons, and use the natural ebb and flow of people and vehicles to cover your movements. In rural areas, stealth might involve using natural cover like trees, hills, and water sources to obscure your movements. Whether you are moving alone or in a small group, maintaining sound discipline—minimizing noise from gear, communications, or footsteps—can prevent detection.

Stealth also extends to how you manage **supply runs and reconnaissance**. Moving discreetly when gathering food, water, or other resources ensures that you do not expose your cache locations or your group's size and capabilities. Keeping your operations under the radar reduces the chance that enemies or rival groups will intercept you during these vulnerable moments.

Once you've mastered mobility and stealth, **hit-and-run strategies** become your most effective offensive tactic. In the face of a superior enemy, direct confrontation is rarely an option. Instead, your objective is to harass and disrupt the enemy without giving them the chance to retaliate. Hit-and-run tactics allow you to strike when the enemy is vulnerable—such as during supply runs, troop movements, or while they are focused on securing a fixed position—and retreat before they can mount a counteroffensive.

Hit-and-run tactics rely on the **element of surprise**. You must gather intelligence on your enemy's movements, routines, and weaknesses to identify the perfect time to strike. The goal is to engage quickly, inflict maximum damage in a short window, and retreat before the enemy can organize a meaningful response. For example, if an armed group regularly uses a certain road to transport supplies, you can set up an ambush by using hidden positions near the route. After launching the attack, your group should immediately fall back to avoid being drawn into a prolonged engagement. The success of these operations doesn't necessarily hinge on destroying the enemy but on disrupting their operations, instilling fear, and forcing them to dedicate additional resources to defense.

In urban environments, hit-and-run tactics can be especially effective when combined with **urban guerrilla tactics**, such as using alleyways, rooftops, and underground tunnels for quick entry and exit points. These environments provide natural cover and make it difficult for the enemy to respond swiftly or pursue you. A hit-and-run attack in an urban setting could involve damaging a key piece of infrastructure—like a communication tower or a fuel depot—and then immediately melting back into the city before the enemy can retaliate.

In rural or wilderness environments, hit-and-run strategies often involve **ambushes and sabotage**. Forests, hills, and other natural landscapes can be used to set traps or lay ambushes at chokepoints, such as narrow mountain passes, bridges, or roadblocks. Once the attack is complete, you use your knowledge of the terrain to escape quickly, making it difficult for the enemy to follow. Sabotage, such as cutting fuel lines or damaging key supply routes, forces the enemy to expend resources on repairs and slows down their advance, giving you time to prepare for future engagements.

It's important to note that the success of hit-and-run operations depends on **maintaining discipline**. Guerrilla fighters must resist the temptation to engage in prolonged firefights, as these can quickly turn the tables in favor of a better-equipped adversary. Once the mission is complete, your group must retreat without hesitation, regrouping at a pre-designated safe location. This requires precise planning, where every member of the group knows their role, the escape routes, and the fallback plan in the event of complications.

A key part of hit-and-run success is also **psychological warfare**. Each attack, though small in scale, has a cumulative effect on your enemy's morale. The constant threat of attack, the knowledge that no place is truly safe, and the feeling of being watched or stalked wear down an enemy over time. While the physical damage of a single hit-and-run raid might be minimal, the psychological impact can force an enemy to divert resources toward defense, limit their movements, or become overly cautious, making them less effective in the field.

To reinforce these tactics, citizen defenders should establish a **network of secure routes and safe houses** to ensure that after an operation, they can retreat to safety without being tracked or ambushed in turn. Establishing multiple fallback positions also prevents the enemy from discovering a central base of operations, allowing your group to remain elusive even after multiple engagements.

Lastly, **speed and adaptability** are critical. Hit-and-run tactics are most effective when your group is able to assess the situation in real time and adjust quickly. Flexibility in planning allows you to capitalize on emerging opportunities or abandon operations when the risk outweighs the reward. Training in rapid decision-making and practicing various retreat strategies ensures that your group can fluidly adapt to changing conditions during an engagement.

For the citizen defender, mastering mobility, stealth, and hit-and-run tactics is essential for surviving and resisting in a collapsed society. These strategies give you the ability to confront stronger opponents without falling into their trap of direct confrontation, allowing you to dictate the terms of engagement and live to fight another day. Through constant movement, careful planning, and well-executed attacks, you can protect yourself and your community from overwhelming forces while keeping the enemy off balance, always one step behind.

CHAPTER 4: SMALL ARMS AND TACTICAL PROFICIENCY

In a collapsed society, where formal security structures have dissolved and the rule of law no longer holds, the ability to defend oneself and one's community becomes paramount. While strategic thinking, mobility, and guerrilla tactics provide the framework for survival, none of these strategies can be executed effectively without a solid grasp of small arms handling and tactical proficiency. This chapter delves into the fundamental skills required to operate small arms safely and efficiently, along with the tactical awareness necessary to ensure that every shot counts.

Small arms—whether they are handguns, rifles, or shotguns—are the primary tools of self-defense in environments where chaos reigns. These weapons are not only crucial for defending against hostile forces but also for establishing a credible deterrent that may prevent attacks from occurring in the first place. However, owning a firearm is not enough. The difference between a survivor and a casualty in such a high-stakes environment often comes down to the operator's skill level and their ability to integrate small arms use into broader tactical plans. Tactical proficiency isn't just about being able to fire a weapon—it's about understanding how, when, and where to employ it effectively under the extreme stress of life-threatening situations.

Understanding the Role of Small Arms in Asymmetric Warfare

In the context of a societal collapse, small arms are typically the most accessible form of defense for civilians. These weapons are portable, versatile, and, when properly used, provide enough firepower to fend off attackers, conduct hit-and-run operations, or protect critical resources. Unlike military-grade equipment, which is often difficult to obtain or maintain in such conditions, small arms can be readily sourced and maintained by individuals or small groups.

The first step to tactical proficiency with small arms is understanding the **specific role they play in asymmetric conflict**. You are not engaging in prolonged firefights with a well-equipped enemy; rather, your objective is to use your weapon as part of a broader strategy of survival and resistance. This means knowing when to fire and when to remain hidden, when to engage directly and when to retreat, and how to use your weapon to protect your mobility and stealth rather than relying on brute force. In asymmetric warfare, each bullet counts, and the noise, attention, and resources used in any engagement must be carefully weighed against the potential gains.

FIREARMS HANDLING AND SAFETY

Before diving into tactical maneuvers, the foundation of all small arms use is **firearms handling and safety**. In a lawless environment, where accidents can have fatal consequences, every member of a defensive group must be well-versed in the safe and responsible handling of firearms. This includes understanding the mechanics of the weapon—how to load, clear, and maintain it—as well as the principles of muzzle discipline, trigger control, and situational awareness. Poor firearms handling can lead to friendly fire incidents, unnecessary noise, or even the loss of your weapon in a critical moment. Mastering these basics ensures that you remain in control of your weapon at all times, reducing the risk of accidents or mistakes under pressure.

MARKSMANSHIP UNDER PRESSURE

In the chaos of a collapsed society, engagements are often fast, unpredictable, and chaotic. The ability to accurately fire your weapon under stress is what separates tactical proficiency from mere possession. **Marksmanship under pressure** involves the ability to quickly acquire targets, maintain control of your weapon during rapid fire, and adjust to moving or obscured threats. In real-world situations, you rarely have the luxury of time or a stable firing position, so your ability to hit targets in dynamic, high-stress environments becomes critical.

This means training with your weapon in conditions that simulate the unpredictability of combat. Shooting while moving, engaging multiple targets in quick succession, and maintaining accuracy in low-visibility or high-stress situations are all skills that must be practiced. Tactical proficiency is not about hitting a stationary target at the range —it's about being able to perform when your life is on the line.

CLOSE-QUARTERS COMBAT (CQC) CONSIDERATIONS

In urban settings or enclosed environments, **close-quarters combat (CQC)** becomes a necessary skill for the citizen defender. This involves maneuvering through tight spaces, such as buildings, hallways, or vehicles, where engagements occur at extremely short ranges. CQC is high-risk and fast-paced, requiring split-second decisions, rapid movement, and precise shooting. Small arms, especially handguns and short-barreled rifles, are ideal for these situations due to their maneuverability in confined spaces.

Tactical proficiency in CQC focuses not only on shooting

accurately but also on maintaining spatial awareness, using cover effectively, and minimizing your exposure to threats. The ability to **clear rooms, move through urban environments**, and engage threats at close range without exposing yourself unnecessarily can often determine whether you survive an ambush or attack in these environments. Defensive techniques such as slicing the pie, using doorways and walls for cover, and communicating with teammates are crucial components of CQC tactics.

FIRE AND MANEUVER: TEAM-BASED TACTICS

For groups defending themselves in a collapsed society, the principle of **fire and maneuver** becomes a central tactic. This involves coordinating the use of small arms to engage an enemy while moving to better positions or retreating. The key to fire and maneuver is teamwork—one part of the group provides suppressive fire, keeping the enemy pinned down, while the other part moves to a more advantageous position, whether to flank the enemy, escape, or find cover. This requires clear communication, trust, and practice, as well as an understanding of how to balance offense and defense.

In fire and maneuver, **covering fire** doesn't need to be accurate —its purpose is to make the enemy hesitant to engage or move. While one group provides this fire, the other moves quickly and quietly, either advancing or retreating as necessary. The ability to perform this tactic well can give small, lightly armed groups the opportunity to survive engagements with larger forces by staying mobile and unpredictable.

AMMUNITION CONSERVATION AND TACTICAL RELOADING

In a collapsed society, ammunition is a finite resource. Each round you fire not only gives away your position, but it also depletes your stock of ammunition, which may be difficult or impossible to replace. **Ammunition conservation** becomes a critical aspect of tactical proficiency, and every shot must be fired with purpose. This means avoiding "spray and pray" tactics and focusing instead on making each shot count. A key part of this discipline is knowing when to engage and when to conserve ammunition by remaining hidden or using alternative defensive strategies.

In addition, **tactical reloading**—the ability to quickly and efficiently reload your weapon during an engagement—can mean the difference between life and death. Reloading under pressure, while still keeping situational awareness, is a skill that must be practiced repeatedly until it becomes second nature. Understanding the balance between using your weapon aggressively and conserving ammo for critical moments is one of the hallmarks of a proficient defender.

WEAPON MAINTENANCE AND RELIABILITY

In a collapsed society, your access to new weapons or professional gunsmiths will be limited or non-existent. This makes **weapon maintenance** a critical survival skill. A firearm that jams or malfunctions in the middle of an engagement is worse than useless—it's a liability. Tactical proficiency means not only knowing how to shoot but also understanding how to keep your weapon in working condition. Regular cleaning, lubrication, and inspection of key components will ensure that your weapon functions when you need it most.

Knowing how to fix common malfunctions, such as clearing jams or replacing worn-out parts, is also essential. Improvised solutions may be required to keep your weapons operational, especially if spare parts are difficult to come by. A reliable weapon is the foundation of all defensive strategies, and maintaining it is your responsibility.

MINDSET AND TACTICAL DECISION-MAKING

Beyond physical skill, tactical proficiency with small arms requires the development of a **combat mindset**. This means staying calm under pressure, thinking critically during engagements, and making quick, informed decisions. In a survival context, every engagement is a high-stakes scenario. The ability to stay focused and make calculated decisions —whether to engage, retreat, or seek cover—ensures that you maximize your chances of survival while minimizing unnecessary risks.

Having a well-honed tactical mindset also involves understanding your own limitations and those of your group. It's about knowing when to take the shot and when to hold back, and always keeping the broader strategy in mind rather than getting caught up in the chaos of the moment. Tactical proficiency is not just a physical skill—it's a mental discipline that will guide every action you take in a collapsed society.

In this chapter, you will learn the skills necessary to handle small arms with confidence and precision, incorporating them into the broader tactics needed for survival in a lawless environment. From close-quarters combat to team-based maneuvers, these techniques will allow you to defend yourself and those you care about, ensuring that you can remain a force to be reckoned with even when the odds are stacked against you.

Mastering Small Arms in Urban and Rural Combat

In a world where the rule of law no longer functions, the ability to effectively wield small arms becomes essential for personal and communal defense. Whether you find yourself navigating the tight, labyrinthine streets of a collapsed urban environment or the open, rugged terrain of rural landscapes, your proficiency with small arms will be the difference between life and death. Urban and rural combat each present unique challenges and advantages, requiring a keen understanding of how to adapt small arms tactics to your surroundings. The citizen defender must be able to fluidly transition between these environments, leveraging the strengths of their weaponry while mitigating its limitations.

URBAN COMBAT: NAVIGATING THE CLOSE-QUARTERS BATTLEFIELD

Urban combat presents one of the most complex and dangerous scenarios for the citizen defender. In densely populated or abandoned cities, streets become chokepoints, buildings become potential strongholds, and every corner could conceal an enemy. The close-quarters nature of urban environments makes engagements fast and brutal, with little room for error. In such scenarios, mastering small arms use is critical not only for survival but also for maintaining mobility and securing key positions within the urban landscape.

The first and most important concept to understand in urban combat is **close-quarters engagement**. Most firefights in urban areas take place at distances far shorter than in rural environments, often within the confines of buildings or streets where visibility is limited, and reaction times are compressed. This means that weapons like handguns, shotguns, and short-barreled rifles become more effective, as they are easier to maneuver in tight spaces and allow for faster target acquisition at short ranges.

As you move through the urban environment, **weapon readiness** is critical. In close-quarters combat, you will have little warning before an engagement begins, meaning that your weapon should always be loaded, with a round chambered, and kept in a ready position. Being caught with your weapon unloaded or holstered could lead to disaster in the split second it takes to draw or chamber a round. You should maintain a low, ready position as you move, allowing you to quickly raise your weapon to fire while still keeping it under control in confined spaces.

Movement through buildings and streets also requires a

nuanced understanding of tactical proficiency. One of the greatest dangers in urban combat is overexposing yourself —whether moving through a doorway or crossing an open street. You must constantly use the environment to your advantage, sticking close to walls, avoiding open areas, and always staying behind cover. For instance, when crossing a street, you should sprint quickly from one point of cover to another, never lingering in the open. When entering buildings, you must be aware of **blind spots**, stairwells, and windows that could expose you to hidden threats.

Small arms tactics in urban environments often involve **room clearing** or engaging enemies from within confined areas like hallways or apartments. In these scenarios, you need to move deliberately and methodically, clearing each section of the room before advancing. The use of techniques such as slicing the pie—where you gradually clear an area by taking small steps around corners, keeping your weapon pointed toward any potential threat—is critical to avoiding unnecessary exposure. When entering a room, your weapon should lead your movements, always ready to fire the moment a threat is detected.

Using cover effectively is another essential aspect of urban combat. Buildings, vehicles, and debris can all provide cover, but not all cover is created equal. Understanding the difference between **cover and concealment**—where cover can stop bullets, while concealment merely hides you—will guide your movement through hostile urban environments. Concrete walls, metal vehicles, or dense structures provide good cover from small arms fire, while wooden fences or drywall may offer little protection beyond hiding your position temporarily.

In urban combat, it's also important to be mindful of **ammunition conservation**. Extended firefights are dangerous in urban areas, as the noise from gunfire will draw other hostile groups or scavengers. If your objective is to escape, make each shot count and disengage as soon as possible to avoid getting pinned down or attracting reinforcements. Running out of ammunition during a prolonged engagement in the middle of a city, where resupply is scarce, can leave you vulnerable. Plan each engagement carefully, and always maintain an escape route.

Lastly, **sound discipline** is critical in urban combat. The sound of gunfire, footsteps, or talking can travel far through streets and alleys, alerting enemies to your presence. Silenced weapons or suppressors, when available, provide a significant advantage, allowing you to neutralize threats without drawing attention. However, even without suppressors, minimizing unnecessary noise—whether from moving quickly through debris or loudly communicating with others—will help you maintain the element of surprise.

RURAL COMBAT: MASTERING DISTANCE AND TERRAIN

In rural environments, combat takes on a different character. Here, engagements tend to occur over longer distances, with terrain playing a critical role in determining the flow of battle. Open fields, forests, hills, and rivers all provide natural obstacles that can either work to your advantage or leave you exposed. In rural combat, the emphasis shifts from close-quarters firefights to engagements where precision, patience, and a strong understanding of your environment are key to success.

One of the defining features of rural combat is **long-range engagement**. Unlike in urban settings, where most firefights occur within a few meters, rural combat often involves targets hundreds of meters away. Rifles and carbines, particularly those with optics or scopes, become the primary weapons of choice due to their range and accuracy. The ability to **engage targets at distance** allows you to harass or eliminate threats before they can close the gap, giving you the upper hand in most rural engagements.

Marksmanship skills take on heightened importance in rural combat. In these environments, you often have time to line up shots, but the margin for error is small, particularly at long distances. Your ability to adjust for wind, bullet drop, and movement over long ranges is critical, and training in these conditions is essential. The use of optics, such as rifle scopes, can dramatically increase your effective range, allowing you to take precision shots from cover without revealing your position.

The **terrain** in rural environments offers both opportunities and challenges. Forests, hills, and ravines provide natural cover and concealment, allowing you to move undetected or set up ambushes. However, open fields, flat plains, or exposed ridgelines can leave you vulnerable to long-range fire. Mastering the art of **using the terrain to your advantage** involves understanding the lay of the land, knowing where to move and where to avoid, and identifying natural chokepoints or defensible positions.

For example, in a wooded area, moving through dense forest offers concealment but limits visibility. You must remain alert for ambushes or enemy movement in such areas, using the cover of trees and foliage to approach undetected. In open fields or mountainous regions, you need to identify **natural cover**, such as large rocks, dips in the ground, or water sources, to avoid being spotted and neutralized by enemy marksmen.

In rural combat, **mobility and patience** are vital. Engaging from a distance allows you to take the initiative, but it also means you must be prepared to **move quickly** once the engagement begins. Remaining in one place for too long in a rural setting increases the likelihood of being flanked or tracked. After taking a shot or engaging the enemy, you should immediately relocate, using the terrain to disappear from sight and prevent your position from being compromised.

Rural combat also offers ample opportunity for **ambushes and hit-and-run tactics**. Isolated roads, bridges, or narrow trails provide perfect chokepoints for ambushing enemies, especially those relying on vehicles or large convoys. Using high ground to gain a tactical advantage, you can fire on unsuspecting enemies and quickly retreat into the natural cover of forests or hills, making it difficult for the enemy to pursue. Rural environments also allow for greater use of camouflage, making it harder for enemies to track your movements or detect your presence.

Weapon maintenance becomes even more critical in rural combat, where environmental factors like mud, rain, dust, and extreme temperatures can affect the reliability of your weapon. Ensuring that your firearm is clean and operational before any engagement will prevent jams or malfunctions that could prove deadly in the field.

Lastly, **resourcefulness** plays a significant role in rural combat. Ammunition, food, and water may be scarce, and resupplying from outside sources might be impossible. Learning to forage, find clean water, and ration ammunition effectively will ensure that you can maintain combat effectiveness over extended periods, especially when retreating into remote or wilderness areas.

For the citizen defender, mastering small arms in both urban and rural combat means understanding how to adapt your tactics, weapon choices, and mindset to the specific challenges of each environment. In urban settings, speed, close-quarters proficiency, and cover are your greatest assets, while in rural areas, patience, precision, and the intelligent use of terrain will help you outmaneuver and outlast stronger forces. Whether navigating through city streets or rugged landscapes, your ability to integrate small arms into your broader tactical strategy is what will keep you alive and able to protect those who rely on you in a lawless world.

Weapon Selection, Maintenance, and Ammunition Conservation

In a world where the rule of law no longer functions, the selection and maintenance of your weaponry, as well as the conservation of ammunition, become critical to your survival. The weapon you choose will determine not only your combat effectiveness but also your ability to defend yourself, your family, and your community in the face of mounting threats. Proper weapon maintenance ensures that your firearm functions when needed, and conserving ammunition ensures that you remain combat-ready in an environment where resupply may be difficult or impossible.

The primary goal is to ensure that every shot, every engagement, and every decision regarding your weapon and ammunition is rooted in practicality, efficiency, and necessity. As a citizen defender, the choices you make in weapon selection, upkeep, and ammunition usage will have long-term consequences for your ability to survive in an unstable and hostile environment.

WEAPON SELECTION: PRACTICALITY AND PURPOSE

The weapon you choose must fit your specific needs, skill level, and environment. In a collapsed society, access to a wide variety of firearms may be limited, so your selection process should prioritize versatility, reliability, and ease of use. Weapons that are prone to malfunctions, hard to maintain, or require specialized ammunition are liabilities that you cannot afford when every encounter could be life-threatening.

For many citizen defenders, the ideal weapon is one that balances **portability, ease of use, and firepower**. While high-caliber weapons or complex systems might offer raw power, they also require more maintenance, tend to weigh more, and often necessitate specialized training. You should aim for a firearm that you can easily carry, handle, and maintain, but one that also provides enough stopping power to neutralize threats in various environments.

1. **Handguns** are often the most accessible and versatile weapons in a collapsed society. Their compact size makes them easy to carry, conceal, and use in close-quarters combat. Handguns are especially useful in urban settings where engagements may occur at short distances, such as inside buildings or narrow alleyways. However, they lack the range and stopping power of rifles or shotguns, making them less effective in open rural environments.

2. **Shotguns** are highly effective at short ranges and ideal for use in close-quarters situations where precision is less critical. Shotguns are also versatile in terms of ammunition—buckshot, slugs, and even less-lethal rounds can be utilized depending on the situation. However, shotguns are heavy, have limited magazine capacity, and are less effective at longer ranges.

3. **Rifles and Carbines** provide greater range, accuracy, and firepower than handguns or shotguns. In rural environments or areas where long-range engagements are likely, a rifle's ability to reach out and engage targets at distance is invaluable. Semi-automatic rifles with detachable magazines are particularly effective for hit-and-run tactics, allowing for rapid fire and quick reloading. However, rifles tend to be heavier and more cumbersome in close-quarters combat, so they must be used in conjunction with good tactical movement.

When choosing a weapon, consider the **availability of ammunition**. In a collapsed society, specific ammunition calibers may be difficult to come by. Opting for common calibers—such as 9mm for handguns, 12-gauge for shotguns, or 5.56mm and 7.62mm for rifles—ensures that you have a better chance of finding or trading for ammo when resupply options are scarce. The last thing you want is to be carrying a powerful weapon that you can no longer feed.

WEAPON MAINTENANCE: ENSURING RELIABILITY

Once you've selected your weapon, keeping it in working condition is your next priority. In a chaotic environment, regular access to gunsmiths or parts will be nearly impossible, meaning that the responsibility for maintaining your weapon falls squarely on your shoulders. **A well-maintained weapon is a reliable weapon**, and reliability is non-negotiable when your life is on the line.

The fundamentals of weapon maintenance include:

1. **Regular cleaning**: Dirt, moisture, and carbon buildup can quickly cause a firearm to jam or malfunction, especially in harsh environments. After every engagement or extended period of use, your weapon should be cleaned and lubricated. This ensures smooth operation and reduces wear on moving parts. If you are in a particularly dirty or wet environment, clean your weapon more frequently.

2. **Inspecting key components**: You must frequently check the **barrel, bolt, firing pin, extractor, and magazines** for any signs of wear, damage, or debris. These components are the most prone to malfunction if not properly maintained. For example, a damaged firing pin or a worn extractor can cause your weapon to fail at the worst possible moment. Regular inspection allows you to address issues before they become critical.

3. **Lubrication**: Friction is the enemy of any mechanical system, and firearms are no different. A well-lubricated weapon will operate more smoothly and be less prone to jamming. However, you need to strike a balance: too much

lubrication in dusty or sandy environments can cause debris to stick to internal components, creating new problems. Understand the conditions in which you're operating and adjust accordingly.

4. **Field repairs and spare parts**: You should be familiar with how to perform **basic field repairs** on your weapon. This might involve clearing a jam, replacing a spring, or reassembling parts after disassembly. In a long-term collapse, you should also **stockpile spare parts**—particularly for critical areas like the firing pin, extractor, or magazines—that are prone to wear over time.

A weapon is only as effective as its operator's ability to maintain it. Familiarize yourself with the **disassembly and reassembly** of your weapon so that you can clean and repair it under any circumstances, even if resources are limited. The more you understand your firearm's mechanics, the better you'll be at keeping it operational in the long term.

AMMUNITION CONSERVATION: MAKING EVERY ROUND COUNT

In a world where ammunition is a finite and precious resource, **conserving ammo** is paramount. The luxury of firing indiscriminately or wasting bullets on low-value targets is something you cannot afford. Each round fired should be calculated and purposeful. Your stockpile may be all you have for the foreseeable future, so it must be preserved carefully.

To conserve ammunition effectively, you need to develop both **discipline and marksmanship**. The first step in conservation is simply learning to resist firing unless absolutely necessary. A few key principles guide this effort:

1. **Aim with intent**: Every shot should be aimed carefully, especially in engagements where ammunition is scarce. Spray-and-pray tactics are a waste of valuable rounds. Developing your **marksmanship skills** so that you can reliably hit your target under pressure is essential. Regular practice

in real-world conditions—moving targets, varying distances, and low-light situations—will help improve your accuracy, reducing the need to fire multiple rounds to neutralize a threat.

2. **Avoid unnecessary engagements**: In a collapsed society, firefights are unpredictable and dangerous. Engaging in a gunfight should be a last resort. If the situation allows, use stealth, mobility, or diplomacy to avoid direct conflict, preserving your ammunition for when it's truly needed. By picking your battles wisely, you can conserve both your bullets and your life.

3. **Fire in controlled bursts or single shots**: In situations where rapid fire is necessary, controlled bursts of 2-3 rounds ensure that you stay on target without emptying your magazine too quickly. Semi-automatic rifles should be fired in single, controlled shots to conserve ammunition and maintain accuracy.

4. **Stockpiling ammunition**: In the lead-up to or aftermath of societal collapse, **stockpiling ammunition** becomes a critical preparation. However, stockpiling doesn't end with simply acquiring rounds; you also need to store them properly. Moisture, extreme temperatures, and improper handling can damage ammunition, rendering it useless. Storing ammunition in dry, cool places, preferably in sealed containers or ammo cans with desiccants to remove moisture, will ensure it remains viable when needed.

5. **Reloading spent casings**: If you have the knowledge and equipment, **reloading spent casings** allows you to extend your ammunition supply. While this requires access to the proper tools, reloading supplies (powder, primers, and projectiles), and time, it is an invaluable skill in long-term survival situations where new ammunition might not be available. Knowing how to safely reload your own rounds can make a significant difference in a prolonged collapse.

6. **Salvaging and scavenging**: In a lawless world, scavenging for ammunition from abandoned buildings, vehicles, or fallen enemies is often a necessity. Understanding the most common calibers in your area and which weapons are most frequently used will help you make decisions about what to search for. However, not all found ammunition is reliable, so inspect any salvaged rounds for signs of moisture damage or degradation before use.

Ammunition conservation, much like weapon maintenance, is a form of discipline. Every round you fire should have a purpose, and every engagement should be weighed against the cost of expending limited resources. Over time, this mindset becomes second nature, ensuring that you remain effective as a defender while minimizing unnecessary waste.

By mastering the principles of **weapon selection, maintenance, and ammunition conservation**, you position yourself to be an effective and reliable defender in a lawless society. Your choice of weapon should reflect the realities of your environment and the availability of ammunition, while your maintenance skills ensure that your firearm remains operational in any situation. Above all, your ability to conserve and use ammunition efficiently guarantees that you can endure over the long haul, continuing to defend yourself and those around you, even when resources grow scarce.

Precision and Discipline in Firefights

In a collapsed society where resources are limited, and every engagement could be your last, the need for precision and discipline in firefights cannot be overstated. The citizen defender must approach every encounter with a mindset that prioritizes efficiency, control, and purpose. Gone are the days of relying on overwhelming firepower or endless supplies of ammunition; in this new reality, each shot matters. Precision and discipline in firefights are what separate those who survive from those who waste their resources, expose their positions, and ultimately fall to stronger forces.

Precision in combat is about more than just marksmanship. It is the ability to remain calm and focused under extreme stress, making calculated decisions and only firing when it's strategically advantageous. Discipline, on the other hand, is the mental and tactical control you exercise throughout a firefight—resisting the impulse to shoot recklessly, managing your ammunition wisely, and maintaining situational awareness to ensure you don't compromise your position or waste valuable resources.

MASTERING PRECISION: MAKING EVERY SHOT COUNT

Precision begins with an understanding of marksmanship, but it extends to every aspect of how you engage the enemy. Every bullet fired must have a purpose, and that purpose must be aligned with your broader strategy. Firing indiscriminately is not only a waste of ammunition, but it also gives away your position and reduces your ability to respond effectively to a dynamic and changing threat environment.

To achieve precision in firefights, you must first focus on **accuracy under pressure**. Combat is chaotic, with unpredictable movements, shifting conditions, and high-stakes threats. Maintaining accuracy under such conditions requires training your body and mind to react instinctively while keeping calm. This means practicing in conditions that simulate real-world engagements, such as firing while moving, engaging multiple targets, and maintaining accuracy in low-light situations.

Your shooting stance, grip, and breathing all contribute to precision. In a firefight, you may not have time to assume a perfect firing stance, but by practicing consistent fundamentals, you can maintain stability and control, even in less-than-ideal situations. When engaging a target, **focus on controlled, accurate shots**, rather than relying on rapid fire. Precision is about minimizing the number of rounds fired while maximizing their effectiveness.

Target identification is another crucial component of precision. In a collapsed society, where various hostile factions, criminal groups, or even other defenders may be present, you cannot afford to engage indiscriminately. Shooting the wrong person—whether a civilian or a potential ally—can have catastrophic consequences. Before you fire, ensure that your target is clearly identified as a threat. In urban environments, where civilians might be present, this becomes especially important.

Fire discipline also extends to understanding your weapon's effective range. Whether you're using a handgun, shotgun, or rifle, know the limits of your firearm's accuracy and stopping power. Engaging targets beyond the effective range of your weapon leads to wasted ammunition and missed opportunities. For example, attempting long-range shots with a handgun when a rifle is required is an exercise in futility and will only serve to expose your position without any strategic gain. Familiarize yourself with your weapon's capabilities and limitations through consistent practice in real-world conditions.

Situational awareness is another critical component of precision. Firing without considering the broader environment—whether it's the position of other defenders, civilians, or hostile groups—can lead to friendly fire incidents or missed opportunities. Before pulling the trigger, assess not just the target, but also the backdrop, the escape routes, and the potential for retaliation. Precision in firefights is about thinking one step ahead: ensuring that each round fired furthers your objectives without unnecessarily escalating the situation or placing you at greater risk.

Fire in controlled bursts if using semi-automatic or automatic weapons. Controlled bursts allow you to keep your weapon on target while preventing overheating or wasting ammunition. If using a rifle with a burst or automatic function, always aim for the upper torso or center mass of the target to maximize your chances of landing effective hits.

DISCIPLINE: KNOWING WHEN AND WHEN NOT TO SHOOT

Discipline in firefights is what allows you to control the engagement, keeping you and your group alive while minimizing unnecessary risks. It's about recognizing that not every situation requires you to fire your weapon. In many cases, staying hidden or retreating may be more advantageous than engaging in a prolonged firefight.

The first step in maintaining discipline is **assessing the tactical situation** before opening fire. Does engaging the enemy at this moment serve your long-term strategy? Will it alert other hostile forces to your presence? Do you have a clear escape route if the firefight escalates beyond your control? Discipline means considering these factors before firing a single shot. If engaging will give away your position or draw in reinforcements, it may be better to remain undetected or find a way to disengage entirely.

In a collapsed society, **managing your ammunition supply** is critical. Ammo is finite, and once it's gone, you may not have the luxury of replenishing it. Discipline in firefights means firing only when necessary, aiming to incapacitate or neutralize threats with minimal shots. Each round should be fired with intent, rather than out of panic or a desire to overwhelm the enemy with noise. The more disciplined you are with your ammunition, the longer you'll be able to sustain yourself through the inevitable conflicts of a lawless world.

Discipline also involves **coordinating with your group**

if you are not fighting alone. A well-coordinated group can alternate between engaging the enemy and reloading, ensuring that someone is always providing cover fire while others reposition or conserve ammunition. **Communication** is key—whether through hand signals, pre-established codes, or verbal commands, ensuring that everyone in your group knows when to fire and when to hold back will prevent chaotic, disorganized engagements.

Another aspect of discipline is understanding **the concept of retreat**. Sometimes, the best course of action is to disengage, fall back, and regroup. This is not a sign of weakness, but a recognition that survival often depends on knowing when to withdraw. If the enemy has superior numbers, firepower, or tactical advantage, holding your ground could lead to unnecessary losses. In a firefight, maintaining the discipline to **break contact** and escape to a safer position is as important as the ability to stand and fight.

Patience and timing are also crucial components of discipline. Rushing into an engagement or firing too early can give away the element of surprise or expose you to counterattacks. Sometimes, the most disciplined action is to wait for the perfect moment to strike—whether it's waiting for the enemy to expose themselves, move into a vulnerable position, or create an opening that you can exploit. The ability to control your impulses and wait for the right time to engage maximizes the effectiveness of your limited resources.

In situations where the enemy is attempting to lure you into an engagement—such as by using decoys or drawing fire to expose your position—**discipline means recognizing these traps** and resisting the urge to react impulsively. By staying calm, evaluating the situation, and maintaining control over your actions, you can avoid being drawn into a disadvantageous firefight.

MAINTAINING EMOTIONAL CONTROL

Firefights, especially in a collapsed society, are emotionally charged. Fear, adrenaline, and anger can cloud your judgment, leading to rash decisions and wasted resources. Maintaining **emotional control** is essential for practicing discipline in firefights. The more you allow your emotions to dictate your actions, the more likely you are to make mistakes—whether it's overextending yourself, firing wildly, or losing focus on the broader tactical picture.

The disciplined defender remains calm, focused, and deliberate. Every decision is made with survival and long-term strategy in mind. Training under stressful conditions, such as timed shooting drills, engaging multiple targets while moving, and practicing low-light combat, helps to build the mental resilience needed to maintain emotional control during a real firefight.

INTEGRATING PRECISION AND DISCIPLINE FOR SURVIVAL

Precision and discipline in firefights are inseparable. Precision allows you to maximize the effectiveness of each shot, while discipline ensures that you only fire when absolutely necessary, conserving resources and maintaining control of the engagement. Together, these principles form the foundation of combat survival in a collapsed society. By integrating both into your approach to firefights, you minimize risks, conserve valuable ammunition, and maintain the ability to fight another day.

In this world, where every engagement could spell life or death, precision and discipline are not optional—they are essential. They ensure that you approach every firefight with the tactical mindset necessary for survival, using your weapon only when it serves your strategic objectives and never allowing yourself to be drawn into reckless or unnecessary engagements. By mastering these principles, you increase your chances of not only surviving each encounter but doing so in a way that strengthens your position in the long-term struggle for survival.

CHAPTER 5: DEFENDING URBAN ENVIRONMENTS

Urban environments present some of the most complex and dangerous challenges for citizen defenders in a collapsed society. Cities, with their dense infrastructure, confined spaces, and large populations, quickly become battlegrounds for control. Streets turn into chokepoints, buildings into defensive positions, and rooftops into vantage points. For the citizen defender, the urban landscape offers both opportunities and risks, providing cover and concealment while simultaneously limiting mobility and increasing the likelihood of close-quarters combat. Successfully defending an urban environment requires an intimate understanding of the terrain, tactical awareness, and the ability to coordinate defense efforts with precision.

Urban defense is fundamentally different from rural or wilderness survival. In cities, the environment itself becomes a weapon. Buildings, alleyways, vehicles, and debris can all be used to block, funnel, or confuse hostile forces. However, these same features can work against you if the enemy understands how to exploit them. The key to defending an urban environment is to control these elements, making the landscape work for you while minimizing the ways in which your opponent can use it to their advantage.

The collapse of society introduces new threats to cities—criminal gangs, rogue militias, and rival factions seeking to control key resources such as food, water, and strategic locations. As a citizen defender, your goal is not only to protect yourself but to secure your environment from these hostile forces. This means understanding the principles of urban defense, including fortifying your position, controlling movement through the city, using chokepoints, and knowing when to engage or retreat.

UNDERSTANDING THE URBAN TERRAIN

Before any defensive strategies can be employed, you must first understand the nature of the urban environment. Cities are a mix of **vertical and horizontal terrain**, with buildings creating layers of potential threats and opportunities. The high ground—rooftops, balconies, or upper floors—provides excellent vantage points for observation or ambush but exposes you to snipers and counterattacks. The streets, meanwhile, are narrow and confined, creating natural chokepoints where defenders can funnel attackers but can also become death traps if not properly secured.

Your ability to **read the terrain** and anticipate how enemies will move through the city is critical. Think of the city as a series of interconnected zones, each with its own tactical significance. Key locations—such as bridges, major intersections, or tall buildings—must be identified early, as controlling these areas allows you to dictate the flow of movement and create defensible perimeters. Securing these positions prevents hostile forces from advancing unchecked and enables you to channel them into zones where they are more vulnerable to ambush or counterattack.

Additionally, the **urban environment's built-in cover and concealment** offers both advantages and dangers. Buildings and vehicles can be used to shield you from enemy fire, but they can also obstruct your line of sight, making it difficult to monitor enemy movements. Windows, doorways, and alleyways are prime locations for ambushes, and your ability to control these areas will determine whether you can hold your ground. By placing sentries or using traps, you can deny the enemy access to key entry points, forcing them into more predictable and controllable pathways.

FORTIFYING YOUR POSITION

In urban defense, fortifying your position is a top priority. Without proper fortifications, even the best tactical planning can quickly unravel in the face of a well-organized attack. Whether you are defending a home, an apartment complex, or a small neighborhood, the first step is to **secure your perimeter** and create defensible positions that minimize your exposure to enemy fire.

Fortifications should focus on **chokepoints and entry points**. These are the locations where attackers are most likely to concentrate their efforts—doorways, windows, stairwells, and narrow streets. Reinforcing these areas with barricades, makeshift walls, or obstacles will slow down enemy advances and provide you with critical time to react. Materials like furniture, sandbags, metal scraps, or even debris from the environment can be used to create barriers that protect you while limiting the enemy's mobility.

In multi-story buildings, **securing stairwells and elevators** is crucial. These areas offer vertical access to your position, and if left undefended, enemies can bypass your front-line defenses by simply moving through different floors. Stairwells should be fortified or even booby-trapped to prevent easy access, while elevators, if still operational, should be disabled or monitored to prevent their use by hostile forces.

Beyond fortifications, **creating fallback positions** within your urban stronghold is critical. In the event that your frontline defenses are breached, you need secondary positions that allow you to continue the fight while retreating in an orderly fashion. These fallback positions should provide cover and a clear line of sight on the enemy's likely approach paths, allowing you to continue defending without being overrun. This layering of defenses ensures that even if one section of your position falls, you can regroup and counterattack from a more secure location.

CONTROLLING MOVEMENT IN URBAN AREAS

In an urban environment, controlling how and where enemies can move is a key defensive strategy. Urban spaces are often dense and cluttered, making it difficult for attackers to move quickly or in large formations without being exposed. As a defender, your goal is to use these features to **channel enemies into predictable routes** where they are vulnerable to ambushes, traps, or concentrated fire.

To achieve this, you must **block or restrict access** to key areas. Simple barriers, such as overturned cars, debris, or barricades, can funnel enemies into narrow streets or alleyways where they have limited mobility and are easy to target. These chokepoints should be strategically placed to maximize your field of fire while minimizing the risk of flanking maneuvers. Controlling movement also means maintaining situational awareness over **key intersections, rooftops, and access points**, using sentries or lookouts to monitor enemy activity and relay critical information about their movements.

If possible, you can use **man-made traps or obstacles** to further limit the enemy's mobility. Spike strips, broken glass, or makeshift barricades can slow down advancing forces, while fire or smoke can obscure their vision and limit their ability to respond to your defensive efforts. By controlling their movement, you force the enemy to fight on your terms, reducing their ability to overwhelm you with sheer numbers.

USING HEIGHT AND CONCEALMENT TO YOUR ADVANTAGE

In urban defense, **height is a significant advantage**. Securing elevated positions, such as rooftops or higher floors of buildings, gives you a better vantage point for monitoring enemy movements and engaging targets at a distance. The high ground provides clear sightlines over streets and alleyways, allowing you to engage enemies before they can get close to your position. However, elevated positions also come with the risk of **exposure to snipers or counterattacks**, so they should be used strategically and only when you can secure your flanks.

From elevated positions, you can deploy **long-range weapons**, such as rifles or marksman rifles, to harass and pick off enemies before they reach your main defenses. Coordinating fire from above with ground-level defenders can create overlapping fields of fire, making it difficult for the enemy to find cover and forcing them to move in the open.

However, concealment is just as important as height. **Blending into the environment**—using shadows, windows, and the natural clutter of the urban landscape—allows you to engage in hit-and-run tactics. If your position is compromised, retreating quickly through back alleys, abandoned buildings, or underground passages will allow you to avoid being surrounded or overrun. Understanding the layout of the city, including alternative routes and hiding places, is essential to maintaining your mobility.

COORDINATING DEFENSE WITH NEIGHBORS AND ALLIES

No defender can hold an urban environment alone. Whether defending a small building or an entire neighborhood, coordinating with others is essential to maintaining a secure defensive perimeter. **Community defense efforts**—where neighbors or small groups pool resources, share intelligence, and take turns standing guard—are the most effective way to maintain 24/7 security in a collapsed society.

Communication is key to coordination. Establishing **secure communication channels**, whether through radios, cell phones, or even runners, allows defenders to share critical information about enemy movements, supply shortages, or breaches in the perimeter. In an urban defense scenario, the ability to call for reinforcements or reposition defenders quickly can make the difference between holding your ground and being overrun.

By working together with others, you can create a **network of defensive position**s throughout the city, ensuring that hostile forces must navigate multiple layers of resistance before reaching key areas. Neighbors and allies also provide additional manpower, allowing for more effective patrols, shared resources, and a greater capacity to engage larger threats.

KNOWING WHEN TO RETREAT

Finally, one of the most important aspects of defending an urban environment is knowing when to retreat. Cities can be overwhelming battlefields, and there may come a time when holding your position is no longer viable. **Retreating strategically**, rather than being overrun, allows you to regroup, live to fight another day, and avoid unnecessary casualties.

When defending in an urban setting, you should always have **multiple exit routes** planned. If your position is breached or the enemy gains the upper hand, having secure fallback positions or escape routes allows you to disengage from the fight without being trapped. These routes should be pre-planned, ideally through concealed alleyways, tunnels, or back doors that are not easily accessible to your adversaries.

In this chapter, you will explore these defensive tactics in greater detail, learning how to read the urban terrain, fortify your position, control enemy movements, and work with others to create a strong and flexible urban defense. The city, with all its complexities and dangers, can become an advantage for those who understand how to turn its features into tools of survival. Through tactical preparation and coordinated defense, even the most chaotic urban environments can be defended effectively.

Urban Fortifications: Turning Your Space into a Defensible Position

In an urban environment where law and order have disintegrated, the ability to transform your home, building, or neighborhood into a defensible position is critical to survival. Urban fortifications allow you to withstand assaults, control the movement of hostile forces, and protect essential resources from looting or occupation. The concept of fortifying a space in a city goes beyond simply building walls or barricades—it's about creating layers of defense that can hold up under sustained pressure while maintaining mobility, visibility, and the ability to retreat when necessary.

Fortifying a position in an urban area requires an understanding of how the environment itself can be used to your advantage. Buildings, vehicles, streets, and natural obstacles can all serve as tools for defense, but without careful planning and strategy, they can also become vulnerabilities. Your goal in creating urban fortifications is to limit your exposure to threats while maximizing your ability to monitor, engage, and, if necessary, escape from enemy forces.

THE IMPORTANCE OF LAYERS IN URBAN DEFENSE

Urban fortifications are most effective when they are layered, meaning that your defenses should be constructed in multiple stages rather than relying on a single barrier or wall. Layers give you the ability to slow down attackers, exhaust their resources, and gain precious time to either engage or retreat. In most cases, attackers will attempt to breach your position multiple times, testing for weaknesses. A layered defense forces them to encounter successive challenges, making it difficult to overwhelm you with a single assault.

The first layer of defense is your **outer perimeter**. This may be the street in front of your building, a courtyard, or a fence. Your goal here is to prevent enemies from approaching unnoticed or without significant difficulty. Barricades made from vehicles, debris, or makeshift barriers can create obstacles that force attackers to expose themselves as they try to navigate or dismantle the outer defenses. Additionally, the outer perimeter should have **visual deterrents**—clear signs that the area is fortified and will not be easily taken. This can discourage opportunistic attackers from even attempting to breach.

The next layer is the **entrance to your building or home**. This area is crucial because once attackers breach the outer perimeter, they will focus their efforts on gaining access to your stronghold. Reinforcing doors, windows, and other entry points with heavy materials—such as metal plates, thick wood, or improvised barriers—will slow their advance. Doors should be fortified with heavy-duty locks, braces, and crossbars that make it difficult to force entry. If possible, **windows should be boarded up or covered with metal grates** to prevent access, but still allow you to observe outside.

Inside the building, you should create **internal fortifications**. These are secondary layers of defense that can be used if the enemy manages to breach the outer barriers. For example, **hallways can be blocked** with furniture, overturned tables, or other heavy objects to create choke points, slowing down intruders and forcing them to expose themselves. Rooms or stairwells can be converted into strongholds where you can retreat, regroup, or launch counterattacks. By fortifying these interior spaces, you add extra layers of security and make it harder for attackers to move through the building uncontested.

FORTIFYING ENTRANCES AND EXITS

The **main entrances** of your building are the most likely points of attack, and they should be fortified with the heaviest barriers possible. In the absence of professionally built fortifications, **makeshift barricades** can be constructed using everyday materials. Heavy furniture, sandbags, scrap metal, and concrete blocks can be arranged to create a formidable obstacle that forces attackers to spend time and effort breaking through.

Whenever possible, **double up on entrances** by reinforcing doorways with secondary barriers—such as braces or doorstops—on the inside. This creates a layered entry that makes it more difficult for enemies to simply kick in the door or break through with tools. Reinforcing hinges and locks with steel plates also ensures that the weakest points of the door are protected.

Windows, particularly those on the ground floor, are another critical vulnerability in urban fortifications. **Boarding up windows** with plywood or metal sheets can prevent intruders from smashing through, while maintaining a few **peepholes or observation slits** will allow you to monitor the outside. If you have access to it, **wire mesh or metal grating** can be installed over windows to provide additional protection. This extra layer makes it harder for attackers to reach the glass and gain entry.

CONTROLLING ACCESS AND CREATING CHOKEPOINTS

While fortifying your position, it's essential to control how attackers move through your space. One of the most effective ways to defend an urban environment is by creating **chokepoints**—narrow areas where enemies are forced to funnel through in single-file or limited numbers. These chokepoints make it easier to defend against larger groups because attackers are more vulnerable when they are restricted in movement.

Stairwells, hallways, doorways, and alleyways are all natural chokepoints that can be **reinforced with barricades or obstacles**. By blocking off wider areas, such as open rooms or large streets, you can guide enemies into these narrower paths, where you are prepared to engage them. **Placing obstacles strategically** at key entry points and intersections slows down the enemy, giving you more time to respond. Chokepoints also allow you to focus your firepower on a smaller area, increasing the effectiveness of your defense.

FORTIFICATIONS IN VERTICAL ENVIRONMENTS

Urban defense often involves using vertical spaces to your advantage. **Multi-story buildings** provide excellent opportunities for defense because they give you the high ground, which is critical in controlling movement and engaging targets at a distance. Fortifying **upper floors** and **rooftops** allows you to set up **vantage points** for observation and engagement, making it difficult for attackers to approach without being seen or fired upon.

When fortifying multi-story buildings, focus on securing **stairwells and elevator shafts**. These vertical access points allow attackers to move between floors quickly, bypassing your ground-level defenses. If stairwells are vulnerable, consider **blocking off or booby-trapping** lower-level stairs to force attackers into bottlenecks, where they can be easily engaged from above. Elevators, if still operational, should be disabled or fortified to prevent enemies from using them to reach upper levels.

Rooftop positions are excellent for **long-range engagement** and observation, but they also expose you to sniper fire from other buildings. When using a rooftop as a defensive position, it's important to set up **cover and concealment**, such as sandbags, barriers, or metal plates, to protect yourself from incoming fire while allowing you to engage targets from a safe position. Additionally, using rooftops allows you to coordinate with other defenders across multiple buildings, creating a **network of elevated defensive positions** that provide overlapping fields of fire.

MOBILITY WITHIN FORTIFICATIONS

Urban fortifications should not be static. While barricades and obstacles are essential for creating defensive layers, **mobility within your fortifications** is equally important. You must always have a plan for **moving between rooms or floors** without exposing yourself to unnecessary risk. This means creating **internal escape routes**, such as connecting tunnels between buildings or backdoors that allow you to retreat without being seen.

Your fortifications should also include **fallback positions**—secondary defensive locations within the building where you can regroup if the front lines are breached. These fallback positions should be well-defended and provide clear lines of sight for defending against attackers as they move deeper into your territory.

In the event of a **full breach**, having an **escape plan** that allows you to abandon your position safely is crucial. This might involve pre-arranged **escape routes** through back alleys, underground passages, or adjacent buildings. Fortifications are only useful as long as they hold, and if a position becomes unsustainable, retreating in an orderly fashion allows you to preserve your resources and regroup for a counteroffensive.

FORTIFICATIONS AS PSYCHOLOGICAL WARFARE

Well-constructed fortifications do more than just provide physical defense—they also serve as a form of **psychological**

warfare. The sight of fortified buildings, blocked streets, and heavily barricaded entrances sends a message to potential attackers that you are prepared, organized, and not easily overcome. This can deter opportunistic looters or gangs from attempting an assault, as they are more likely to target weaker, less defended areas.

Maintaining a visible **presence of strength**, such as armed sentries or clear signs of fortification, projects an image of control and power. In a collapsed society, where fear and uncertainty dominate, your ability to convey strength through fortifications can prevent conflict before it even begins.

By turning your space into a defensible position, you gain the upper hand in any urban conflict scenario. Through careful planning, strategic use of the environment, and constant awareness of your vulnerabilities, you can create a fortified position that not only holds against assaults but also gives you the tactical advantage. Your fortifications are more than just walls—they are the first line of defense in protecting your life and the lives of those around you in a chaotic and lawless world.

Tactics for Navigating Streets and Buildings Under Siege

In a collapsed society, where hostile forces may roam unchecked, navigating streets and buildings under siege is one of the most dangerous and critical skills a citizen defender must master. When the urban environment becomes a battleground, moving through streets or entering buildings can expose you to sniper fire, ambushes, and other deadly traps. To survive in these hostile settings, you need to employ advanced tactics that prioritize stealth, speed, and constant situational awareness. The chaotic nature of a city under siege presents unique challenges—crowded streets, narrow alleyways, and multi-story buildings all become potential hazards as well as opportunities for defense or escape.

The key to surviving in such a scenario is to control the movement through these urban spaces, using the environment to your advantage while minimizing your exposure to threats. By mastering tactics that allow you to effectively navigate through streets and buildings, you improve your chances of avoiding detection, neutralizing enemies, and reaching your destination safely.

NAVIGATING STREETS UNDER SIEGE

Streets in a besieged city are rife with danger. They often serve as the main routes for hostile forces, criminals, or rival groups to move through the urban landscape. Whether it's a narrow alleyway or a wide boulevard, streets become chokepoints where ambushes are common, and there is little cover for those caught out in the open. The following tactics help reduce your vulnerability when navigating streets that are under siege:

1. Stick to the Shadows and Avoid Open Spaces

When navigating streets, your goal is to remain unseen as much as possible. This means **staying out of open spaces**, which expose you to gunfire or surveillance from high vantage points. Stick to **shadows, building walls, and alleyways** to minimize your profile. Move alongside structures, hugging the walls and avoiding windows, balconies, or rooftops where snipers or enemy lookouts may be positioned.

Whenever possible, travel during **low-visibility conditions**, such as at night or in fog, to reduce the chance of detection. Streets that are well-lit or heavily exposed should be avoided, as they are prime targets for ambushes or sniper fire.

2. Move in Short, Controlled Bursts

Speed and unpredictability are crucial when crossing streets under siege. Instead of sprinting across long distances, move in **short, controlled bursts** between cover points. Identify objects such as cars, debris, or doorways that can serve as temporary shelter, and use these as staging points to assess the next section of the street. Your movement should be fast but calculated—always knowing your next destination before you make a move.

The concept of "**bounding overwatch**" can be useful if you're traveling in a group. In this technique, one person moves forward while the others cover them, and then the roles reverse. This ensures that someone is always scanning for threats while others are on the move.

3. Maintain Low Profile and Concealment

Always maintain a **low profile** when moving through streets, crouching or crawling if necessary to avoid being spotted by elevated threats like snipers. **Concealment** should be your priority, even if it means taking longer to reach your destination. Using trash piles, parked cars, or even damaged infrastructure to block enemy sightlines is critical. Urban environments often have **plenty of clutter**, from downed power lines to abandoned vehicles, which you can use as natural cover while moving.

4. Watch for Ambushes and Booby Traps

Streets under siege are often riddled with **ambush points and booby traps**. Narrow alleyways, street corners, and intersections are prime locations for attackers to lie in wait. Always approach these areas cautiously, assuming that the enemy could be waiting to strike. If you must move through a narrow street or alley, **scan the upper floors of buildings**, windows, and doorways for signs of movement or traps. Taking the long way around may seem counterproductive but can often be the safer option if you suspect an ambush.

Be aware of **tripwires, hidden explosives, or traps** that could be set to target anyone moving through the street. If you detect anything suspicious, such as wires or unusual debris, avoid the area and find an alternative route.

5. Use Distraction Tactics

In some cases, creating a **distraction** can help you navigate streets under siege by drawing attention away from your position. This might involve creating noise or movement in one area to force the enemy to investigate while you move through another. Tossing objects, using flares, or triggering alarms can momentarily divert attention, giving you an opportunity to cross exposed areas or bypass dangerous intersections.

NAVIGATING BUILDINGS UNDER SIEGE

Buildings offer both refuge and risk in an urban siege scenario. While they provide cover and concealment, they are also confined spaces where traps, ambushes, and enemy forces may lie in wait. Navigating through a building requires careful planning and precise tactics, as each room or hallway presents potential threats. The following strategies help you move safely through buildings that are under siege:

1. Approach Every Building as Hostile

When entering a building in a besieged city, you must **assume the worst**. Treat every building as a potential enemy stronghold, with traps, ambushes, or snipers hidden inside. Before entering, **survey the exterior** of the building for signs of occupancy or danger—such as barricaded windows, recent footprints, or open doors. If possible, use binoculars or a spotting scope to assess the building from a distance before approaching.

2. Clear Rooms Methodically

Once inside a building, move with deliberate caution. **Clear each room methodically** before proceeding to the next, ensuring there are no enemies hiding or traps lying in wait. This is where the concept of "**slicing the pie**" comes into play—moving slowly around doorways or corners in small increments, with your weapon aimed toward any potential threat. This technique minimizes your exposure while giving you a clear view of the room or hallway before you enter.

Avoid rushing into rooms blindly, as this can expose you to ambushes from concealed attackers. If you're moving with a group, coordinate your movements so that no one enters a room alone, and ensure that each team member covers a different section of the room as it's cleared.

3. Utilize Vertical Movement Carefully

Many buildings in an urban siege environment are multi-story, and **vertical movement** through stairwells and elevators introduces additional risks. **Stairwells** are prime ambush locations, as they force you to move in a single direction with little cover. Always ascend or descend with caution, keeping your weapon ready and scanning each floor for threats as you move. Avoid using **elevators** unless absolutely necessary, as they can be disabled or sabotaged, trapping you inside.

When possible, **use alternative vertical routes**, such as fire escapes, ropes, or even holes in the floor or ceiling, to avoid predictable entry points like stairwells. These alternative routes can allow you to surprise the enemy or bypass heavily guarded areas.

4. Use Cover and Concealment Indoors

Just like on the streets, **cover and concealment are critical indoors**. Furniture, pillars, and doorways can provide makeshift cover as you move through rooms and hallways. Keep to the sides of rooms, avoiding open spaces where you can be easily targeted. Always remain conscious of windows and other openings that might expose you to snipers or gunfire from outside.

Avoid **standing directly in doorways**, as they are natural sightlines for anyone trying to track your movements. Instead, move through doorways quickly and at an angle to minimize your exposure. Similarly, **windows should be approached with extreme caution**—use mirrors, scopes, or even broken pieces of glass to check for threats outside without exposing yourself.

5. Secure Key Locations Within the Building

In a building under siege, **securing key locations** like stairwells, choke points, and rooftops is essential. These areas control the movement of both defenders and attackers, giving you the advantage in deciding where and when to engage. **Rooftops**, while dangerous, provide a vantage point for spotting enemy movements, while stairwells serve as critical choke points that can be easily defended or sabotaged to prevent enemy advancement.

Blocking off unnecessary exits and securing rooms with multiple entry points helps you **control the flow of movement** within the building. **Barricades** made from furniture, debris, or other materials can prevent attackers from moving freely while allowing you to stage counterattacks from defensible positions.

6. Establish Escape Routes

Navigating a building under siege requires an understanding that no position is impregnable. Always have **multiple escape routes** in case your position is compromised. These routes should be pre-planned, taking you through less obvious exits such as back doors, basements, or neighboring buildings connected by fire escapes or rooftops.

By maintaining flexible, **secondary exit plans**, you can avoid being trapped or surrounded during an enemy assault. Knowing when to **retreat** and re-position yourself in another part of the building or neighborhood is crucial to long-term survival in a siege.

7. Manage Noise Discipline

Indoors, noise travels easily and can give away your position to enemies both inside and outside the building. Practice **noise discipline** by moving quietly, avoiding loud conversations, and minimizing any unnecessary sounds, especially if you're trying to remain concealed. Pay attention to creaking floors, doors, or windows, and use padded shoes or socks to reduce the noise of footsteps. Silence can often be your greatest asset in a building under siege, allowing you to hear the movements of attackers before they know you're there.

Navigating streets and buildings under siege is an exercise in precision, discipline, and constant vigilance. Whether moving through the open danger of a street or the confined risk of a building, every step you take must be calculated to minimize exposure, anticipate threats, and maintain the element of surprise. The key to survival lies in your ability to use the urban environment to your advantage, turning potential hazards into defensive assets and making every movement count in a hostile, unpredictable world. By mastering these tactics, you increase your odds of surviving even the most dangerous urban environments.

Ambushes, Choke Points, and Defensive Traps

In a world where the rule of law no longer exists, effective defense is not about brute strength or sheer firepower. It's about strategy, using the environment to your advantage, and employing tactics that maximize your ability to control the battlefield. Ambushes, choke points, and defensive traps are the critical tools at your disposal for creating strategic advantages, even when you're outnumbered or outgunned. These methods rely on careful planning, deep knowledge of the terrain, and the ability to anticipate enemy movements.

Ambushes and traps allow you to disrupt the enemy's plans, inflict maximum damage with minimal exposure, and maintain the upper hand in defensive situations. Choke points, meanwhile, funnel enemy forces into narrow areas where they are most vulnerable, turning the chaos of urban or rural warfare into a controlled engagement on your terms. These tactics are designed to give you a strategic edge by turning the environment into a weapon that neutralizes the enemy's numerical or technological superiority.

AMBUSHES: MAXIMIZING THE ELEMENT OF SURPRISE

Ambushes are among the most effective and devastating tactics for a citizen defender. When properly executed, an ambush allows you to strike a more powerful force from a position of concealment, inflicting heavy damage before the enemy can react. Ambushes are particularly useful in environments where mobility and stealth are key—whether in urban streets, rural pathways, or inside a fortified building.

The power of an ambush lies in the **element of surprise**. The goal is to attack your enemy when they are least prepared and most vulnerable, often in a location where they feel relatively safe or are moving through a confined space. This tactic works best when you have a clear understanding of the enemy's movement patterns, allowing you to predict when and where they will pass through a predetermined kill zone.

1. Location, Location, Location

The success of an ambush depends heavily on choosing the right **location**. Ideally, the ambush site should provide you with clear lines of sight, multiple firing angles, and sufficient cover and concealment to protect your group both during and after the attack. In urban environments, alleyways, narrow streets, stairwells, and abandoned buildings offer excellent opportunities for ambushes. In rural areas, thick forests, ravines, and bridges serve the same purpose, allowing you to use natural or structural cover to hide your presence.

The best locations for ambushes also limit the enemy's ability to maneuver or escape. **Choke points**, such as narrow corridors, staircases, alleyways, or mountain passes, are prime locations for ambushes because they force the enemy to funnel into a small, confined area where they are most vulnerable. Ambush locations should always include a pre-planned **escape route** for your team, ensuring that you can disengage quickly if the enemy manages to mount a counteroffensive.

2. Concealment and Preparation

In an ambush, **concealment is everything**. The enemy must not know they are walking into a trap until it's too late. Proper concealment means blending into the environment so thoroughly that even if the enemy is scanning the area, they see nothing unusual. This might involve hiding behind debris in an urban environment, using natural foliage in rural areas, or even staging in a location such as a basement or rooftop where the enemy is unlikely to look.

Once the ambush is set, you must remain **patient**. Ambushes require discipline—waiting for the right moment when the enemy is fully committed to the kill zone before launching your attack. Premature action or noise can alert the enemy, causing them to retreat or mount a defense before they enter the kill zone.

3. The Kill Zone

The **kill zone** is the area where the enemy is most vulnerable and where your ambush will have the greatest impact. It should be a confined space where the enemy has limited movement options, and ideally, where their escape routes are restricted. Ambushes should be **synchronized and sudden**, with your team launching a coordinated attack from multiple directions to overwhelm the enemy in a short period of time.

For example, in an urban environment, setting up an ambush in a narrow alley allows your team to fire on the enemy from multiple angles—windows, rooftops, and doorways—while they are confined to a limited path of movement. In rural environments, ambushing a convoy as it moves through a narrow pass or dense forest allows you to strike hard and fast before they can mount a counteroffensive.

4. Follow-up and Retreat

An ambush is designed to be quick and decisive. **Once the attack is launched**, it's important to retreat before the enemy can recover or bring reinforcements. Ambushes should rarely result in a prolonged firefight—your goal is to inflict damage and then disappear. Pre-planned escape routes through alleyways, rooftops, or forest trails allow you to withdraw from the engagement safely while avoiding pursuit.

CHOKE POINTS: CONTROLLING ENEMY MOVEMENT

Choke points are a critical component of urban and rural defense, allowing you to funnel enemy forces into narrow, controlled spaces where they can be easily targeted. In a collapsed society, controlling choke points is often the difference between holding your position or being overrun by a larger force. By forcing the enemy to move through narrow, restricted areas, you negate their numerical advantage, making it easier to engage them with limited resources.

1. Identifying Natural and Artificial Choke Points

Choke points can be **natural features** of the landscape—such as narrow streets, bridges, tunnels, or mountain passes—or they can be **artificially created** by blocking off certain areas with barricades or obstacles. In urban environments, narrow alleyways, stairwells, and hallways act as natural choke points that force the enemy to advance in single-file or small groups, making them easy to engage with minimal risk to the defenders.

In rural environments, chokepoints can be created by blocking roads with debris, downed trees, or vehicles, forcing enemy convoys or troops to slow down or dismount from their vehicles. These chokepoints should be **pre-identified and reinforced**, giving you time to prepare traps or ambush positions around them.

2. Fortifying and Defending Choke Points

Once you've identified a choke point, **fortifying the area** with barricades, debris, or obstacles is essential for maximizing its defensive potential. Barricades slow down the enemy, force them to expose themselves while clearing obstacles, and give you time to engage them from a secure position. Choke points should be **reinforced with crossfire positions**, allowing you to engage enemies from multiple angles while they are confined to a narrow path.

Stairwells, for example, can be turned into deadly choke points by blocking the lower stairs and positioning defenders on upper floors with clear sightlines on the entrance. In rural environments, blocking a road with debris while positioning snipers or ambushers in concealed positions around the choke point allows you to decimate a convoy or patrol as they attempt to clear the obstruction.

3. Ambushes at Choke Points

Combining **choke points with ambush tactics** is one of the most effective ways to engage larger forces with limited resources. By forcing the enemy into a choke point and then launching an ambush from multiple concealed positions, you can strike with overwhelming force before the enemy can retreat or regroup. This tactic works especially well in urban environments where movement is already restricted by narrow streets and dense buildings, giving you the advantage of surprise and firepower.

DEFENSIVE TRAPS: TURNING THE ENVIRONMENT INTO A WEAPON

Defensive traps are a low-cost, high-impact tactic for slowing down or neutralizing enemy forces. In urban and rural environments, traps can be used to **inflict casualties, slow down enemy advances, or create confusion and panic**. When combined with ambushes and choke points, defensive traps become a powerful tool for controlling the battlefield and buying time to retreat or reposition.

1. Types of Defensive Traps

Defensive traps come in many forms, depending on the environment and available resources:

- **Booby traps**: These can include tripwires connected to explosive devices, such as grenades or improvised explosive devices (IEDs), placed in areas where the enemy is likely to pass. Booby traps are effective for targeting key chokepoints, entryways, or areas that are difficult to guard directly.

- **Spike strips or caltrops**: These can be laid across roads or pathways to puncture the tires of vehicles or slow down foot soldiers. Placing these in chokepoints where the enemy must advance on foot ensures that their movement is restricted, making them easier targets for ambush.

- **Noise traps**: These are designed to create confusion or panic by triggering loud noises, such as bells, cans, or alarms, when tripped. Noise traps can be used to distract the enemy, forcing them to investigate while you prepare an ambush or retreat.

- **False cover trap**s: In urban environments, placing booby traps under debris, such as under rubble or behind doors, can lure the enemy into a false sense of security. When they take cover behind these objects, the trap is triggered, causing chaos and disruption.

2. Placement and Concealment of Traps

The key to effective traps is **placement and concealment**. Traps should be hidden in areas where the enemy is likely to pass, such as doorways, stairwells, or narrow streets. They should be concealed using debris, foliage, or other natural cover to ensure that the enemy does not spot them until it's too late. Traps are most effective when used in conjunction with **ambushes or defensive positions**, slowing down or confusing the enemy long enough for you to strike.

3. Psychological Impact of Traps

In addition to their physical effects, traps have a significant **psychological impact** on the enemy. The constant threat of traps forces enemy forces to move more cautiously, slowing down their advance and putting them on edge. This psychological pressure can lead to mistakes, hesitancy, and a general sense of fear, making it easier to control the battlefield and dictate the terms of engagement.

By combining ambushes, choke points, and defensive traps, you transform the environment into a weapon that neutralizes the enemy's advantages and puts you in control of the battle. Whether defending a building, a street, or a rural outpost, these tactics allow you to punch far above your weight, turning even a small group of defenders into a formidable force.

CHAPTER 6: RURAL SURVIVAL AND DEFENSE

While urban environments may become the epicenters of chaos during a societal collapse, rural areas pose their own unique challenges and opportunities for survival. In many ways, rural survival and defense differ fundamentally from their urban counterparts. The open spaces, forests, farmlands, and remote terrain found in rural settings provide both advantages and risks for the citizen defender. The relative isolation of rural areas can offer a degree of safety from the concentrated threats that dominate cities, but it also means fewer resources, limited access to critical infrastructure, and the ever-present danger of roving groups intent on seizing control of remote territories. The ability to survive and defend oneself in rural environments requires adapting to the natural landscape, mastering self-sufficiency, and employing tactics that turn the vastness of the countryside into an advantage.

Rural defense is characterized by longer engagement distances, increased reliance on stealth and camouflage, and the necessity of resourcefulness. Defenders must be prepared for extended periods of isolation, ensuring that they can live off the land, protect key resources like food and water, and secure their position against both organized attackers and opportunistic raiders. In this chapter, you will explore the key principles of rural survival and defense, learning how to leverage the terrain, fortify remote positions, and build self-reliance in a world where outside help may never come.

UNDERSTANDING THE RURAL LANDSCAPE: THE NATURAL ADVANTAGE

In rural environments, the terrain is your greatest asset. Whether it's dense forests, rolling hills, rivers, or mountains, the natural features of the countryside provide cover, concealment, and defensive opportunities that are far more difficult to exploit in urban settings. The wide-open spaces and relative isolation make it easier to detect incoming threats, giving defenders time to prepare and respond. However, these same features also mean that once an attack begins, reinforcements or supplies may be difficult to come by.

The key to rural survival and defense lies in understanding the landscape and using it to your advantage. Forests can serve as both cover and concealment, allowing you to move undetected or set up ambushes. Hills and ridgelines provide vantage points for spotting enemies at a distance, while rivers and bodies of water can create natural barriers that slow down attackers. Knowing the terrain intimately—every path, trail, and hidden route—is essential for maintaining mobility and security.

ISOLATION AS BOTH STRENGTH AND WEAKNESS

Rural environments offer a degree of isolation that can be both a blessing and a curse. On the one hand, the relative remoteness of rural areas means you are less likely to encounter the concentrated dangers found in cities, such as large criminal gangs or organized militias. The lack of dense population centers reduces the risk of random violence or looting, and the wide-open spaces allow for greater visibility and situational awareness.

On the other hand, isolation means that you are often on your own. The absence of nearby allies or law enforcement makes it difficult to call for help if you come under attack, and the limited access to resources—such as medical supplies, fuel, or ammunition—means that self-sufficiency is a critical aspect of rural survival. You must be prepared to survive for long periods without external assistance, relying on your ability to secure food, water, and shelter from the environment around you.

SELF-SUFFICIENCY AND RESOURCE MANAGEMENT

In a collapsed society, **self-sufficiency** becomes the cornerstone of rural survival. Unlike in urban areas, where scavenging or bartering may still be possible, rural environments require you to be largely independent, capable of sustaining yourself and your group with minimal external support. This means mastering the skills necessary to procure food, water, and shelter from the natural environment, as well as stockpiling critical supplies well in advance of any breakdown in societal order.

1. **Food and Water**: In rural environments, access to fresh water and sustainable food sources is paramount. Rivers, streams, and rain collection systems can provide drinking water, but they must be carefully filtered and purified to avoid contamination. Food can be sourced through hunting, fishing, foraging, and small-scale farming. Learning the basics of agriculture—such as growing vegetables, raising livestock, and managing crops—will ensure that you can maintain a reliable food supply over the long term. Knowledge of local edible plants, game, and fishing opportunities will also be critical for immediate sustenance.

2. **Energy and Fuel**: With limited access to traditional energy sources like electricity or gas, rural survival often depends on alternative energy systems. Solar panels, wind turbines, or even wood-burning stoves can provide basic heating and cooking capabilities. Stockpiling fuel—whether it's firewood, propane, or gasoline—ensures that you can maintain basic

living conditions even if you are cut off from regular supply chains.

3. **Tools and Maintenance**: Maintaining your equipment, weapons, and shelter over long periods is critical to rural defense. Tools such as axes, saws, knives, and basic repair kits allow you to build or reinforce structures, maintain your weapons, and repair essential items. Stockpiling spare parts, seeds, and basic medical supplies will also ensure that you are prepared for the inevitable wear and tear that comes with extended isolation.

FORTIFYING REMOTE POSITIONS

In rural environments, **fortifying your position** becomes critical to withstanding any assault. Remote homesteads, farms, or cabins must be reinforced with both natural and artificial defenses, ensuring that attackers cannot simply walk up to your doorstep unnoticed or unopposed. The open nature of rural areas requires a different approach to fortification than in urban settings, where buildings and streets create natural barriers.

1. **Perimeter Defense**: The first line of defense in rural areas is the outer perimeter—the area surrounding your home or base. This can be secured by using fences, walls, or natural barriers like thorn bushes or water features. Perimeter defenses should include early warning systems, such as noise traps, motion detectors, or even guard dogs, which alert you to the presence of intruders before they reach your position. In dense forested areas, clearing an area around your home provides a clear line of sight, reducing the chances of enemies sneaking up undetected.

2. **Fortifying the Structur**e: Your main shelter should be **reinforced to withstand attacks**, whether from raiders or natural threats. Windows should be boarded up or covered with metal grates to prevent easy entry, while doors should

be reinforced with heavy locks, crossbars, or braces. The use of **hidden compartments or escape routes** allows you to avoid capture or to secure valuables, weapons, or food in case your main defenses are breached.

3. **Control of High Ground**: In rural areas, **high ground** is a strategic asset. Securing ridgelines, hills, or elevated areas near your position gives you a tactical advantage, allowing you to spot incoming threats and engage from a distance. Establishing **overwatch positions** or lookouts on high ground ensures that you always have eyes on your surroundings, giving you valuable time to prepare or escape if necessary.

4. **Concealment and Camouflage**: Unlike urban environments, where fortifications are often visible to deter attackers, rural defense relies heavily on **concealment**. Hidden bunkers, shelters, or supply caches that blend into the natural environment can provide long-term security. Camouflaging your position with natural materials, such as foliage or dirt, ensures that attackers have difficulty spotting your base from a distance. In some cases, **false trails or decoy structures** can be used to mislead attackers, diverting them away from your true position.

HIT-AND-RUN TACTICS AND GUERRILLA WARFARE

In rural environments, the vast open spaces and natural terrain lend themselves to **hit-and-run tactics**—the cornerstone of guerrilla warfare. Rather than engaging in prolonged firefights, defenders in rural areas must rely on **mobility, speed, and surprise** to outmaneuver attackers. The goal of hit-and-run tactics is to inflict damage on the enemy while minimizing your own risk, striking quickly and retreating before the enemy can regroup or retaliate.

1. **Using the Terrain**: The terrain in rural environments provides **numerous opportunities for ambushes and hit-and-run tactics**. Forests, valleys, and ridgelines create natural

chokepoints where attackers can be funneled into narrow paths, making them vulnerable to ambush. By setting up temporary positions in these areas, you can launch surprise attacks on enemy forces, striking hard and disappearing before they can respond.

2. **Mobility and Escape**: Mobility is key to rural defense. **Staying on the move** prevents attackers from pinning you down, and knowing the terrain intimately allows you to retreat or relocate quickly. Pre-established **escape routes** through forests, across rivers, or over mountains ensure that you always have a way out if your position becomes untenable.

3. **Ambushes and Traps**: Ambushes are highly effective in rural settings, where natural cover and concealment allow you to strike from hiding. Setting up **booby traps**—such as spike strips, noise traps, or simple IEDs—along commonly traveled paths or near your perimeter can disrupt enemy movements and slow their advance, making them easier to engage. Ambushes should be **quick and decisive**, hitting the enemy hard before retreating to avoid prolonged engagements.

COMMUNITY DEFENSE AND ALLIANCES

In many cases, survival in rural areas depends on **community defense**—banding together with other homesteads, farms, or small groups to create a n**etwork of defenders**. By working together, you can pool resources, share intelligence, and mount a more coordinated defense against outside threats. Establishing **alliances** with other rural communities allows you to defend larger areas more effectively, ensuring that no single homestead is left isolated or vulnerable.

Community defense requires careful **coordination and communication**. Establishing secure methods of communication—whether through radios, signal fires, or runners—ensures that you can call for help in the event of an attack. By creating a **mutual defense pact**, you can share the burden of patrolling the area, manning lookout posts, or stockpiling critical resources.

Through a combination of self-sufficiency, strategic fortifications, hit-and-run tactics, and community alliances, rural defenders can protect themselves from the dangers of a collapsed society. While rural environments present unique challenges, they also offer a degree of freedom and mobility not available in urban settings, allowing defenders to turn the natural landscape into their greatest asset. This chapter will provide you with the knowledge and tactics needed to thrive and defend effectively in the vast, untamed world beyond the city's reach.

Leveraging the Natural Environment for Defense

In rural survival and defense, the natural environment becomes one of your most powerful allies. Unlike the urban landscape, where human-made structures define the battleground, rural settings offer vast, dynamic terrains that can be shaped to your advantage. Forests, mountains, rivers, and other natural features provide both concealment and barriers, allowing you to craft defensive strategies that maximize the strengths of the terrain while minimizing your exposure to risk. Understanding how to harness the land for defensive purposes is key to protecting your homestead, preserving your resources, and surviving in a world where external help is no longer available.

In a collapsed society, when attackers or hostile forces seek to dominate rural areas, those who can effectively integrate the natural environment into their defense plans will have a significant advantage. The key lies in blending your defenses into the terrain, turning natural features into defensive tools, and making it difficult for the enemy to detect your presence or launch a direct assault on your position. By doing so, you can outmaneuver more powerful enemies, create chokepoints and kill zones, and maintain mobility, all while remaining hidden from those who would do you harm.

CONCEALMENT: USING NATURE TO DISAPPEAR

One of the greatest advantages the natural environment offers is **concealment**. Unlike the hard lines of buildings or city streets, rural environments—forests, hills, tall grasses, and rocky outcrops—naturally provide cover and camouflage, making it much more difficult for attackers to locate you. By blending into the environment, you can move undetected, set up defensive positions, or stage ambushes with little risk of being seen.

1. Camouflage and Blending with the Terrain

To remain undetected, you must **camouflage yourself, your shelter, and your supplies**. Start by adapting your clothing and equipment to match the local terrain. In forests, use natural foliage, dirt, and mud to break up the outline of your body and equipment. Earth-toned clothing, camouflage nets, and ghillie suits help you blend into your surroundings, making it difficult for enemies to spot you from a distance.

Your **defensive structures and supplies** should also be camouflaged. Buildings, bunkers, or supply caches should be covered with natural materials—branches, leaves, rocks, or dirt—to ensure they are hidden from aerial surveillance or ground patrols. If you're using vehicles, cover them with tarps that match the surrounding landscape or park them in dense underbrush where they can't be seen. The key is to **mimic the environment**, making it difficult for anyone to identify your position as a defensive stronghold.

2. Concealed Defensive Positions

The natural environment offers numerous places to build

concealed defensive positions. Forests provide the perfect cover for sniper nests or hidden firing points. By positioning yourself in dense foliage or behind rocks, you can fire on advancing enemies without giving away your exact location. Even in more open terrain, you can dig shallow **fighting positions** and cover them with grass or debris to remain hidden while still maintaining a clear line of sight.

When creating these positions, think strategically about how they fit into the larger environment. For example, placing a firing position at the base of a hill allows you to shoot upward, while using the hill as a natural shield from enemy return fire. **Elevated positions**, such as ridges or tree stands, give you a commanding view of the surrounding area, making it easier to spot approaching threats without exposing yourself.

3. Using Waterways and Lowlands

Rivers, creeks, and marshlands provide natural **concealment and barriers**. Dense vegetation often surrounds waterways, offering an excellent hiding place for both people and supplies. You can use these areas to move undetected or set up temporary defensive positions along the water's edge. Attackers are less likely to search these locations thoroughly, and the water serves as an additional barrier to foot soldiers or vehicles.

Waterways also allow for **covert movement**. Using boats, rafts, or even swimming, you can move along rivers or creeks without leaving tracks or making noise that would give away your position. In marshy or swampy areas, the difficult terrain makes it nearly impossible for large groups to move quickly, giving you the advantage of mobility and defense in these areas.

CREATING NATURAL BARRIERS: SLOWING DOWN THE ENEMY

The natural landscape can serve as an effective tool for **slowing down enemy movement** and controlling their approach to your position. Whether you're defending a homestead, a farm, or a remote shelter, using the environment to create **natural barriers** will make it difficult for hostile forces to advance without exposing themselves to danger.

1. Defensive Use of Forests and Vegetation

Forests and dense vegetation naturally create chokepoints that can be used to your advantage. By **funneling the enemy** into narrow paths or through thick underbrush, you make it difficult for them to move quickly or stay organized. This allows you to stage ambushes or force them into vulnerable positions where they are more exposed to your defenses.

You can also **reinforce these natural barriers** by creating **deadfalls or ditches** filled with sharp branches or spikes, slowing down foot soldiers or vehicles trying to move through wooded areas. Cutting down trees to block roads or trails makes it difficult for vehicles to pass, while still allowing you and your group to move through the forest on foot.

2. Using Hills and Elevation to Control Movement

Hills and ridgelines are natural barriers that slow down attackers and give you the advantage of height. **Controlling the high ground** is one of the oldest and most effective military strategies, and it applies just as well in a rural defense scenario. Positioning your shelter or defensive post on elevated ground ensures that any attackers must approach uphill, making them slower and more exposed targets. The steeper the incline, the more vulnerable they become to gunfire or traps as they struggle to climb.

Placing **chokepoints at the base of hills**—such as narrow trails or valleys—forces the enemy into predictable paths where you can engage them from an elevated position. By reinforcing these natural chokepoints with traps or obstacles, you further slow their advance and make it easier to defend your position.

3. Rivers, Lakes, and Waterways as Natural Barriers

Rivers and lakes naturally serve as **defensive barriers**, slowing down attackers and limiting their options for advancing. Use these water features to your advantage by placing your position on the far side of a river or along the banks of a lake, forcing any attackers to cross the water before they can reach you. **Bridges or narrow crossing points** become natural chokepoints that can be easily defended, and you can use the water itself as a natural moat to prevent direct assaults.

If you control the crossing points—whether they're bridges, fords, or makeshift rafts—you can decide when and where to allow movement across the water. **Blowing up or disabling a bridge** cuts off access to your position, while using hidden boats or rafts allows you to move across the water undetected.

TURNING TERRAIN INTO DEFENSIVE KILL ZONES

By understanding the layout of the natural environment, you can turn certain areas into **defensive kill zones**—places where the enemy is forced into a vulnerable position, allowing you to inflict maximum damage with minimal risk. Kill zones are most effective when attackers are forced to funnel into a confined space, such as a valley, ravine, or narrow trail, where their movement is restricted and they are exposed to your fire.

1. Funneling the Enemy into Predictable Paths

The first step in creating a kill zone is to control how and where the enemy moves. Use natural features like cliffs, rivers, or thick forests to **funnel the enemy into a single path**. If the natural terrain doesn't provide this funneling, you can create it by blocking off alternative routes with debris, trees, or other obstacles. The goal is to force the enemy into an area where you can engage them from multiple angles with minimal risk to your position.

Once the enemy is confined to this path, you can **set up ambush positions** on the high ground or in concealed locations around the kill zone. Your firing points should be well-concealed, allowing you to strike before the enemy knows they're in danger. If possible, **control both ends of the kill zone**, cutting off the enemy's ability to retreat or regroup.

2. Trapping the Kill Zone

The effectiveness of a kill zone can be greatly increased by **placing traps or obstacles** in the path of the enemy. **Booby traps**, such as spike pits, tripwires, or explosive devices, can be hidden along the path, forcing the enemy to slow down or stop altogether. The more the enemy is delayed, the more exposed they become to your defensive fire.

In addition to traps, you can use natural features like **rockslides or avalanches** to further disrupt the enemy's movement. If your position is located above a ravine or steep hill, **triggering a rockslide** as the enemy moves through can cause massive damage, cutting off their escape route and trapping them in a vulnerable position.

ADAPTING TO SEASONAL CHANGES

Rural environments are subject to **seasonal changes** that can affect both your defensive strategies and the movement of enemy forces. Snow, rain, and changing foliage all impact visibility, mobility, and the effectiveness of traps or barriers. As seasons shift, your approach to defense must adapt.

1. Winter Defense

In the winter, **snow and ice** create unique challenges and opportunities. Deep snow can slow down attackers and make it difficult for vehicles to move through the terrain. However, it also makes it harder for you to remain concealed, as footprints and movement through snow are easy to track. You can use snowdrifts to **create barriers** or cover your defensive structures, but you must also plan for the increased difficulty of movement.

2. Spring and Summer Camouflage

In the spring and summer, the increased vegetation provides excellent **camouflage**, allowing you to blend into the environment more easily. Use the dense foliage to conceal defensive positions, traps, and supply caches. However, the thick vegetation can also obscure your view of approaching threats, so **clearing select areas** around your position while maintaining cover is essential for balancing concealment and visibility.

3. Flooding and Wet Weather

In regions prone to **flooding or heavy rains**, waterways can quickly change, creating new barriers or opening new paths for attackers. If your position is near a river, ensure that you have contingency plans in place for rising water levels. **Mud and rain-soaked ground** can also slow down movement, making it harder for attackers to move quickly while giving you the chance to set up more traps or ambush points.

Leveraging the natural environment for defense requires a deep understanding of the terrain and how it can be used to slow down, confuse, and ultimately defeat an enemy. Whether you're using forests for concealment, rivers as barriers, or hills to create kill zones, the land itself becomes your strongest weapon. By mastering these tactics, you turn the open spaces and wild terrain of rural environments into formidable defensive tools, allowing you to protect your home, your resources, and your life in a lawless world.

Camouflage, Tracking, and Evasion in Rural Settings

Camouflage, tracking, and evasion are essential skills for anyone navigating rural environments in a lawless society. In these open and often hostile landscapes, the ability to blend into the surroundings, avoid detection, and evade pursuit is crucial for survival. The wide expanses of nature offer both opportunities and dangers. While the terrain can provide ample cover and concealment, it can also leave you exposed to those with tracking skills or superior knowledge of the area. Mastering these elements allows you to move through the environment undetected, ambush enemies with precision, and escape when pursued by those intent on harm.

Camouflage in rural settings requires understanding how to manipulate the environment to blend seamlessly into it. The natural landscape, from forests and hills to fields and rivers, offers a variety of materials and features that can be used to your advantage. Clothing, gear, and shelters should match the colors and textures of the surrounding terrain. In wooded areas, earth tones—such as greens, browns, and dark grays—are ideal for mimicking the forest floor or tree cover. Adding natural elements like leaves, twigs, and dirt to your gear can further break up your outline, making you less noticeable to anyone scanning the area for movement. In open fields or barren areas, where foliage is sparse, wearing colors that mimic the sky or surrounding rocks is essential. Movement should be slow and deliberate to avoid attracting attention, especially when moving through an area with limited natural cover.

Tracking is a double-edged skill. While understanding how to track others allows you to gain valuable information about enemy movements and location, it also teaches you how to avoid leaving signs of your own presence. When tracking someone, careful observation of footprints, broken branches, disturbed soil, and subtle changes in the environment can reveal the path they have taken. Different terrains leave different clues: in soft, muddy ground, footprints are more obvious, while in rocky or hard soil, the signs may be limited to slight disturbances in the earth. Understanding these nuances is essential for following a trail without being detected yourself. When you are the one being tracked, avoiding such signs becomes a matter of survival. Moving over hard, dry ground or rocky surfaces minimizes footprints. In forested areas, stepping lightly to avoid breaking branches or trampling plants helps conceal your passage. Doubling back on your path, crossing water, or climbing rocky terrain are all effective strategies to throw off pursuers.

Evasion in rural settings depends on your ability to outthink and outmaneuver those pursuing you. It requires not only physical agility but also mental discipline and strategic planning. When escaping from a potential threat, the first step is to break the line of sight. Quickly finding cover behind trees, rocks, or in thick brush prevents enemies from following your exact movements. Once out of sight, changing direction frequently and using natural obstacles, such as rivers or steep hills, helps confuse anyone attempting to track you. Moving through difficult or uneven terrain is tiring, but it can give you an advantage by slowing down your pursuers. Navigating through areas that are hard to traverse, like dense underbrush, swampy land, or steep ravines, buys you time and can exhaust or frustrate those chasing you. In some cases, moving at night or in low-visibility conditions, like fog or rain, can provide additional cover, allowing you to slip away unnoticed.

The rural environment also provides unique opportunities for using deception in evasion. Setting false trails, such as walking in one direction for a short distance and then backtracking along your own path before branching off, can lead trackers astray. Creating disturbances in the environment, like scattering leaves or dragging branches behind you to mask footprints, can help confuse those following you. In cases where pursuit is imminent, setting up simple traps or noise distractions—such as tying branches together to fall and create noise—can divert attention long enough for you to escape to a safer location.

Below are practical examples of camouflage, tracking, and evasion in rural settings that illustrate how these skills are applied in real-world situations where survival depends on your ability to remain unseen, avoid capture, and outmaneuver potential threats.

Imagine you're moving through a dense forest, attempting to avoid detection by a hostile group. To effectively blend into the environment, you would start by ensuring that your clothing and gear match the surrounding terrain. In a forest setting, wearing green or brown clothing that mimics the colors of the trees and underbrush would be critical. You could further enhance your camouflage by attaching local foliage to your clothing and equipment—tying small branches or leaves to your pack or helmet to break up your silhouette. As you move, keep low to the ground and use the terrain to your advantage by sticking close to tree trunks, staying in the shadows, and moving slowly to avoid sudden movements that could catch the attention of anyone watching from a distance.

Now, let's say you come across signs that the hostile group has passed through the area recently. Observing subtle changes in the forest floor—such as displaced leaves, broken twigs, or fresh footprints in a patch of mud—would give you clues about their direction and numbers. By studying the depth and size of the footprints, you could estimate how many people passed through, whether they were moving quickly or cautiously, and how recently they were there. If you notice branches broken at shoulder height, that might indicate the group was moving through the forest without regard for stealth, which could mean they are unaware of your presence or confident in their strength.

As you decide to move away from the area to avoid potential contact, the principles of evasion become vital. Your first goal is to break any line of sight. If you suspect someone might be following you, quickly step behind a tree or into a thicket to obscure yourself. Once hidden, don't continue in the same direction you were originally moving. Instead, change your route, perhaps circling back slightly before moving at an angle to your previous path. This can throw off anyone trying to follow your movements. As you move, be careful not to create obvious signs of your passage. Step lightly on solid ground, avoid walking through wet or muddy areas where your footprints would be visible, and take care not to break branches or disturb the underbrush.

If you're being actively pursued, understanding how to use the natural environment to slow down or mislead your enemies becomes critical. For instance, crossing a small stream can help hide your tracks, as footprints in waterlogged ground are harder to trace. Once you've crossed the water, you could walk along the edge of the stream for a while before re-entering the forest in a different direction, making it difficult for pursuers to pick up your trail. Another tactic would be to head towards an area of thick underbrush or rocky terrain. While these areas are harder to traverse, they also offer excellent opportunities for hiding, and the difficulty of movement could discourage anyone from continuing the pursuit.

In addition to terrain, you can use noise and distractions to your advantage. Suppose you reach a narrow ravine and suspect that your pursuers are closing in. Dropping a heavy branch or dislodging a pile of rocks on one side of the ravine could create a sudden noise, drawing their attention while you quietly slip away on the other side. Simple tricks like these can disorient or confuse your enemies, buying you valuable time to put more distance between you and them.

If the pursuit intensifies and you find yourself needing to set up a defensive point while evading, the use of terrain becomes even more important. Position yourself on higher ground, such as a hill or ridge, where you have a better vantage point and where attackers would have to expose themselves to approach you. Choose a location where you can see approaching threats from multiple directions, but where you can also remain hidden behind natural cover like boulders, dense foliage, or a fallen tree. Setting simple traps—such as creating noise traps with strings tied to cans or branches—can alert you to an approaching enemy and give you time to escape.

Finally, using decoys or false trails can further mislead those tracking you. For example, if you need to stop for a short rest, leave a few false clues of your direction by pressing down branches or scattering a few items to suggest you've headed in one direction. Then, move in the opposite direction or take a more difficult route that would make tracking you harder. These small, deceptive actions can cause your pursuers to waste time and energy following a false trail while you make a clean escape.

These practical examples highlight the importance of camouflage, tracking, and evasion in rural settings. Whether you are hiding in dense forests, moving across open fields, or navigating rivers and rocky terrain, your ability to manipulate the environment, understand the signs of movement, and stay one step ahead of your enemies will determine your success in a collapsed and dangerous world.

Camouflage, tracking, and evasion are complementary skills. Together, they allow you to disappear into the environment, avoid detection, and evade capture in rural settings. By mastering these techniques, you not only protect yourself from threats but also gain the ability to observe others without being seen, strike when the moment is right, and retreat when the situation turns against you. These skills are critical to maintaining control of your surroundings and ensuring your survival in the unpredictable and often dangerous world of rural conflict.

Establishing Hidden Bases and Supply Caches

Establishing hidden bases and supply caches in rural settings is a critical strategy for long-term survival in a collapsed society. When access to resources becomes scarce and lawlessness prevails, having a secure location where you can rest, regroup, and resupply without being easily detected provides a crucial advantage. Hidden bases serve as operational hubs, while supply caches ensure you have access to essential goods like food, ammunition, and medical supplies in case your primary base is compromised or travel becomes necessary. The key to creating these hidden assets lies in their secrecy, strategic placement, and adaptability to the natural environment.

A hidden base must offer both concealment and defensibility. When scouting for a suitable location, the goal is to find an area that is difficult to detect but offers enough natural protection and resources to support prolonged stays. Remote areas, such as dense forests, rocky cliffs, caves, or even abandoned rural buildings, are ideal for setting up hidden bases. The surrounding terrain should act as a natural barrier to prevent easy access, with elevation providing the advantage of visibility over a wide area. Placing the base on high ground or tucked within a natural hollow, such as beneath a ridgeline or near a secluded water source, adds layers of security. Ideally, the location should offer access to fresh water and be close enough to areas rich in game or edible plants, allowing you to remain self-sufficient.

Once a location is chosen, building or adapting the base requires discretion. If using natural materials, such as wood or stone, make sure the structure blends seamlessly into the environment. Shelter should be constructed in a way that it remains hidden from aerial surveillance and difficult to spot from a distance. Camouflage techniques—such as covering the base with natural foliage, tree branches, or mud—help ensure it remains undetectable. If the base is set near a rock face, painting or covering the exterior to match the natural colors of the landscape further enhances its invisibility. The entrance should be concealed, with vegetation or debris hiding any signs of human activity. Paths leading to and from the base must be indirect, using routes that leave minimal tracks and avoid exposing the location.

The interior of a hidden base should be practical, with storage for essential supplies, sleeping areas, and, if possible, basic defensive features like reinforced walls or lookout points. Keeping the base small and compact reduces its visibility and makes it easier to maintain. Ventilation and insulation are important to manage smoke, heat, and scent that could give away your position. Any fires for cooking or warmth should be small and well-contained, ideally using a rock or earth barrier to mask smoke.

In addition to the hidden base, supply caches serve as lifelines in times of crisis. Caches are small, hidden stockpiles of essential supplies placed in various locations throughout your operating area. The primary purpose of these caches is to provide backup resources in case your main supplies are lost, your base is compromised, or you need to move quickly through different terrains. By spreading out your supplies in multiple secret locations, you reduce the risk of losing everything in one attack or discovery.

Supply caches must be carefully concealed, ideally located in places that are difficult for others to stumble upon but easy for you to access. Natural features, such as hollowed-out trees, caves, or buried containers, provide excellent hiding places. You can also create caches within natural debris—such as inside a pile of rocks or buried under fallen branches—where they appear to blend in with the environment. When choosing cache locations, ensure they are spaced out across a wide area but not too far from known routes or places you might travel in an emergency.

The contents of a supply cache should be tailored to meet specific survival needs. Essential items include non-perishable food, clean water, medical supplies, ammunition, fire-starting tools, and extra clothing. In rural environments, having basic hunting or trapping gear, such as snares or fishing equipment, can extend your ability to procure food without depleting your main resources. Each cache should contain enough supplies to sustain you for several days, allowing you to recover, resupply, and make it to the next cache or your hidden base.

Durability is a critical factor when building supply caches. Using airtight, watertight containers helps protect the contents from moisture, animals, and environmental decay. Military-grade storage containers, PVC pipes sealed with end caps, or even heavy-duty plastic bins buried underground ensure that supplies remain intact for long periods. Labeling the exterior of caches with markers that only you can identify —such as scratches on a nearby tree or a rock arranged in a specific pattern—allows you to find them without drawing attention to their location.

The most effective use of supply caches involves placing them along strategic routes. In rural settings, these might be along hunting paths, riverbanks, or forested areas that provide natural cover. The caches should be positioned far enough away from main roads or well-traveled areas to avoid accidental discovery but close enough to be reached in case of a quick escape or during long-distance travel. If you plan to relocate or traverse different environments, having caches in each terrain ensures you are never far from essential resources.

Both hidden bases and supply caches are integral to long-term survival. The base provides you with a secure, concealed location to rest and plan your actions, while caches ensure that no matter what happens, you have access to critical supplies. The success of this strategy depends on your ability to keep these assets secret, well-maintained, and adaptable to the ever-changing dangers of a collapsed society. By leveraging natural concealment and carefully planning their placement, you can create a network of hidden resources that will sustain you through even the most challenging conditions.

CHAPTER 7: INFORMATION WARFARE AND COMMUNICATIONS

In a world where society has collapsed and chaos reigns, the battle for survival extends beyond physical confrontations and the control of resources. Information, the ability to communicate, and the power to influence perceptions become just as crucial as weapons and supplies. The collapse of traditional forms of governance and law enforcement leaves a vacuum not only in security but also in the flow of reliable information. In this environment, those who control the narrative, manage intelligence, and manipulate information will have a significant strategic advantage. Information warfare, often thought of as a tool of states and organized militaries, now becomes a vital tactic for the citizen defender navigating a fractured society.

In times of societal collapse, communication systems, the spread of rumors, misinformation, and propaganda become as dangerous as physical threats. People, desperate for guidance and leadership, turn to any available source of information, often believing whatever they hear without verifying its truth. Those who can leverage this chaotic information landscape can shape the behavior of others, influence movements, and, more importantly, control the environment in ways that brute force cannot. Information warfare is the new battlefield—one where knowledge, communication, and deception determine who survives and who succumbs to the uncertainty of the times.

Understanding the principles of information warfare and communications is essential in this new reality. It involves not only managing your own flow of information—protecting your intelligence from falling into enemy hands—but also manipulating what others know, think, and believe. Whether it's spreading disinformation to mislead potential enemies, securing sensitive communications to prevent interception, or monitoring enemy movements through surveillance and intelligence gathering, mastering the flow of information becomes critical for defending your position and achieving your strategic objectives.

At its core, information warfare in a collapsed society revolves around three key principles: intelligence gathering, secure communication, and the dissemination of influence. Each of these principles must be understood and applied in order to create a solid foundation for managing the flow of knowledge in a world where trust is broken, and deception is a weapon.

Intelligence gathering is the first and most vital step in information warfare. To survive and protect your group, you need to know what is happening in your immediate environment—whether it be the movements of hostile forces, the locations of resources, or the activities of rival groups. In a collapsed society, traditional sources of intelligence, such as news media or government broadcasts, may no longer exist. You are left with whatever fragmented information you can collect from the streets, the radio waves, and the rumors whispered between survivors. The ability to sift through this often unreliable data, separating fact from fiction, and gathering useful, actionable intelligence becomes critical.

The key to effective intelligence gathering is establishing a network of trusted sources and developing the skills to observe and analyze patterns of behavior. In urban environments, this might involve infiltrating or eavesdropping on rival groups, establishing informants, or monitoring the movements of hostile forces through surveillance. In rural settings, it might mean using scouts, patrols, or listening to radio frequencies to pick up transmissions. Knowing where your enemies are, what they are planning, and how they intend to act gives you the upper hand in deciding when to engage, when to retreat, and how to prepare.

The second pillar of information warfare is secure communication. In the chaos of a collapsed society, communication networks are vulnerable to interception, sabotage, or manipulation. Whether you are coordinating with allies, passing intelligence to your group, or issuing orders, ensuring that your communications remain private and secure is essential. An intercepted message could reveal your location, plans, or weaknesses, leading to devastating consequences. Developing secure channels of communication, such as encrypted radio transmissions, coded messages, or physical couriers, allows you to protect sensitive information from prying eyes.

Digital communication, while potentially powerful, becomes a double-edged sword in a collapsed society. Any device transmitting radio signals, mobile data, or GPS locations can be tracked or intercepted by hostile forces. Using technology for communication requires careful planning and the implementation of secure protocols to prevent outsiders from accessing your data. If using electronic devices, minimizing your digital footprint—by limiting transmissions, avoiding unencrypted messaging, and using anonymous methods—reduces the risk of interception. On the other hand, low-tech methods, such as hand-delivered messages or coded signals, offer a more secure way to communicate, albeit with the added difficulty of ensuring those methods are reliable and efficient.

The third and final aspect of information warfare is the dissemination of influence—shaping the beliefs, decisions, and actions of those around you. In times of collapse, fear and uncertainty grip the population, and those who can offer certainty—whether true or false—can control the narrative. Propaganda, disinformation, and psychological operations (PSYOPS) become weapons in your arsenal, allowing you to mislead your enemies, build loyalty among allies, and project strength even when your resources are limited. Information becomes a currency of power, and by controlling what others believe, you gain leverage over their behavior.

For the citizen defender, disinformation can be used to great effect in confusing or demoralizing rival groups. False reports of troop movements, fake warnings of impending attacks, or planted rumors of hidden resources can send your enemies on wild goose chases or cause them to overextend their forces. Propaganda aimed at demoralizing opponents—spreading doubts about their leadership, capabilities, or strength—can weaken their resolve without a shot being fired. At the same time, you must protect your own group from falling prey to similar tactics. Rumors, especially in a fractured society, spread like wildfire, and the ability to control the narrative within your group prevents division and panic.

Psychological operations go hand in hand with information warfare, using fear, uncertainty, and hope to manipulate the minds of both enemies and allies. By projecting an image of strength, even when you are outnumbered or undersupplied, you can dissuade potential aggressors from attacking or weaken their will to fight. For example, setting up decoy fortifications, playing loud noises to simulate larger forces, or broadcasting fake radio transmissions can give the illusion of greater power than you actually possess. On the other side, the careful use of rumors and misinformation can lead rival groups into conflict with each other, allowing you to maintain your position while they weaken one another.

It is not enough to simply gather information, secure your communications, and manipulate the narrative. To truly succeed in information warfare, you must also develop the skills of **counter-intelligence**. Knowing that your enemies are likely to employ the same tactics against you, you must take steps to protect your group from surveillance, infiltration, and psychological manipulation. Developing strong internal security measures—vetting new members, monitoring communications for signs of interception, and training your group to recognize disinformation—ensures that your operations remain protected. Information, once compromised, can be as deadly as a breach in physical security, and vigilance in this area is key to long-term survival.

As technology evolves, the nature of information warfare shifts, even in a collapsed society. Drones, for instance, can be used for reconnaissance, spying on enemy positions from a distance or gathering data about movements in your area. They also serve as powerful psychological tools, instilling fear simply by their presence overhead. Similarly, radio and communication jammers, while advanced, become important in disrupting enemy communications during critical moments. If you have access to such technology, learning how to operate it gives you a distinct advantage on the battlefield of information.

As you navigate the unpredictable environment of a post-collapse world, remember that the strength of your group depends not only on the resources you control or the weapons you possess, but on your ability to outthink and outmaneuver enemies in the information domain. Managing the flow of knowledge—what you know about others and what they know about you—will determine whether you can maintain order within your ranks, protect your group from threats, and ultimately, influence the world around you.

In the end, information warfare is about survival on multiple levels—physical, psychological, and strategic. By controlling how information moves, how it is communicated, and how it is used, you ensure that even in a lawless and fractured world, your group has the upper hand. The power of knowledge, well-used, can decide the course of any conflict, making it one of the most essential elements in your survival toolkit.

Controlling the Narrative: Disinformation and Psychological Tactics

In a world where traditional structures of authority have crumbled and society is embroiled in conflict, controlling the narrative becomes a decisive weapon. In the absence of formal governance, trust is shattered, and misinformation spreads like wildfire. In such an environment, disinformation and psychological tactics are not merely tools—they are essential strategies for survival. For the citizen defender, mastering these techniques allows for the manipulation of both adversaries and potential allies, crafting a narrative that enhances security and builds influence in a world devoid of order.

Disinformation, as a deliberate act of spreading false or misleading information, functions as a powerful tool for creating confusion, division, and uncertainty within hostile forces. Psychological tactics, meanwhile, are the calculated application of fear, hope, doubt, and authority to manipulate how others think and act. Both strategies revolve around one crucial principle: perception is reality. Whoever controls what people see, hear, and believe controls the battlefield, no matter how limited their resources may be.

In the context of a collapsed society, where communication networks are fragile and rumors dominate the airwaves, disinformation can shape entire communities 'actions. It can cause enemies to retreat or overextend, diverting them away from your true locations. It can plant the seeds of fear, creating hesitation or fostering internal dissent within hostile groups. At the same time, carefully crafted psychological operations can win over neutral parties, turning potential threats into allies or discouraging future attacks. The battle for survival, therefore, is not fought only with weapons and tactics—it is fought with stories, ideas, and the strategic dissemination of lies and half-truths.

ROLE OF DISINFORMATION IN A COLLAPSED SOCIETY

In the chaos of societal collapse, reliable information is a scarce commodity. Without centralized institutions to provide consistent news or updates, individuals and groups are left to rely on fragmented reports, hearsay, and rumors. This information vacuum provides the perfect opportunity for those skilled in disinformation to manipulate perceptions and shape outcomes. Disinformation works because it takes advantage of two human tendencies: the need for certainty in uncertain times, and the impulse to act on incomplete information when clarity is lacking.

For the citizen defender, disinformation can be deployed to disorient and mislead adversaries. False reports of troop movements, hidden caches of resources, or impending attacks can cause hostile groups to waste time and energy on phantom threats. For example, planting a rumor that a well-armed faction is amassing near a key resource hub can send enemies on a wild goose chase, allowing you to secure valuable supplies uncontested. Similarly, spreading false information about your own strength or position can cause rivals to hesitate or withdraw.

In this sense, disinformation is a form of **asymmetric warfare**. It allows those with fewer resources to punch above their weight by exploiting the enemy's lack of information. If executed correctly, disinformation can lead enemies to make fatal mistakes—whether that means committing too many resources to an irrelevant area or attacking a position they wrongly believe to be undefended.

PRACTICAL APPLICATION OF DISINFORMATION

The first step in executing effective disinformation is identifying your target's informational weaknesses. In a fractured society, different factions, criminal gangs, and rogue militias are likely to have limited means of verifying information. This creates fertile ground for introducing falsehoods that appear credible enough to be acted upon. However, disinformation must always be tailored to the psychology of your adversary. If the lie is too outrageous or contradictory to their existing beliefs, it will be quickly dismissed.

Start by crafting a false narrative that aligns with the fears or desires of your target. For example, if you know that a hostile faction is desperate for supplies, you can plant information about a valuable resource depot in a remote location. The more believable the lie, the more likely they are to take the bait. Use intermediaries, third-party contacts, or even intercepted communications to "leak" this false intelligence. The goal is to ensure that the information appears organic—something they stumbled upon themselves, rather than something fed to them by an adversary.

To sustain the credibility of disinformation, it is often necessary to introduce elements of truth. If you're misleading an enemy about the size of your forces, for instance, it may help to stage visible but controlled movements near their territory—just enough to suggest activity without revealing your true strength. The use of visual deception—such as setting up decoy camps, burning fires without the presence of troops, or planting fake radio communications—reinforces the false narrative. The objective is to create a complex web of lies and truths that is difficult to unravel.

PSYCHOLOGICAL OPERATIONS AND THE POWER OF FEAR

Psychological operations (PSYOPS) are a natural complement to disinformation, and they are just as vital in controlling the narrative. Where disinformation misleads the enemy, psychological tactics manipulate their emotions—particularly fear and uncertainty. In a society where order has collapsed, fear is a pervasive force, one that can be leveraged to dissuade attacks, demoralize opponents, and project strength.

Fear operates on both an individual and collective level. Individually, fear paralyzes decision-making, making adversaries hesitant to act. Collectively, fear can lead to disunity, panic, and infighting within enemy ranks. For the citizen defender, exploiting fear means presenting your group as a far greater threat than it actually is, or alternatively, positioning yourself as an ally too dangerous to provoke.

The use of fear-based messaging can be highly effective. For example, spreading rumors of booby-trapped roads, hidden snipers, or deadly ambushes can cause hostile forces to approach cautiously, slowing their advance and allowing you to prepare defenses or retreat. Additionally, carefully placed signs, warning shots, or even staged events—such as a fake attack that leaves behind obvious signs of violence—can create the impression that your territory is heavily fortified and patrolled, even if your forces are limited.

Fear is also used to amplify the effectiveness of disinformation. A rumor alone may not be enough to sway an enemy's decision-making, but combined with the fear of an unknown threat, it can lead them to make rash choices.

For instance, spreading the belief that your group possesses advanced weaponry, coupled with staged incidents that "prove" its destructive power, can create hesitation or push adversaries to abandon their plans.

CREATING DOUBT AND DIVISION THROUGH PSYCHOLOGICAL TACTICS

Beyond inducing fear, psychological tactics are also used to create doubt and division among your enemies. A unified enemy is strong; an enemy riddled with doubt, questioning its leadership, or plagued by internal conflict is weak. The goal of psychological warfare in this context is to plant the seeds of uncertainty and mistrust, disrupting the enemy's cohesion and effectiveness.

One effective tactic is to target the enemy's leadership. Disinformation campaigns that suggest incompetence, betrayal, or even corruption among rival leaders can cause their followers to question authority. For instance, planting rumors that a rival leader is secretly negotiating with other factions can foster suspicion, leading to internal fractures. Once doubt is introduced, it can spread rapidly in a context where communication is limited and trust is already fragile.

Psychological tactics are particularly useful in situations where you lack the manpower or resources for direct confrontation. Rather than engaging in a full-scale conflict, you can use disinformation to pit enemy factions against each other, letting them weaken themselves while you remain out of the fray. If, for example, two rival groups are vying for control of a key resource, spreading false reports that one group is planning an ambush against the other can lead to pre-emptive strikes, forcing them into conflict.

In addition to targeting leadership, psychological operations can focus on eroding group morale. For example, leaving behind carefully constructed signs or messages that highlight the hopelessness of their cause can have a powerful demoralizing effect. Simple graffiti, notes, or even intercepted radio communications that suggest the futility of their struggle can cause lower-level fighters to desert or refuse to fight.

CONTROLLING THE NARRATIVE AMONG ALLIES

While disinformation and psychological tactics are often used to weaken enemies, they are just as critical in maintaining the cohesion and morale of your own group. In a collapsed society, maintaining unity and preventing fear or doubt from taking hold in your ranks is essential for survival. Disinformation can be used internally to prevent panic or foster loyalty among group members.

For example, if your group is facing shortages or setbacks, it may be necessary to downplay the severity of these issues or shift blame to an external threat. Psychological tactics can also be used to reinforce confidence. By controlling what your group knows—carefully managing reports of successes, downplaying losses, and exaggerating the enemy's weaknesses—you can create an atmosphere of determination and strength.

At the same time, it is vital to inoculate your group against enemy disinformation. In a world where trust is easily eroded, encouraging open communication, loyalty, and vigilance within your ranks helps prevent outside attempts to sow division. Training your group to recognize signs of disinformation and ensuring they are well-informed about your overall strategy protects against infiltration and keeps morale high.

DEFENSIVE INFORMATION WARFARE: PROTECTING YOUR OWN NARRATIVE

While controlling the narrative against others is essential, protecting your own narrative from being manipulated by rival groups is just as critical. The collapse of society means that information warfare flows in both directions. Adversaries will be just as eager to spread disinformation and psychological attacks to undermine your efforts, and it is essential to remain vigilant against these tactics.

One of the first lines of defense against enemy disinformation is controlling the flow of information within your own group. Centralized command of information prevents rumors from spreading unchecked, and establishing a clear chain of communication ensures that your group receives accurate updates. Regular briefings that provide truthful, but framed, versions of events help to counter any external attempts to sway your group's perceptions. At the same time, remaining transparent enough to maintain internal trust ensures that doubts don't creep into your ranks.

Psychological resilience is another defense against enemy tactics. Training your group to withstand fear and uncertainty, emphasizing discipline and trust in leadership, prevents morale from breaking down when faced with enemy PSYOPS. Encouraging a mindset of skepticism toward outside information—while promoting unity and shared purpose—helps inoculate your group against psychological manipulation.

In the end, controlling the narrative through disinformation and psychological tactics is about controlling the minds of both your adversaries and your allies. It is about shaping what they see, think, and feel, influencing their actions without direct confrontation. In a world where information is fragmented and unreliable, those who master these skills gain a critical advantage, using perception as a weapon just as powerful as any firearm. The ability to manipulate information—to make the enemy believe what you want them to believe—can turn the tide in a world where survival depends not only on strength but on the ability to outthink and outmaneuver those who seek to do you harm.

(For more on this topic, see 'Controlling the Narrative: The Definitive Guide to Psychological Operations, Perception Management, and Information Warfare' by the author)

Creating Encrypted and Covert Communication Channels

In a world where the rule of law no longer holds, and traditional infrastructure has collapsed, communication becomes both a lifeline and a potential vulnerability. Maintaining reliable, secure, and covert channels of communication is essential for any citizen defender operating in a chaotic environment. Without effective communication, your ability to coordinate with allies, share critical information, and stay ahead of adversaries is severely compromised. But in a fractured society, any message you send could be intercepted, decoded, and used against you if not properly secured. Creating encrypted and covert communication channels becomes an essential skill, protecting your operations from enemy interference while ensuring that your movements and plans remain confidential.

In such a volatile landscape, communication cannot rely solely on technology. While digital encryption provides powerful tools for securing messages, you must also develop non-digital, low-tech methods of covert communication that can be used when technology fails or is too dangerous to employ. Whether you are passing messages within a trusted group, coordinating movements with distant allies, or sending critical information without leaving a trace, the key lies in mastering both high-tech encryption and old-fashioned covert techniques.

The primary goal of creating secure communication channels is to prevent interception. Enemies may attempt to monitor radio frequencies, hack into digital devices, or even plant informants within your group to gain access to your intelligence. To combat this, encrypted communication ensures that even if a message is intercepted, it cannot be easily deciphered. Meanwhile, covert communication allows you to send and receive information in ways that are difficult to detect or trace.

BASICS OF ENCRYPTED COMMUNICATION

Encryption refers to the process of converting information or messages into a code, unreadable to anyone without the key to decode it. In a collapsed society, digital encryption can be used to secure electronic messages sent over long distances, particularly via radio, text, or satellite communications. However, relying on digital systems introduces risks, as skilled adversaries might have the tools to intercept or jam electronic communications.

When using encryption for communication, choosing the right encryption method is crucial. Some modern encryption algorithms—such as Advanced Encryption Standard (AES) or end-to-end encryption apps like Signal—are designed to be extremely difficult to crack. These systems work by encoding your messages so that only the intended recipient, with the correct decryption key, can read them. While the strength of these encryption methods makes them useful in protecting your digital communications, it's important to minimize the number of transmissions sent. The more often you use these channels, the more likely you are to attract attention.

To set up an encrypted communication network, begin by distributing secure encryption keys to trusted members of your group. These keys should be kept confidential and regularly changed to reduce the risk of compromise. If possible, use multiple layers of encryption to ensure that even if one method is compromised, another layer of protection still exists. For instance, encrypt a message using one system, then re-encrypt it with a second layer before sending it. This ensures that even if an adversary intercepts part of the communication, they will not have access to the entire message.

Another option is to use **one-time pads** for encryption. A one-time pad is an encryption technique that uses a random key to encode each message. The key is used only once and then discarded, making it impossible to crack without the specific key. While highly secure, the downside is that both sender and recipient must have access to the same key, which must be exchanged securely beforehand.

Digital encryption, however, should be used sparingly, especially in environments where electronic signals are easily tracked or jammed. Wireless transmissions leave a trace, and even encrypted messages can attract attention if an adversary is monitoring frequencies for activity. This makes it critical to combine digital encryption with **radio discipline** —limiting the frequency and duration of transmissions, using directional antennas to reduce signal detection, and varying communication times and frequencies to avoid pattern recognition.

LOW-TECH COVERT COMMUNICATION

While digital encryption offers robust security, low-tech methods of covert communication are equally important, especially in environments where electronic transmissions are unsafe. Covert communication relies on discretion, ingenuity, and the use of non-verbal signals, dead drops, and coded messages to pass information without revealing that a message has been sent.

One of the most effective low-tech methods is the use of **prearranged signals or codes**. These signals are simple, yet effective, means of communication that don't involve the direct transmission of information. For example, a specific arrangement of objects—such as a stone placed on a fence post or a flag draped in a particular way—can signal to an ally that an area is safe or that an agreed-upon action should be taken. These signals should be subtle, blending into the natural environment or urban landscape so that only those familiar with the code can interpret them.

Another covert method involves the use of **dead drops**, where messages or items are left in hidden locations for retrieval by others. This method avoids the need for face-to-face communication or electronic transmission, greatly reducing the risk of interception. Dead drops can be hidden in everyday objects, such as hollowed-out tree trunks, hidden compartments in walls, or under stones in a specific location. The key to a successful dead drop is ensuring that both the sender and receiver know the precise location and time to retrieve the message without being observed.

To further secure dead drop communications, messages can be **coded or concealed** within seemingly innocuous items. A book, for example, can be used to hide a message by underlining specific words on different pages that spell out the actual content. This technique—known as a **book cipher** —uses a predetermined text shared between the sender and receiver. The sender marks certain words or letters in the text, which the receiver decodes based on their knowledge of the code.

In addition to coded messages, physical **steganography**—the art of hiding messages within other objects—can be used. For instance, a message can be written in invisible ink or microfilm, then hidden inside a common object like a piece of clothing or a household item. By using ordinary items as containers for covert communication, you can avoid drawing attention to the fact that a message is being passed.

RADIO COMMUNICATION AND DIRECTIONAL TRANSMISSIONS

In a collapsed society, radio communication becomes one of the most accessible forms of long-distance messaging, but it also presents significant risks. Radio frequencies are easy to monitor, and unencrypted messages can be intercepted by anyone with a receiver. Even encrypted radio transmissions can attract attention, as adversaries may monitor the airwaves for activity.

To mitigate these risks, **radio discipline** is essential. When using radio communication, keep transmissions short and infrequent to reduce the chances of interception. Use code words and predetermined signals to convey meaning without revealing too much information. For example, instead of stating your exact location, use a code that only trusted members understand, such as referring to a certain area by an innocuous name. Change these codes regularly to avoid giving enemies time to decipher them.

Additionally, using **directional antennas** for radio transmission can reduce the range at which signals can be intercepted. A directional antenna focuses the signal in a specific direction, minimizing the likelihood that someone outside of that range will pick up the communication. This method is particularly useful for communicating with allies at known locations while reducing the risk of nearby enemies listening in.

IMPORTANCE OF OPERATIONAL SECURITY (OPSEC)

Creating secure communication channels, whether digital or low-tech, requires strict adherence to **operational security (OPSEC)** principles. OPSEC is the practice of safeguarding critical information and ensuring that your group's activities remain concealed from adversaries. In a collapsed society, where surveillance is constant and resources are scarce, maintaining OPSEC is essential to keeping your communications private and your operations secure.

One of the most important OPSEC practices is limiting who has access to sensitive information. Only those who absolutely need to know a piece of intelligence should be privy to it. This principle, known as "need-to-know," prevents unnecessary leaks and ensures that even if one member of your group is compromised, they won't be able to divulge critical information about the entire operation.

Another crucial aspect of OPSEC is **compartmentalization**. This involves dividing information into isolated compartments so that no single individual has access to everything. For example, if you are coordinating a multi-step operation, ensure that different teams only know the details of their specific tasks, not the entire plan. This reduces the risk of an enemy capturing all the information if one team is compromised.

Finally, **minimizing your digital footprint** is a vital part of OPSEC in the modern age. Even when using encrypted communications, consider the possibility that your devices could be compromised. Regularly switch communication methods, change passwords, and avoid storing sensitive information on devices that could be lost or stolen. Using physical tokens—such as handwritten notes or prearranged signals—provides an additional layer of security.

In the chaos of a collapsed society, secure communication becomes a matter of life and death. Whether using encrypted digital messages or low-tech covert techniques, the ability to communicate without being intercepted by adversaries is a fundamental part of surviving and defending your group. By mastering encryption, developing covert communication channels, and adhering to OPSEC principles, you ensure that your operations remain confidential and your movements unpredictable. These skills, while often overlooked, are as critical to your survival as any weapon or fortification. In a world where information is a powerful currency, controlling how it flows and who receives it is the key to staying one step ahead of the threats around you.

Sabotaging the Enemy's Communications and Intelligence

In a collapsed society where traditional institutions no longer function,. In the absence of centralized authority, rival groups, hostile factions, and even well-organized militias rely heavily on their ability to gather and disseminate information. By sabotaging these channels, you cripple their ability to coordinate attacks, defend resources, and respond to threats. Sabotaging communications and intelligence not only weakens the enemy tactically but also sows confusion, panic, and mistrust among their ranks. This gives the citizen defender a powerful advantage, turning the enemy's reliance on information against them.

In any conflict, control over the flow of information determines who holds the strategic upper hand. Disrupting your adversary's ability to communicate internally or externally limits their decision-making capacity and makes them vulnerable to both direct and psychological attacks. In a collapsed society, this can be done through both digital and physical means, leveraging a combination of sabotage, deception, and infiltration. The goal is to break down the enemy's information infrastructure, leaving them blind, disoriented, and uncoordinated.

IDENTIFYING THE ENEMY'S COMMUNICATION CHANNELS

Before you can effectively sabotage an enemy's communications, you need to identify the channels they rely on for transmitting information. In a post-collapse environment, these channels might include radio communications, digital devices, physical messengers, and even informal networks of spies and informants. The first step in a successful sabotage campaign is to observe and analyze how your adversary communicates, gathering as much intelligence as possible about their methods, frequencies, and vulnerabilities.

Radio frequencies are often the most common form of communication in such settings, particularly for groups that rely on long-distance coordination. Monitoring these frequencies and identifying patterns in transmission gives you valuable insights into how their communication network functions. Digital communications, if available, may include encrypted messaging apps, emails, or even social media platforms. While more difficult to intercept directly, these can still be sabotaged if you understand the enemy's technological infrastructure.

Physical methods of communication, such as messengers carrying notes or verbal orders between camps, are slower but offer valuable opportunities for interception. If the enemy relies on human messengers, sabotaging this link in the communication chain can prevent critical information from reaching its destination, delaying enemy action or forcing them to revert to slower and more vulnerable methods.

RADIO SABOTAGE AND JAMMING

One of the most effective ways to sabotage the enemy's communications is through **radio jamming**. In a collapsed society, where communication infrastructure is fragile, radio jamming can paralyze an enemy's ability to coordinate, causing chaos and confusion. Radio jamming works by broadcasting interference on the same frequencies that the enemy uses for communication, rendering their transmissions unreadable. This can be done using relatively simple equipment—a radio transmitter that broadcasts static or noise on the target frequency.

The key to successful radio jamming is timing. Continuous jamming may alert the enemy to your interference, allowing them to adapt by changing frequencies or communication methods. Instead, consider intermittent jamming, disrupting their communications at critical moments—such as during attacks, troop movements, or strategic meetings—so that they cannot effectively respond to developments. This creates disorientation, delays in decision-making, and prevents them from issuing orders or calling for reinforcements.

For more targeted interference, **directional jamming** allows you to focus your disruption on specific locations, such as enemy strongholds or command centers, without broadcasting across an entire region. This method minimizes the risk of alerting other groups to your actions and allows you to disrupt communication only where it matters most. To implement this, you would need equipment capable of focusing the jamming signal in a specific direction, further isolating your enemy's communications.

INTERCEPTING AND MANIPULATING ENEMY COMMUNICATIONS

Beyond jamming, intercepting and manipulating enemy communications can offer both tactical and psychological advantages. **Radio interception** allows you to listen in on the enemy's transmissions, gathering valuable intelligence about their movements, plans, and weaknesses. Once you've identified the frequencies they use, you can monitor their communications, giving you insight into their strategy while remaining hidden.

The next step is **manipulating these communications**. Once you understand their patterns, you can introduce false information or create confusion by transmitting misleading messages over their frequency. For instance, during a coordinated attack, you could broadcast false orders in the enemy's own language, instructing their units to retreat or regroup in a vulnerable position. This tactic plays on the enemy's reliance on their communication network, turning their own tools against them.

Alternatively, by intercepting their communications without altering them, you can set traps based on the information you gather. If you overhear plans for an ambush or resource convoy, you can pre-emptively strike or set up your own ambush, leveraging the enemy's operational security failure.

SABOTAGING DIGITAL COMMUNICATIONS AND DATA NETWORKS

In a modern collapsed society, adversaries may still rely on digital communications for coordination, particularly if they have access to mobile networks, internet, or satellite communications. Sabotaging these digital channels requires a different approach, involving cyber tactics such as **hacking, spoofing, or disrupting servers**. If you have access to digital warfare tools, even basic hacking skills allow you to compromise the enemy's digital infrastructure, intercepting or altering messages, planting false information, or disabling their communication systems entirely.

One of the most effective methods for sabotaging digital communications is to **disrupt the network infrastructure** that supports these transmissions. This can be as simple as physically destroying key communication hubs—such as satellite relays, cell towers, or data servers—or using **denial-of-service (DDoS) attacks** to flood the enemy's network with traffic, rendering their systems inoperable. By forcing the enemy offline, you cut them off from external resources, leaving them isolated and vulnerable.

Another tactic is to plant **malware or spyware** within the enemy's digital systems. If you can gain access to their devices—either through physical infiltration or by hacking—

implanting malicious software allows you to monitor their communications, steal data, or even control their systems remotely. This covert form of sabotage is less likely to be detected and can provide long-term strategic advantages as you gather intelligence without revealing your presence.

INFILTRATION AND PSYCHOLOGICAL SABOTAGE

While technology offers numerous avenues for sabotaging communications, sometimes the most effective method is through **infiltration and psychological sabotage**. Placing an informant within the enemy's ranks allows you to disrupt their communication network from the inside. This infiltrator can pass false information, misinterpret orders, or delay the transmission of critical intelligence, causing confusion and mistrust within the enemy group.

Psychological sabotage goes hand in hand with infiltration. By spreading disinformation internally—such as rumors of spies, betrayal, or leadership failures—you can erode the enemy's confidence in their own communication systems. This can lead to internal fractures, with different factions questioning the authenticity of the messages they receive or the loyalty of those transmitting them. A fractured enemy, unable to trust its own sources of information, becomes significantly easier to defeat.

Another form of psychological sabotage is creating **false communications** that appear to come from enemy leadership. By intercepting and replicating the style and format of their messages, you can transmit false orders that undermine their operations. For example, sending a false order to retreat or change course can derail an offensive, buying you time to regroup or set up an ambush. The key here is subtlety—false communications must appear authentic enough to be trusted by enemy forces.

DISRUPTING PHYSICAL INTELLIGENCE NETWORKS

In addition to digital and radio communications, many factions in a collapsed society will rely on **physical intelligence networks**, including spies, scouts, and human messengers. Sabotaging these networks can be as simple as intercepting messengers en route, either by ambushing them or bribing them to work as double agents. Disrupting the flow of physical messages—whether by intercepting couriers or creating false checkpoints—slows down the enemy's operations and leaves them cut off from critical intelligence.

In the case of spies and scouts, counterintelligence becomes a key tool for identifying and neutralizing these threats. Regularly changing your own communication methods, using **disinformation traps** (planting false intelligence to see if it's passed back to the enemy), and closely monitoring new members of your group all help to disrupt physical intelligence gathering. Eliminating enemy spies or turning them into double agents can sow discord within enemy ranks, making them question the reliability of their own intelligence sources.

SABOTAGING THE ENEMY'S TRUST IN THEIR INTELLIGENCE

Ultimately, the most powerful form of sabotage is not simply cutting off the enemy's communication channels but making them doubt the reliability of their own intelligence. This form of **psychological warfare** undermines the enemy's decision-making at a fundamental level. By manipulating their information streams—through false reports, misleading intelligence, and contradictory messages—you create an environment of uncertainty. Once the enemy starts questioning the validity of their own information, they become paralyzed, unable to act decisively.

An effective method for this is the introduction of **consistent, subtle disinformation** over time. Rather than blatant lies, feed the enemy half-truths—mixing accurate reports with slight exaggerations or misleading details. This creates a pattern of confusion that slowly erodes their confidence in the intelligence they receive. As the enemy begins to suspect that their information has been compromised, they will hesitate, second-guess orders, and ultimately lose trust in their leadership.

By strategically sabotaging communications and intelligence, you weaken the enemy from within, leaving them blind and vulnerable in a hostile environment. Whether through jamming radio frequencies, hacking digital networks, or infiltrating their intelligence operations, the citizen defender can turn the flow of information into a weapon. Sabotage not only disrupts the enemy's tactical operations but also undermines their psychological stability, leading them to question their own capabilities and decisions. In a world where survival depends on controlling information, mastering the art of sabotage ensures that your adversaries remain in the dark while you move forward with precision and purpose.

CHAPTER 8: LOGISTICS IN A COLLAPSED SOCIETY

In the chaotic aftermath of a societal collapse, where law and order have disintegrated, the importance of logistics becomes both paramount and existential. Logistics—the efficient coordination and management of resources—determines not just the success of military operations, but the very survival of individuals and groups. In a world where traditional supply chains no longer function, access to basic necessities like food, water, medical supplies, fuel, and ammunition is unpredictable. In such an environment, mastering the art of logistics means not only knowing how to acquire resources but also how to store, transport, and protect them from theft or destruction.

Without a functioning government or commercial infrastructure, everything from resupplying a small group of defenders to maintaining an operational stronghold requires careful planning and strategy. The ability to secure vital resources while managing their distribution efficiently becomes the backbone of survival. A single miscalculation in logistical planning—whether due to a lack of fuel, dwindling food supplies, or exposure to the elements—can be as lethal as an enemy attack.

In this chapter, we will examine the core principles of logistics in a collapsed society. From establishing supply networks to maintaining secure stockpiles, the focus is on how to manage resources in a hostile and unpredictable environment. The breakdown of transportation systems, the unreliability of modern technology, and the constant threat of looting or raids mean that you must be adaptable and resourceful. The ability to think several steps ahead, anticipating future shortages while securing what's immediately needed, is key to keeping your group alive and operational.

The foundation of effective logistics in a collapsed society lies in understanding that survival is a long game. Whether you're scavenging from abandoned cities, repurposing old infrastructure, or bartering with other groups, the goal is to build a sustainable, self-reliant system that can withstand both internal challenges and external threats. Critical decisions about what to store, how to move supplies, and where to establish secure depots become a matter of life and death. In this hostile world, the ones who master logistics—those who can plan, adapt, and secure what they need—are the ones most likely to endure.

RESOURCE ACQUISITION AND BARTERING

In a world where currency may no longer hold value, logistics begins with resource acquisition. The collapse of centralized systems means that supply sources—like supermarkets, gas stations, pharmacies, and factories—may be abandoned, depleted, or controlled by hostile forces. As a result, scavenging, foraging, and bartering become primary means of obtaining necessary resources. However, in many cases, finding the right balance between risk and reward is critical. Venturing too far into urban areas or unsecured regions for supplies may expose your group to attacks, while missing opportunities to scavenge could leave you under-resourced.

Scavenging in collapsed cities or towns offers a short-term supply of goods, but these resources will quickly become scarce as other groups engage in the same hunt for survival. You must therefore focus not only on gathering supplies but on building sustainable methods of acquisition. Identifying sources of renewable resources—such as farmland for food or natural water sources—is crucial. In some cases, forming alliances with local farmers, hunters, or skilled craftsmen who can produce goods becomes a strategic necessity. These relationships are often built on bartering, where goods, services, or protection are exchanged for resources.

Bartering will likely become one of the primary methods for acquiring what cannot be scavenged or produced. Successful bartering depends on the value of your goods and services, as well as your negotiation skills. Items that become high-value in a post-collapse world—such as medical supplies, antibiotics, fuel, tools, and weapons—can be exchanged for food, shelter, or protection. However, establishing reliable trading partners is essential, as bartering carries the inherent risk of deception or robbery. Clear agreements and mutual trust, as well as the ability to defend yourself, are critical in ensuring successful exchanges.

STOCKPILING AND STORAGE

Once resources are acquired, the next challenge is stockpiling and storage. In a collapsed society, supplies are finite, and hoarding may seem tempting. However, indiscriminate stockpiling can lead to waste, spoilage, or theft if not carefully managed. Properly storing resources in a way that ensures longevity and security is the foundation of any long-term survival strategy.

Non-perishable goods—such as canned food, dried grains, and seeds—must be prioritized for their long shelf life. Perishable items like fresh meat or dairy will quickly spoil unless preserved through methods like salting, smoking, or dehydration. Knowing how to preserve and store food properly extends the usefulness of limited supplies and prevents spoilage from becoming a threat to survival.

Water, one of the most critical resources, presents its own logistical challenges. Access to clean, potable water may be limited, especially in urban areas where infrastructure has collapsed. Stockpiling water requires large, secure containers and filtration systems, ensuring that contamination doesn't occur over time. In rural areas, establishing reliable water collection and filtration systems—such as rainwater collection, wells, or natural springs—becomes a priority. Protecting these water sources from contamination or sabotage is vital to sustaining your group in the long term.

Ammunition and weapons must also be carefully stored to prevent deterioration and to ensure they remain accessible when needed. Ammunition should be stored in dry, cool environments to prevent degradation, and weapons should be maintained regularly to ensure functionality. Misfires or malfunctions due to poorly stored firearms or ammunition can be catastrophic in defensive situations.

Security of stockpiles is another pressing concern. Supply caches must be hidden and guarded, especially in areas where rival groups or hostile forces may attempt to raid your supplies. Distributing caches across multiple locations reduces the risk of total loss if one depot is discovered or compromised. These locations should be concealed in a way that doesn't draw attention, using natural terrain features or disguised entryways to blend into the environment. The goal is to secure enough resources to survive while minimizing the risk of theft or destruction.

TRANSPORTING SUPPLIES: MOBILITY AND RISK

In a collapsed society, transporting supplies presents one of the greatest logistical challenges. Without functional infrastructure—such as roads, fuel stations, or transportation hubs—moving resources from one location to another requires significant planning. The key to successful transportation is balancing mobility with security. Vehicles, while faster and more efficient for transporting large quantities of supplies, also become vulnerable targets for ambushes, especially in open or contested areas. Using vehicles means ensuring they are well-maintained, fueled, and able to traverse rugged terrain in case of blocked or damaged roads.

When vehicles are unavailable or impractical, moving supplies on foot becomes necessary. While slower and more labor-intensive, foot-based transportation reduces the likelihood of detection by hostile forces and allows for greater stealth in contested environments. The use of **pack animals**, such as horses or donkeys, becomes invaluable in rural areas, where roads are impassable or fuel is unavailable. These animals can carry heavier loads over difficult terrain, providing a more sustainable transport option for long-distance movements.

The primary risk in transporting supplies is exposure. The more visible your movement, the more likely you are to be targeted by hostile groups looking to seize your resources. Planning **secure transportation routes**—which avoid known enemy territory, ambush points, or open spaces—minimizes the risk of attack. Alternative routes, including back roads, forest paths, or waterways, provide opportunities to transport goods without drawing attention. In some cases, it may be necessary to **move at night** or during low-visibility conditions to further reduce the risk of interception.

MAINTAINING OPERATIONAL SUPPLY CHAINS

In a collapsed society, maintaining a functional supply chain —no matter how rudimentary—ensures your group has continued access to essential goods. This requires more than just hoarding supplies; it involves building a network of acquisition, storage, and distribution that can adapt to changing circumstances. A disrupted supply chain can cripple an otherwise functional group, leading to shortages and collapse.

To maintain operational supply chains, it's critical to **diversify sources of supply**. Relying on a single source for food, fuel, or other resources creates a dangerous dependency. Establishing multiple channels of acquisition—whether through scavenging, trade, or alliances—ensures that you have options when one source runs dry. Additionally, planning for **seasonal fluctuations** in food availability, water access, and weather conditions ensures that your supply chain remains resilient even in the face of environmental challenges.

Regular **inventory checks** and audits of your stockpiles are essential to ensure that you are aware of what's available, what's running low, and what needs to be replenished. Rotating supplies, particularly food and water, prevents spoilage and waste. Effective logistics management also involves planning for the unexpected—whether it's a sudden influx of people needing shelter or an unexpected raid that depletes resources. Flexibility and foresight are key to surviving logistical challenges in an unpredictable world.

PROTECTION OF SUPPLY LINES

Once supply chains are established, their protection becomes a top priority. In a collapsed society, rival groups and hostile forces will inevitably target supply lines in an attempt to seize resources or weaken your group's ability to function. Ensuring that your supply lines remain secure involves a combination of **stealth, deception, and force**.

Supply routes should never be predictable. Constantly changing the timing, route, and method of transport minimizes the likelihood of ambush or interception. Additionally, decoy operations—where false supply convoys are sent out to draw enemy attention—can be used to protect critical supply lines. In cases where your supply lines are under constant threat, **armed escorts** may be necessary to guard critical shipments. However, armed transport increases the visibility of your operations and should be used strategically, rather than as a default approach.

Ultimately, logistics in a collapsed society is not just about managing supplies—it's about ensuring that your group remains resilient, adaptable, and prepared for both immediate and long-term survival. Mastering the art of logistics means thinking several moves ahead, planning for contingencies, and securing the resources needed to weather an uncertain future. In this chaotic environment, those who can efficiently manage and protect their resources will have the best chance of survival, while those who falter in logistics risk being left at the mercy of both scarcity and conflict.

Securing and Managing Essential Resources

Securing and managing essential resources in a collapsed society is fundamental to survival. Without a functioning infrastructure or reliable supply chains, every necessity —food, water, fuel, medical supplies, and ammunition— must be treated as a precious commodity. The collapse of modern logistics means that securing these resources is not just a matter of acquiring them but also ensuring their longevity, preventing spoilage or theft, and managing their consumption to meet immediate and future needs. Effective resource management requires strategic foresight, disciplined planning, and the ability to adapt to a constantly shifting environment.

One of the primary challenges in securing resources in a collapsed society is that scarcity is pervasive, and competition for those resources is fierce. What was once abundant may now be rationed or hoarded by rival groups or hostile forces.

Stockpiling is only part of the solution; to ensure your group's survival, it's essential to implement a system that accounts for replenishment, proper storage, and efficient allocation. The risks of overconsumption or poorly managed supplies are significant—without careful planning, a cache of supplies that should have lasted months can be depleted in a matter of weeks, leaving your group vulnerable to hunger, thirst, or even exposure.

The first step in securing resources begins with assessing your current environment. In urban areas, resource collection may involve scavenging from abandoned stores, offices, or homes. However, these initial gains are finite, and urban centers can quickly become dangerous due to the concentration of competing groups. As such, rural areas, where natural resources like food and water can be found more readily, may offer a more sustainable long-term solution, though these areas present their own logistical challenges, such as transport and storage over longer distances.

FOOD AND WATER SECURITY

In a post-collapse world, access to food and water becomes the highest priority for survival. Food, particularly perishable items, will quickly disappear from shelves or spoil without refrigeration. Ensuring a steady supply of sustenance requires a combination of scavenging, farming, and possibly bartering. Initially, scavenging in urban areas might provide some relief, but this is short-lived. Canned goods, dried grains, and non-perishable items will run out, and as competition increases, so will the risk of violence over these resources.

Long-term food security requires diversifying your supply. Small-scale agriculture—growing vegetables, raising livestock, or even fishing—becomes essential to sustaining a group over extended periods. In rural settings, this might mean establishing a garden or hunting for wild game, but even urban areas offer potential for rooftop gardens or cultivating unused plots of land. Seeds for crops should be stockpiled, and knowledge of farming techniques is critical. The ability to grow your own food provides both security and independence from the chaos that often follows a resource collapse.

Water security is just as crucial, if not more so. Without access to clean water, dehydration and disease will quickly follow. In urban environments, water sources may be contaminated or unreliable, while in rural areas, natural sources like rivers, lakes, or rainwater collection systems can be set up and used if properly filtered. It's important to stockpile both water and water filtration systems—simple water purification tablets, filtration devices, or boiling methods can mean the difference between life and death when clean water is scarce. Long-term solutions, like building wells or setting up large-scale rainwater collection systems, are essential for providing sustainable access to potable water.

MANAGING SUPPLIES: RATIONING AND STORAGE

Once resources have been secured, managing them effectively is the next challenge. In a collapsed society, wastefulness is deadly. Rationing becomes a central strategy in ensuring that supplies last as long as possible. This means calculating the bare minimum of food, water, and other resources that individuals need to stay healthy and dividing supplies accordingly. Strict control over distribution prevents hoarding, overconsumption, and internal conflict within your group.

Storage of supplies is another critical consideration. Food, water, and ammunition must be stored in secure, controlled environments to prevent spoilage, theft, or loss. Food storage requires dry, cool spaces, protected from pests and rodents. Canned goods can last for years if kept in the right conditions, while dried goods like rice and beans must be protected from moisture and contamination. Ammunition and weapons must be stored in a way that ensures they remain functional and are not subject to degradation.

In addition to proper storage, hiding supply caches in multiple locations is a strategic necessity in a collapsed society. Having all of your supplies in one place makes them vulnerable to theft or raids. By distributing caches in various, well-hidden locations, your group can still access vital resources even if one site is compromised. These caches should be concealed using natural terrain, buried underground, or hidden in abandoned structures, making them difficult for others to find. The location of these caches should only be known to trusted members of your group, ensuring that if one member is captured or compromised, the entire supply chain isn't jeopardized.

FUEL AND ENERGY MANAGEMENT

Fuel and energy are critical resources that often go overlooked in the early stages of collapse, but without them, the ability to move, generate power, or stay warm becomes severely limited. Fuel, especially gasoline, will be in short supply, and once the infrastructure breaks down, there will be no more shipments coming in. Stockpiling fuel becomes essential, but fuel is volatile and difficult to store safely. Containers must be sealed and kept in well-ventilated areas away from open flames to prevent accidents.

Alternative energy sources, such as solar panels, wind turbines, or wood-burning stoves, offer more sustainable solutions for the long term. Setting up solar panels to power basic devices or building a wind turbine can provide much-needed electricity, while wood-burning stoves offer a reliable source of heat and cooking in colder climates. The ability to harness these renewable energy sources becomes a significant advantage in maintaining your group's long-term viability.

Transportation becomes another logistical challenge without fuel. In urban environments, bicycles, carts, or even pack animals may replace vehicles as a primary means of moving supplies. In rural settings, horses or mules may become vital for transporting goods over long distances where roads are impassable or fuel is unavailable. Planning routes that avoid conflict zones or areas controlled by hostile groups becomes essential to preserving both your supplies and your group's safety.

SECURING MEDICAL SUPPLIES

Access to medical supplies in a collapsed society is often a matter of life and death. Hospitals and pharmacies will be quickly stripped of essential items, and any existing stockpiles will become targets for looting. Securing medical resources such as antibiotics, bandages, antiseptics, and painkillers should be an immediate priority. These supplies will be needed not only for treating injuries but for preventing infection and disease, which become rampant in environments where sanitation and access to clean water are compromised.

Stockpiling medical supplies early and distributing them across multiple caches reduces the risk of losing everything in a raid or theft. Additionally, learning basic first aid and medical procedures, such as how to treat wounds, disinfect injuries, and administer CPR, is essential. In the absence of professional medical care, the ability to provide emergency treatment becomes a survival skill in itself.

Beyond basic medical supplies, acquiring knowledge about natural remedies and herbal medicines becomes increasingly valuable as pharmaceutical supplies run out. Certain plants and herbs, like aloe for burns or garlic for its antimicrobial properties, can be used to treat illnesses and injuries when conventional medicines are no longer available. Understanding how to identify and harvest these natural resources becomes part of your overall strategy for maintaining health within your group.

GUARDING AGAINST THEFT AND RAIDS

In a collapsed society, your greatest threat often comes not from the scarcity of resources but from others who seek to take them. As supplies dwindle, theft and raids become more frequent, with rival groups or individuals resorting to violence to secure what they need. Protecting your resources from these threats requires vigilance, fortification, and, in many cases, armed defense.

Securing your main base of operations against intruders is essential. This means fortifying entrances, setting up perimeter defenses, and maintaining constant surveillance. Those in urban environments may need to barricade windows and doors, while those in rural settings can use natural barriers like rivers, forests, or cliffs to help defend their positions. Early warning systems—such as tripwires, noise alarms, or motion sensors—provide advance notice of an approaching threat, allowing your group time to respond.

Defensive measures extend to protecting supply caches as well. As mentioned, distributing supplies across multiple locations reduces the impact of a single raid, but it's equally important to keep these locations hidden and inaccessible. Using decoy caches—less valuable supplies left in an obvious location—can divert attackers away from the more critical stores, buying you time to relocate or defend your main supplies.

Ultimately, securing and managing essential resources in a collapsed society is a continuous balancing act between acquisition, rationing, storage, and defense. Every resource must be treated as vital to survival, and every decision about how to use or protect it can have long-lasting consequences. With strategic planning, adaptability, and careful management, you can ensure that your group has the supplies needed not only to survive but to thrive in a world where scarcity is the new normal.

Food, Water, Medical Supplies, and Ammunition Storage

In a collapsed society, where law and order have disintegrated and resources have become scarce, proper storage of essential supplies is vital for survival. The effective storage of food, water, medical supplies, and ammunition can mean the difference between life and death for your group. In a hostile environment, these supplies are not only necessary for immediate survival but also serve as a buffer against future uncertainty. Whether you are defending a small community, a family, or a group of citizen defenders, having a secure, well-managed stockpile ensures that you can withstand the challenges of scarcity, defend against hostile forces, and maintain operational capability in the face of ongoing threats.

The key to successful storage is to ensure longevity, accessibility, and protection. Each type of resource has specific needs to remain usable over time. Improper storage can lead to spoilage, contamination, or degradation, rendering vital supplies useless when they are needed most. Moreover, stockpiles are vulnerable to theft, raids, and environmental factors such as weather or pests. Planning for these threats and safeguarding your stockpiles is essential for ensuring that your resources last as long as possible.

FOOD STORAGE

In a world where grocery stores and supply chains are no longer functioning, having a secure, well-organized food stockpile is crucial to sustaining life. However, food is inherently perishable, and improper storage can lead to spoilage, contamination by pests, or degradation due to environmental factors such as heat and humidity. In a collapsed society, the availability of refrigeration and modern preservation methods may be limited or nonexistent, so special care must be taken to ensure that your food stores remain viable for extended periods.

The first step in managing food storage is selecting the right types of food. Focus on non-perishable and easily preserved items, such as canned goods, dried grains, beans, lentils, and freeze-dried or dehydrated food. These items have long shelf lives and can be stored in a variety of environments with minimal risk of spoilage. Canned goods, for example, can last for several years if kept in a cool, dry place, while grains and beans can remain viable for even longer if stored properly.

STORAGE TECHNIQUES FOR LONGEVITY

Storing food requires not only selecting the right types of provisions but also ensuring that they are kept in an environment that minimizes exposure to the elements. Food should be stored in a cool, dark, and dry place, ideally underground or in a climate-controlled area to avoid heat and moisture, which can lead to spoilage and mold growth. For dried goods like rice, beans, and flour, vacuum-sealing or storing them in airtight containers, such as Mylar bags with oxygen absorbers, extends their shelf life by preventing exposure to oxygen, moisture, and pests.

For longer-term food storage, consider creating **food caches** in multiple hidden locations. These caches act as a safeguard in case your primary food supply is discovered, raided, or destroyed. Distribute the caches across various, secure sites—underground bunkers, hidden compartments within walls, or remote areas where access is restricted. This ensures that even if one cache is compromised, you still have access to other supplies.

Preserving perishables without refrigeration presents additional challenges, but traditional methods can be employed. **Canning**, **pickling**, **smoking**, and **drying** food are effective preservation techniques that have been used for centuries to extend the shelf life of fruits, vegetables, and meat. Smoking or salting meat, for example, prevents bacteria from growing, while drying fruits and vegetables removes moisture, which inhibits mold and decay. These preservation techniques are valuable in rural areas where foraging and hunting provide fresh resources, but refrigeration is not an option.

PROTECTING FOOD FROM PESTS AND CONTAMINATION

In a collapsed society, one of the greatest threats to food storage is the invasion of pests—rodents, insects, and other vermin that can contaminate or destroy your stockpiles. Securing your food from these pests requires careful planning and the use of proper containers. Airtight, rodent-proof containers made of metal or heavy-duty plastic help protect food from rodents, while keeping food caches elevated or hanging in trees reduces the risk of ground-based vermin accessing them. Additionally, regular inspection of food stores for signs of infestation—such as droppings, gnaw marks, or insect activity—ensures that any contamination is caught early before it spreads.

Sanitation is another critical factor in food storage. In a collapsed society, the risk of contamination from improper handling or unsanitary storage conditions is much higher, leading to foodborne illnesses that could decimate a group. Ensure that food is stored in clean, dry environments, and that members of your group understand the importance of washing hands and maintaining basic hygiene when handling or preparing food. Regularly rotating food stores—using the oldest items first—helps prevent food from going bad, while keeping an accurate inventory of your stockpile ensures that nothing is left forgotten or wasted.

WATER STORAGE

Access to clean, drinkable water is one of the most immediate survival concerns in any collapsed society. Without reliable infrastructure, water supplies from cities and towns can quickly become contaminated or cease to function altogether. Securing a long-term, sustainable water source is essential, but having an emergency water supply that is safely stored is critical for periods when access to natural water sources is limited or compromised.

Water storage requires careful planning, as it takes up more space and is more difficult to secure than other supplies. The best approach is to store water in **large, food-grade containers** that are made of durable plastic, stainless steel, or glass. Containers should be airtight to prevent contamination from bacteria, algae, or chemicals. For large groups, **water barrels or tanks** are ideal for storing large quantities of water, while smaller containers such as jugs or canteens can be used for individual transport.

Water must also be treated before storage to ensure that it remains safe to drink. Using water purification methods —such as boiling, using purification tablets, or filtering —eliminates harmful bacteria and pathogens. Additionally, treating stored water with small amounts of unscented bleach or using commercial water treatment solutions extends its shelf life and helps prevent contamination over time.

Like food caches, **water caches** should be established in multiple locations to protect against the loss of your primary water supply. If your base of operations is attacked or compromised, having access to alternative water sources, such as nearby streams, lakes, or rainwater collection systems, ensures that you can maintain a reliable supply. Keep these water sources hidden or well-protected from contamination and sabotage, as access to clean water becomes one of the most valuable resources in a collapsed society.

For longer-term water security, consider setting up **rainwater collection systems** or drilling wells in rural environments. Rainwater collection, particularly when coupled with proper filtration, provides a renewable water source that can sustain your group for long periods. Storing rainwater in covered barrels or tanks, with appropriate filtration systems, ensures a steady supply of potable water without needing to rely on outside sources.

MEDICAL SUPPLIES STORAGE

In the chaos of a collapsed society, access to medical care becomes extremely limited, and having a well-stocked cache of medical supplies is crucial for treating injuries, preventing infections, and managing illnesses. Medical supplies, however, are highly perishable and prone to degradation if not stored correctly, which makes proper storage essential to ensuring their viability over the long term.

Basic medical supplies—bandages, antiseptics, painkillers, antibiotics, and surgical tools—should be stored in a cool, dry place to prevent contamination or spoilage. Temperature fluctuations and humidity can reduce the effectiveness of many medications, particularly antibiotics and vaccines, so storing them in temperature-controlled environments is essential. In the absence of refrigeration, insulation or underground storage can help stabilize the temperature and extend the shelf life of critical medicines.

SECURING MEDICAL RESOURCES AGAINST SPOILAGE AND THEFT

A key factor in the long-term management of medical supplies is keeping an organized, detailed inventory of what you have on hand. In a collapsed society, medical supplies are difficult to replace, so waste or misuse must be avoided. Track the expiration dates of medications, rotating stock and using items before they expire. For items like antibiotics, painkillers, or blood pressure medications, storing multiple types or brands helps ensure that you have alternatives available in case one type is ineffective or unavailable.

Like food and water, medical supplies are prime targets for theft, and stockpiles should be well-hidden or stored in secure locations. A small, easily accessible cache of basic medical supplies can be kept near your primary base of operations, while more specialized or larger stores should be concealed in hidden caches or in fortified rooms. This ensures that you have immediate access to basic first aid but don't risk losing all your supplies in a single raid.

AMMUNITION AND WEAPONS STORAGE

In any situation where societal order has collapsed, securing and storing weapons and ammunition is critical for defending your group and maintaining operational readiness. Ammunition, however, is sensitive to environmental conditions and can degrade if not stored properly. Ensuring that your ammunition remains dry, clean, and protected from the elements is key to maintaining its effectiveness over time.

Ammunition should be stored in **airtight, waterproof containers**, such as metal ammo boxes or plastic storage bins, which prevent moisture from seeping in and causing corrosion or damage to the cartridges. The storage location should be cool and dry, away from extreme heat, which can cause ammunition to degrade or misfire. Ammunition stored underground or in climate-controlled spaces lasts significantly longer than ammunition stored in fluctuating temperatures or humid environments.

DISTRIBUTING AND HIDING AMMUNITION

Just as with food and water, it is essential to avoid keeping all your ammunition in one place. Spread out your ammunition across different caches, ensuring that you have access to it no matter where you are operating. Hidden caches of ammunition can be concealed in remote locations, disguised under rocks or in hollowed-out trees, or buried underground. These caches should be accessible but well-hidden, reducing the risk of discovery by enemy forces.

When storing ammunition, it's important to keep track of the different types and calibers. Organizing your storage based on the type of weapon ensures that you have the right ammunition available when you need it. Regularly inspect ammunition caches for signs of damage or degradation and rotate your stock to ensure the oldest ammunition is used first.

In a collapsed society, protecting your ammunition stores from theft or enemy seizure is as important as maintaining their condition. Securing the entrance to storage rooms, installing surveillance or alarm systems, and keeping weapons and ammunition stored separately can reduce the risk of your resources being stolen. In the event of a raid, having backup caches ensures that you can continue to defend your group even if some supplies are compromised.

In a world without functioning systems, storing food, water, medical supplies, and ammunition becomes the cornerstone of survival. Each of these resources requires careful management and planning to ensure that they remain viable, accessible, and protected from both environmental degradation and hostile forces. The key to success lies in proper preparation—organizing caches, preserving supplies, and securing stockpiles against theft or loss. With these strategies in place, your group can weather the challenges of a collapsed society, ensuring that you have the means to survive for the long term, no matter what threats arise.

Bartering, Raiding, and Self-Sufficiency

In a collapsed society, survival hinges on the ability to adapt, innovate, and secure essential resources by any means necessary. With the breakdown of traditional supply chains, currency may lose its value, and communities will revert to more primitive forms of economic exchange, often involving bartering or raiding. However, neither bartering nor raiding can guarantee long-term survival on their own. True resilience comes from cultivating self-sufficiency—being able to produce, store, and protect resources without reliance on others. By balancing these three strategies—bartering, raiding, and self-sufficiency—a group can maximize its chances of survival in a lawless and resource-scarce environment.

BARTERING AS AN ECONOMIC STRATEGY

In the absence of formalized currency or functioning markets, bartering becomes one of the primary methods of exchange in a collapsed society. Bartering allows individuals and groups to trade goods or services for essential resources that they cannot produce themselves. This system can foster cooperation and the exchange of valuable skills between groups, but it also requires a keen understanding of the relative value of resources in a world where supply and demand shift constantly.

To engage in successful bartering, it's important to recognize that the value of items changes drastically in a collapsed society. Luxury goods or entertainment items, once highly sought after in a functional society, quickly lose value. Instead, survival necessities such as food, water, medical supplies, fuel, ammunition, and tools become the primary commodities for trade. The ability to acquire, produce, or stockpile these essential items gives you leverage in barter negotiations. Skills —such as medical expertise, mechanical repair, or weapon maintenance—also become valuable bargaining chips, as they provide ongoing utility in exchange for immediate goods.

Successful bartering depends on building relationships and alliances with neighboring groups or individuals. Trusted trading partners reduce the risk of betrayal or deception, and ongoing barter arrangements can provide a steady flow of necessary resources. However, every barter interaction comes with inherent risks. It's critical to approach bartering cautiously, always prepared for potential theft or ambush. Engaging in trades in neutral, open areas, with a backup security plan, can reduce the likelihood of falling into a trap.

Having a deep understanding of supply shortages and the needs of other groups is also crucial in bartering. By anticipating which items will become more valuable—whether due to seasonal changes, geographic limitations, or societal shifts—you can secure a strong position in future trades. For example, stockpiling medical supplies or fuel early on, when they are still somewhat available, allows you to barter at a premium when these items become increasingly scarce.

RAIDING AS A LAST RESORT

While bartering offers a more cooperative path to securing resources, raiding represents the more aggressive alternative. In a collapsed society, many groups will inevitably resort to violence to survive, targeting stockpiles, vulnerable groups, or isolated homesteads to seize necessary supplies. Raiding, while often viewed as morally ambiguous, may become a necessary option for survival, particularly when resources are unattainable by other means. However, raiding carries significant risks—both to the raiders and to the stability of the society they inhabit.

Raiding can be strategic and limited, targeting enemy groups or stockpiles that pose an immediate threat or represent a concentrated supply of critical resources. Rather than engaging in indiscriminate attacks, raiding should be carefully planned, with reconnaissance on the target's weaknesses, supply quantities, and defensive capabilities. A successful raid requires coordination, speed, and stealth, aiming to overwhelm the target before they can mount a defense or call for reinforcements.

One of the most important aspects of raiding is determining when and where to strike. Targeting poorly defended areas or enemy factions that already view your group as hostile minimizes the risk of diplomatic fallout. However, raiding should never be undertaken lightly, as it can lead to ongoing conflicts or the creation of powerful enemies. If a raid results in the death of civilians or destruction of property, your group could become the target of retribution, leading to escalations in violence that threaten long-term survival.

Moreover, raiding presents its own logistical challenges. Transporting stolen goods, especially large quantities of food, fuel, or ammunition, requires planning and preparation. Moving quickly is essential to avoid counterattacks or rival groups intercepting the stolen supplies. Additionally, securing and hiding stolen resources is just as important as acquiring them. A poorly defended or obvious stockpile will quickly become a target, leading to further raids against your group.

In many cases, raiding becomes a vicious cycle. Groups that rely on raiding to survive often deplete local resources quickly, forcing them to move farther afield to find new targets. This can leave them vulnerable to retaliation or overextension, and the more raids they conduct, the more enemies they create. Therefore, raiding should be viewed as a short-term solution —a means to gain critical supplies in an emergency, not a sustainable method of survival.

CULTIVATING SELF-SUFFICIENCY

While bartering and raiding may provide short-term access to resources, neither method guarantees long-term survival. In a collapsed society, the only truly sustainable approach is self-sufficiency—the ability to produce, store, and manage the resources you need without relying on external sources. Self-sufficiency allows your group to minimize interactions with potentially hostile factions, reduce dependence on volatile trade networks, and insulate itself from the unpredictability of the broader environment.

Self-sufficiency begins with securing access to basic resources, such as food and water. Growing your own food—whether through gardening, farming, or raising livestock—ensures a renewable supply that is independent of external forces. Even in urban environments, rooftop gardens, hydroponic systems, or the repurposing of abandoned land can provide critical food sources. In rural areas, larger-scale agriculture, hunting, and fishing become primary means of sustenance, allowing your group to maintain a steady supply of protein and crops.

Water security is equally important. Setting up sustainable water collection systems, such as rainwater harvesting, wells, or filtration of natural water sources, ensures that your group has access to clean drinking water without relying on outside sources. Water filtration and purification techniques must be employed to prevent illness, especially when dealing with natural water sources that may be contaminated.

Fuel and energy present a unique challenge in self-sufficiency. Traditional fuel sources, like gasoline and propane, will become increasingly scarce as the collapse progresses. Renewable energy sources, such as solar panels, wind turbines, or wood-burning stoves, offer more sustainable solutions. Solar panels can provide electricity for lighting, communication devices, or small tools, while wind turbines can generate power for larger systems if properly constructed. Wood-burning stoves, while basic, provide both heat and cooking capabilities, especially in colder climates.

Another aspect of self-sufficiency is building a sustainable defense. Producing and maintaining weapons and ammunition—whether through reloading ammunition, crafting basic weapons, or repairing existing firearms—

is critical for defending your resources. Blacksmithing skills or the ability to manufacture rudimentary weapons using scavenged materials can become invaluable when conventional weapons run low.

Developing a self-sufficient medical supply is also critical. Stockpiling medical supplies early on is a priority, but it is equally important to understand how to use natural remedies and herbal medicine when pharmaceuticals are unavailable. Many common plants have medicinal properties that can treat infections, alleviate pain, or reduce inflammation. Learning how to identify and cultivate these plants ensures that your group is not reliant on quickly depleting medical resources.

BALANCING BARTERING, RAIDING, AND SELF-SUFFICIENCY

Survival in a collapsed society requires flexibility, and each of these strategies—bartering, raiding, and self-sufficiency—must be employed at different times depending on circumstances. A balanced approach that leans on bartering for rare items, uses raiding in emergencies, and prioritizes self-sufficiency provides the best chance of long-term survival. Bartering allows for cooperation and reduces the need for conflict, while raiding can provide a quick influx of resources when there is no alternative. However, the cornerstone of any survival strategy must be self-sufficiency, which ultimately insulates your group from the external volatility of a fractured world.

By cultivating a diverse range of skills—gardening, foraging, hunting, water purification, and weapon maintenance—your group can produce what it needs to survive, minimizing dependence on others. Building alliances through bartering helps maintain peace with neighboring factions, while raiding, used sparingly, can bolster supplies in times of crisis. Ultimately, balancing these methods ensures that your group remains resilient, adaptable, and ready for whatever challenges come its way in a post-collapse world.

This strategic flexibility ensures that, even in the most desperate situations, your group has options. The ability to barter for what you cannot produce, the capacity to raid for immediate needs, and the discipline to develop self-sufficiency allows for a multifaceted survival strategy. In a world of limited resources and constant danger, those who can navigate these strategies with precision and foresight will be best equipped to thrive in the long term.

CHAPTER 9: ORGANIZING CITIZEN DEFENSE UNITS

In a society that has collapsed, where law enforcement and military protection are no longer reliable or even present, the survival of a community or group often depends on its ability to organize its own defense. The chaos and violence that follow societal breakdown create an environment where individuals, families, and small communities are forced to fend for themselves. In such an environment, ad hoc groups and informal militias begin to form to fill the security vacuum. These **citizen defense units** become the first line of protection against threats—whether from criminal gangs, rival factions, or hostile external forces.

Organizing a citizen defense unit requires structure, discipline, and strategy, even though these groups may be made up of civilians with little or no prior military experience. The strength of such units lies not in advanced weaponry or military training but in their cohesion, adaptability, and deep knowledge of their environment. For a defense unit to be effective, it must be well-organized, well-led, and able to operate in a variety of settings, from urban street skirmishes to rural ambushes. More importantly, it must be built on a foundation of trust, solidarity, and a shared commitment to protect the group's collective interests.

The key to building a successful citizen defense unit lies in understanding that defense is not solely about repelling attackers. It also involves maintaining internal security, gathering intelligence, setting up early warning systems, and ensuring that your group remains operational in times of stress or conflict. In this chapter, we will explore the fundamental principles of organizing and leading a citizen defense unit in a collapsed society, focusing on everything from recruitment and leadership to tactics, communication, and logistics.

RECRUITMENT AND BUILDING TRUST

The first step in organizing a citizen defense unit is assembling a group of people willing and capable of defending the community. Recruitment begins with identifying individuals who possess the physical and mental resilience to engage in defense activities, but more importantly, those who can be trusted. In a collapsed society, trust becomes the most valuable asset, as the risks of infiltration, betrayal, or cowardice can destroy a group from within.

When recruiting, look for individuals with skills that are valuable in a defensive context. Prior military or law enforcement experience is an obvious advantage, but do not overlook those who possess other critical skills. Hunters, mechanics, medics, and even engineers can contribute to the overall effectiveness of the unit. A well-rounded group will have members who can provide tactical support, maintain weapons and equipment, administer first aid, and handle the logistical aspects of defense, such as transportation, food, and communication.

Recruitment should also focus on building a group that can work well together under pressure. A defense unit composed of individuals who are uncooperative or prone to panic will be ineffective, no matter how well-armed or trained they are.

Building trust is a slow process, but one that is essential for group cohesion. Start by establishing small units within your group—pairing or assigning people to work together on tasks such as patrols, fortification, or supply runs. This allows members to develop trust through shared experiences and responsibilities.

Once a core group is assembled, recruitment can expand beyond the immediate circle to include the broader community. However, this must be done carefully, ensuring that new members are vetted thoroughly and integrated slowly. A rushed recruitment process can lead to security breaches or internal conflict, so it is important to balance the need for manpower with the necessity of maintaining a trusted, reliable group.

LEADERSHIP AND COMMAND STRUCTURE

An effective citizen defense unit requires strong, clear leadership. Without a defined command structure, a group can easily descend into chaos during moments of crisis. Leadership does not necessarily have to be based on military hierarchy, but there must be a clear chain of command that is respected and followed by all members. The leader of the unit must be decisive, competent, and capable of making tough calls under pressure, but also approachable and respected by the group.

The leader's role is not just to direct the unit in combat or during defensive operations but to maintain morale, discipline, and cohesion. In a collapsed society, the psychological toll of ongoing conflict and insecurity can wear down even the most resilient individuals. A strong leader will recognize when members of the group are reaching their breaking point and take steps to provide rest, support, or rotations to prevent burnout.

In addition to the overall leader, each defense unit should

be divided into smaller squads or teams, each with its own squad leader. These squad leaders are responsible for the day-to-day management of their teams, ensuring that tasks are completed, supplies are maintained, and communication with the rest of the unit is kept open. The structure should be flexible enough to adapt to changing circumstances, with each squad capable of operating independently if necessary, but integrated into the larger defense strategy.

The command structure must also allow for feedback and input from the rank-and-file members. While the leader has the final say, a healthy defense unit is one where decisions are informed by the expertise and observations of all its members. Encouraging open communication within the unit fosters a sense of ownership and responsibility among the group, ensuring that everyone is invested in the success of the unit's defense efforts.

TRAINING AND TACTICAL READINESS

Even if a group has no prior experience in combat, training is essential to prepare for the inevitable conflicts that will arise in a collapsed society. Training does not need to be highly specialized or formalized, but it must focus on core competencies that will enhance the group's ability to defend itself. These include basic firearms training, close-quarters combat, ambush tactics, patrol and reconnaissance operations, and emergency medical procedures.

Firearms training should be a top priority, as many individuals in a collapsed society will have access to small arms but may lack the knowledge or experience to use them effectively. Training should cover not only the basics of handling and firing weapons but also maintenance, ammunition conservation, and tactics for using firearms in both urban and rural settings. Emphasizing accuracy over volume of fire is critical, as ammunition will be a limited resource, and every shot must count.

Training in small-unit tactics, such as how to move as a group through different environments, set up ambushes, or defend a fixed position, is also essential. These tactical skills increase the group's ability to respond effectively to threats, whether they come in the form of small raiding parties or larger organized forces. Regular drills, including simulated attacks or raids, help solidify these tactics and ensure that the group can react quickly and coherently under pressure.

Beyond combat training, every member of the defense unit should be trained in basic first aid and trauma care. Injuries are inevitable in a conflict, and the ability to administer emergency medical care can save lives. Training members to apply tourniquets, treat gunshot wounds, and manage shock or trauma ensures that the group can sustain itself even in the face of significant casualties. Having a dedicated medic or medical team within the unit is ideal, but in their absence, every member should be prepared to handle medical emergencies.

DEFENSIVE TACTICS AND FORTIFICATIONS

Organizing a citizen defense unit goes beyond preparing individuals for combat. It also involves planning and implementing defensive strategies to protect the group's base of operations, whether it's a homestead, neighborhood, or larger community. Effective fortification and the strategic use of terrain are critical for defending against both organized attacks and opportunistic raids.

The first step in fortification is understanding the environment. In an urban setting, buildings, streets, and infrastructure can be used to create defensible positions, chokepoints, and barriers. Barricading entry points, reinforcing doors and windows, and using rooftops for observation and defense give a significant advantage in urban combat. In rural environments, natural barriers like rivers, forests, and hills provide cover and concealment, while fences, trenches, and elevated watchtowers offer additional layers of defense.

Defense units should prioritize setting up **early warning systems**—simple alarms or tripwires that alert the group to approaching enemies. These systems provide critical time to prepare defenses or execute evacuation plans. The placement of lookouts or scouts around the perimeter of the base also increases the unit's ability to detect and respond to threats before they arrive at the gates.

While defense is important, the unit must also be prepared for **offensive action** when necessary. This includes setting up ambushes, launching preemptive strikes on enemy positions, and engaging in hit-and-run tactics that weaken hostile forces without risking large-scale engagements. The unit's leadership must balance the need for defense with the strategic advantage of seizing opportunities to diminish the strength of adversaries.

LOGISTICS AND SUSTAINING OPERATIONS

A successful defense unit does not operate on tactics and strategy alone; it requires a logistical backbone to sustain operations over the long term. This includes securing food, water, medical supplies, and ammunition, as well as managing transportation and communication. Organizing the logistics of the defense unit ensures that it remains operational in the face of prolonged conflict.

Establishing a supply chain—whether through foraging, farming, or scavenging—guarantees that the group has access to the resources it needs. Regular resupply missions should be planned and conducted by smaller teams, minimizing the exposure of the main unit while ensuring that critical supplies are replenished. Storing these supplies in secure locations, distributed across multiple caches, reduces the risk of losing everything to a single raid or attack.

Ammunition management is also a key part of logistics. While stockpiling is essential, careful rationing of ammunition is necessary to prevent waste. Every member of the defense unit should be trained in conserving ammunition and making every shot count. Fire discipline during engagements —ensuring that only necessary shots are fired and that there is no panic fire—prolongs the viability of the unit's defensive capabilities.

Additionally, establishing reliable communication within the unit and with neighboring groups is critical for maintaining coordination and intelligence. Radios, signal fires, or other low-tech communication methods can be used to relay information about enemy movements or request reinforcements. Keeping communication secure is paramount to preventing the enemy from intercepting messages or identifying weaknesses in the group's defenses.

MORALE AND PSYCHOLOGICAL RESILIENCE

The psychological health of a defense unit is just as important as its tactical readiness. Prolonged conflict, constant threats, and the stress of living in a collapsed society can erode morale and lead to internal conflict or breakdowns in discipline. Leaders must recognize the importance of maintaining morale by fostering a sense of purpose and solidarity within the group.

Providing regular breaks from high-stress activities, rotating members between different duties, and encouraging downtime for rest and recovery are essential for maintaining psychological resilience. Celebrating small victories, whether in securing resources or repelling an attack, helps reinforce the group's unity and commitment to its defense mission.

Ultimately, organizing a citizen defense unit is about building a resilient, adaptable group that can protect its community, sustain its operations, and respond effectively to the myriad challenges of a collapsed society. By focusing on recruitment, training, leadership, tactics, and logistics, a citizen defense unit can become a formidable force in maintaining security and survival in the most uncertain and dangerous of times.

Forming and Leading Small Defensive Teams

Forming and leading small defensive teams in a collapsed society is essential for maintaining security and ensuring the survival of a group or community. In a hostile and resource-scarce environment, smaller teams offer flexibility, mobility, and the ability to react quickly to emerging threats, making them more effective in guerrilla-style warfare or decentralized defense. These teams are often tasked with patrolling, reconnaissance, and engaging in defensive or offensive actions on behalf of the larger group, and their success depends on careful organization, strong leadership, and tactical efficiency.

A small defensive team typically consists of a handful of individuals who can operate independently or in coordination with larger units. The formation and leadership of these teams require a balance of strategic planning, the selection of skilled and trustworthy members, and a command structure that ensures each team can function autonomously while still contributing to the overall defense strategy. Effective small defensive teams must be versatile, capable of executing various missions, and able to make quick decisions under pressure without relying on constant communication with a central command.

To lead such a team successfully, a leader must foster cohesion, maintain discipline, and ensure that every member understands their role and the larger objective. This section explores how to form, structure, and lead small defensive teams, focusing on the critical aspects of team dynamics, communication, tactical readiness, and leadership strategies.

SELECTING TEAM MEMBERS

The first step in forming a small defensive team is the careful selection of its members. In a collapsed society, where trust is paramount, team selection must focus on individuals who not only possess the necessary physical and tactical skills but also demonstrate reliability, loyalty, and the ability to function under extreme stress. While prior military or law enforcement experience is an advantage, it is not always a requirement. What matters most is each member's ability to contribute to the team's mission and work cohesively with others.

When selecting team members, consider the unique skills that each individual brings to the group. A well-rounded small defensive team benefits from a diverse set of capabilities, including marksmanship, hand-to-hand combat, first aid, mechanical skills, and reconnaissance. Assigning roles within the team based on these skills allows for greater operational efficiency. For example, a team might consist of a team leader, a scout or tracker, a designated marksman, and a medic. While every member should be cross-trained in essential survival and combat skills, these specialized roles help the team respond more effectively to various scenarios.

Trust is the cornerstone of any defensive unit, but it is especially important in small teams. Each member must be able to rely on the others to perform their duties and remain calm under fire. Any sign of unreliability, disobedience, or lack of mental toughness can undermine the entire team's effectiveness, leading to failure in critical missions. Leaders should conduct informal evaluations of potential team members, observing how they perform under pressure and how well they integrate into the team dynamic before finalizing their selection.

TEAM STRUCTURE AND ROLES

Once the team members have been selected, it's important to establish a clear structure within the group. While small teams are more flexible than larger units, they still require defined roles to ensure that tasks are distributed efficiently and that command is followed without hesitation. A typical small defensive team consists of a leader and three to five additional members, each assigned to a specific role.

- **Team Leader**: The team leader is responsible for planning missions, making tactical decisions, and maintaining overall coordination. This person must have strong leadership skills, the ability to remain calm under pressure, and the respect of the other team members. The team leader ensures that everyone knows their role in the mission, communicates with the larger defense unit when necessary, and makes quick decisions in the field.

- **Scout/Reconnaissance**: This role focuses on gathering intelligence about enemy movements, terrain, and potential threats. The scout often moves ahead of the team, using stealth to observe the environment and report back with critical information. This role requires strong situational awareness, tracking skills, and the ability to remain undetected.

- **Designated Marksman**: The marksman is tasked with providing long-range support during engagements, offering precision fire when needed. This role requires excellent marksmanship, patience, and the ability to pick off high-value targets from a distance without exposing the team's position.

- **Medic**: The team's medic is responsible for providing emergency medical care in the event of injuries. This role requires a solid understanding of trauma care, wound management, and basic field surgery. The medic must carry medical supplies and be ready to stabilize injured team members during or after a conflict.

- **Riflemen/Support**: Depending on the mission, the remaining members of the team function as riflemen or provide additional support, such as carrying extra ammunition, food, or specialized equipment like radios or demolition tools. These members are the backbone of the team during combat, responsible for engaging enemies, providing cover fire, and maintaining the team's overall mobility.

While each team member may have a specialized role, cross-training is essential to ensure that the team can continue operating if one member is incapacitated. Every member should have a basic understanding of medical procedures, reconnaissance tactics, and marksmanship to maintain team cohesion and readiness under any circumstances.

COMMUNICATION AND COORDINATION

Effective communication is critical to the success of any defensive team, especially when operating in small units where every decision and movement must be coordinated with precision. In a collapsed society, communication networks may be limited or compromised, requiring teams to rely on secure, low-tech methods of communication to avoid detection and ensure operational security.

Within the team, clear communication protocols must be established from the outset. Each team member should know when and how to communicate during an engagement, whether through verbal commands, hand signals, or radio transmissions. The use of **radio discipline**—short, clear transmissions that minimize the risk of interception—ensures that the team remains covert while maintaining contact with the rest of the unit or command structure.

When operating in hostile environments, maintaining **line-of-sight communication** through hand signals or visual cues is often preferable to radio communications, especially in situations where stealth is critical. Hand signals can relay information about enemy positions, movement, or commands to fire without alerting the enemy. Establishing these silent communication protocols during training ensures that every member of the team can respond instantly to commands without needing to speak.

Communication also extends to coordination with other teams or the larger defense unit. Small teams are often part of a broader defense network, and their actions must align with the group's overall strategy. This requires regular check-ins with command, the use of secure communication channels, and the ability to relay intelligence about enemy movements or threats quickly and accurately. In situations where communication is compromised or unavailable, contingency plans should be in place so that each team knows how to act autonomously.

TACTICAL READINESS AND MOBILITY

The strength of a small defensive team lies in its mobility and ability to engage in rapid, flexible operations. Unlike larger units, which may be slower to move and more cumbersome, small teams can take advantage of guerrilla tactics—striking quickly and retreating before the enemy can mount a counterattack. To maintain this tactical advantage, the team must prioritize mobility, both in terms of physical movement and operational flexibility.

Mobility means staying light, carrying only essential supplies, and being ready to move at a moment's notice. Every team member should be equipped with the basic gear needed for survival and combat, but overburdening the team with unnecessary equipment will slow them down and make them vulnerable to ambush. Pack organization is critical—each member should carry only what is essential for the mission, with food, water, ammunition, and medical supplies distributed evenly among the team to ensure that no one is carrying too much.

Tactical readiness also involves constant **situational awareness**. The team leader and the scout must assess the terrain, the enemy's capabilities, and potential escape routes at all times. This level of awareness allows the team to exploit the environment—using natural cover, choke points, or ambush positions to their advantage. Regular training in navigating different types of terrain (urban, forest, mountainous) ensures that the team can operate effectively in a variety of settings.

Another key element of tactical readiness is the ability to **shift from defense to offense** seamlessly. In some cases, the best defense is a well-timed attack, and small teams are particularly suited to engaging in **hit-and-run tactics**. By striking at vulnerable points in the enemy's defenses or supply lines, small teams can create confusion and weaken the enemy without committing to prolonged engagements. These tactics require speed, coordination, and the ability to retreat quickly before the enemy can organize a response.

LEADERSHIP AND DECISION-MAKING

Leading a small defensive team is a unique challenge that requires a combination of tactical expertise, quick decision-making, and emotional intelligence. The team leader must be able to assess threats in real time, make decisions that maximize the team's strengths, and adapt to rapidly changing circumstances. In a high-stress environment, the ability to remain calm, focused, and decisive is critical.

Decision-making within a small team is often fast-paced, with little time for debate or deliberation. The team leader must trust their instincts, rely on the information provided by the scout or other members, and make split-second decisions about whether to engage, retreat, or maneuver into a better position. The success of these decisions depends on the team's training and preparation—if the team is well-trained, every member will know their role, and decisions will be executed swiftly and without hesitation.

However, leadership is not just about making tactical decisions. It's also about maintaining the team's morale, discipline, and trust. A good leader ensures that every team member feels valued, understands their role, and has the confidence to perform under pressure. Leaders must also be attuned to the mental and emotional state of their team, providing rest or relief when needed to prevent burnout or breakdowns.

In a collapsed society, where the future is uncertain, and every day brings new challenges, leading a small defensive team requires both strategic vision and tactical precision. The ability to balance aggression with caution, maintain discipline under fire, and adapt to the constantly shifting landscape of threats makes the difference between success and failure. With strong leadership, a cohesive structure, and clear communication, small defensive teams can serve as the foundation of a larger defense strategy, protecting their community and ensuring survival in a hostile world.

Maintaining Morale and Cohesion Under Extreme Conditions

Maintaining morale and cohesion under extreme conditions is one of the most challenging yet essential tasks for any leader in a collapsed society. When society crumbles, and chaos becomes the norm, the psychological strain on individuals and groups intensifies. Fear, uncertainty, deprivation, and constant threats from hostile forces can erode the unity and willpower of even the most well-prepared defense units. In such an environment, morale is not just a matter of emotional well-being; it becomes a strategic asset. A group that loses its sense of purpose and unity is vulnerable to collapse from within, even if it is physically well-supplied and well-defended. Therefore, ensuring that morale and cohesion are maintained is just as crucial as logistical planning or tactical readiness.

The psychological resilience of a group is built on several pillars: trust, shared purpose, leadership, discipline, and the ability to cope with adversity. These elements, when combined, create a foundation that allows individuals to endure extreme conditions without breaking apart. While maintaining morale in a collapsed society is a complex task that requires vigilance and constant effort, it can be achieved through effective leadership, regular communication, fostering a sense of belonging, and providing opportunities for rest and recovery. A group that feels connected and supported, despite the hardships, will remain more resilient and cohesive under the most difficult circumstances.

LEADERSHIP AND THE ROLE OF COMMAND

Leadership plays a critical role in maintaining morale, especially under extreme conditions. A strong leader sets the tone for the entire group, modeling calmness, resilience, and decisiveness even in the face of adversity. Leaders who maintain their composure inspire confidence and trust, which, in turn, keeps morale high. In contrast, a leader who appears uncertain, indecisive, or overly emotional can quickly erode the group's confidence, leading to internal conflict or a breakdown in discipline.

Effective leaders understand that morale is not just about keeping spirits high during easy times; it's about managing fear, stress, and fatigue during difficult times. To achieve this, leaders must communicate clearly and honestly with their group. Transparency, even about difficult truths, is essential. People can endure harsh realities if they feel they are being treated with respect and are part of the decision-making process. Regular updates on the situation, the group's objectives, and any threats on the horizon allow members to feel informed and engaged, reducing anxiety that comes from uncertainty.

Leaders must also ensure that each member of the group has a clear role and understands how their contribution fits into the broader mission. This sense of purpose is crucial in maintaining morale. People need to feel that their actions matter, that they are part of something larger than themselves, and that their efforts contribute directly to the group's survival. By reinforcing the value of each individual's role, leaders foster a sense of belonging and responsibility, keeping cohesion intact.

DISCIPLINE AND ROUTINE

Maintaining a sense of order and routine is essential in extreme conditions. Chaos breeds fear, and fear can quickly lead to panic or disarray within a group. Discipline, both mental and physical, acts as a stabilizing force, giving individuals something to hold onto when everything else seems to be falling apart. Regular schedules, even for basic tasks like eating, sleeping, patrolling, and cleaning, provide a sense of normalcy that helps to combat the psychological effects of uncertainty and disorder.

Discipline also ensures that standards are maintained even in the most trying circumstances. Group members must be held accountable for their actions, and any deviations from established protocols—whether it's failing to perform a duty or acting out of panic—should be addressed immediately. While discipline must be enforced, it should not be harsh or overly punitive. The goal is to build a culture of responsibility and mutual respect, where each individual understands the importance of their role and feels supported by the group.

Training plays an essential role in maintaining discipline under stress. Regular drills, including those that simulate high-stress situations, prepare the group to respond to real threats without losing cohesion. Familiarity with procedures, whether in combat or in managing everyday tasks, reduces the likelihood of panic or disobedience when the group faces real danger. The more familiar people are with their duties, the more automatic their responses will be, even under intense pressure.

COMMUNICATION AND TRANSPARENCY

In extreme conditions, rumors, misinformation, and the lack of clear communication can destroy morale. In the absence of reliable information, individuals tend to fill in the gaps with their worst fears. Leaders must counteract this by maintaining open, transparent lines of communication with the group. Regular briefings on the current situation—whether it's about enemy movements, the state of supplies, or internal challenges—are essential in keeping everyone informed and focused.

In times of crisis, communication should be direct and honest. Sugarcoating bad news or withholding information in an attempt to protect morale can backfire, especially if the truth eventually surfaces. When people feel that they are being kept in the dark, trust erodes, and resentment can grow. By contrast, even difficult information, if delivered with honesty and a clear plan of action, reinforces the idea that the group is in control of its situation, no matter how dire.

Leaders should also encourage communication between group members, fostering an environment where people feel free to express concerns, ask questions, or offer suggestions. This horizontal communication strengthens bonds between individuals and helps to resolve small conflicts before they escalate. It also ensures that everyone is contributing to the group's overall mission, providing feedback and offering solutions to ongoing challenges.

REST AND RECOVERY

One of the most overlooked aspects of maintaining morale under extreme conditions is ensuring that members of the group have opportunities for rest and recovery. Exhaustion—both physical and mental—can severely undermine cohesion and decision-making ability. No matter how disciplined or motivated a group is, individuals need time to rest, recuperate, and decompress. Denying rest for too long can lead to breakdowns in mental health, mistakes in judgment, and even internal conflict.

Leaders must recognize when individuals or the group as a whole are reaching their limits. Rotating shifts for high-stress tasks, such as patrols or guard duty, ensures that no one person is overworked. Additionally, designating safe periods for sleep and relaxation, even if only for short stretches, helps mitigate the toll of prolonged stress.

Creating small opportunities for "normal" activities—whether it's sharing a meal, engaging in light conversation, or engaging in hobbies—allows the group to maintain a sense of humanity amidst the chaos. These moments of respite remind individuals that they are still living, not merely surviving. They provide an outlet for stress and create a psychological buffer against the constant tension of the environment.

BUILDING A SENSE OF COMMUNITY AND SOLIDARITY

Morale is deeply tied to the sense of community within the group. When individuals feel that they are part of a collective that cares for their well-being, they are more likely to endure hardships without becoming demoralized. Leaders can foster this sense of community by encouraging mutual support, empathy, and shared responsibility. This begins with ensuring that every member of the group feels valued and respected, regardless of their specific role or rank.

Shared rituals or traditions, such as debriefing after a mission, eating meals together, or even maintaining a small space for prayer or reflection, can strengthen these bonds. Such activities reinforce the idea that the group is united in both its goals and its challenges. It also gives people a sense of continuity in the face of upheaval, helping them to connect emotionally with their fellow members.

Leaders should also address any internal conflicts immediately and constructively. Tensions are inevitable under extreme conditions, especially when people are scared, hungry, or fatigued. However, left unaddressed, these tensions can escalate into serious conflicts that undermine the group's cohesion. By maintaining open communication and encouraging conflict resolution, leaders can ensure that disagreements are resolved before they fester.

ADAPTING TO LOSS AND SETBACKS

In a collapsed society, setbacks and losses—whether of supplies, territory, or even lives—are inevitable. These moments can be devastating for morale, especially when they come unexpectedly or seem insurmountable. Leaders must be prepared to manage the psychological impact of such losses, keeping the group focused on its long-term survival rather than succumbing to despair or panic.

One way to manage loss is to frame it within the broader context of the group's mission. Every setback, no matter how serious, should be viewed as a challenge to be overcome rather than a definitive defeat. Leaders can use setbacks as teaching moments, emphasizing what the group can learn from the experience and how it will adapt in the future. By focusing on resilience and problem-solving, leaders help the group to maintain a sense of agency even in the face of adversity.

Additionally, acknowledging and processing grief after a significant loss—such as the death of a group member—is essential. Ignoring or suppressing grief can lead to emotional disengagement or resentment. Instead, leaders should provide time and space for individuals to process their emotions, whether through group discussions, rituals, or private reflection. Addressing grief openly reinforces the humanity of the group and strengthens its emotional bonds, rather than allowing loss to fragment morale.

CELEBRATING SMALL VICTORIES

While extreme conditions are marked by constant challenges, leaders must also recognize and celebrate the small victories along the way. These moments, whether it's securing a much-needed resource, successfully completing a mission, or simply surviving another day, provide psychological boosts that help sustain morale over the long term. Celebrating victories reminds the group of its capability and resilience, fostering a sense of pride and accomplishment.

These celebrations do not need to be elaborate, nor do they need to come at the expense of operational security or discipline. A brief acknowledgment, a shared meal, or a few moments of rest can serve as a reminder of the group's strength and determination. Such moments of recognition reinforce the idea that progress is being made, even if the larger picture remains bleak.

In a world where survival is the daily struggle, maintaining morale and cohesion under extreme conditions becomes as important as securing food, water, or ammunition. A group that remains unified and psychologically resilient will outlast one that succumbs to fear, doubt, or infighting. By fostering trust, discipline, communication, and community, leaders can create a foundation of morale that allows their group to weather even the most difficult circumstances. In doing so, they ensure not only survival but the possibility of thriving in a hostile, collapsed world.

Rotations, Rest, and Managing

Psychological Fatigue

In the harsh and unpredictable environment of a collapsed society, where the constant threat of violence, deprivation, and exhaustion looms, managing psychological fatigue becomes a critical part of maintaining both individual and group effectiveness. The relentless pace of survival takes its toll not only physically but mentally, eroding the decision-making abilities, morale, and cohesion of even the most disciplined defense units. Recognizing and addressing the need for rest, recovery, and mental resilience is not just a matter of compassion—it is a strategic necessity. Proper rotations and structured rest periods are crucial to ensuring that every member of the group remains sharp, focused, and capable of handling the intense pressures of ongoing conflict or uncertainty.

Fatigue, particularly psychological fatigue, weakens not only the individual but the entire unit. A tired group is a vulnerable one, prone to mistakes, poor judgment, and internal conflicts. Exhaustion diminishes the ability to respond to threats, erodes morale, and can lead to more serious mental health issues, including anxiety, depression, and in extreme cases, complete mental breakdowns. To prevent these outcomes, leaders must establish a system of rotations that ensures members of the group are regularly rested and given the time to recover both mentally and physically. Managing psychological fatigue is about more than just providing sleep—it's about creating a culture that recognizes the importance of mental resilience, offers opportunities for decompression, and prevents burnout.

ESTABLISHING ROTATIONS FOR CRITICAL TASKS

The first and most obvious step in managing psychological fatigue is to establish a rotation schedule for critical tasks such as patrols, guard duty, reconnaissance, and resource gathering. These are the high-stress activities that demand constant vigilance and quick decision-making, placing a heavy burden on those responsible. Without proper rotations, the individuals tasked with these roles can quickly become exhausted, making them less effective and increasing the risk of mistakes that could endanger the entire group.

Rotations ensure that no one person is overburdened for too long. This involves creating a roster system where each member of the group is assigned specific duties on a rotating basis, with clear expectations about the length of each shift and when rest periods will occur. The length of shifts should be determined by the nature of the task, the level of danger involved, and the available personnel. High-intensity duties, such as guarding a vulnerable location or conducting reconnaissance in enemy territory, should have shorter shifts compared to less stressful tasks like maintaining equipment or cooking.

Leaders must be mindful of how they assign rotations. While every member of the group should share the burden of high-stress tasks, it's important to consider each individual's capacity for handling specific types of duties. Some individuals may excel at long-range scouting but may not have the temperament for long shifts of static guard duty, and vice versa. By aligning strengths with tasks while ensuring equitable distribution of the workload, leaders can prevent both physical and psychological burnout.

Beyond just rotating the individual members, groups should rotate between different types of duties as well. This prevents monotony and reduces the mental strain that comes with performing the same task over and over. For example, a member who has just completed a patrol shift might spend their next rotation working on less intense tasks, such as repairing equipment, before being assigned back to the front line of defense.

SCHEDULING REST AND RECOVERY

Rest is the most fundamental element in maintaining psychological resilience, but it goes beyond just sleep. Structured rest periods should be integrated into the group's schedule, ensuring that every individual has sufficient downtime to recover from both physical exertion and mental strain. These rest periods should be protected from interruptions unless there is an immediate threat. Ensuring the sanctity of rest times demonstrates to the group that their well-being is a priority and helps maintain trust in leadership.

Rest schedules should take into account the natural rhythms of the body, allowing for both short breaks during long tasks and extended periods of sleep when necessary. While it might be tempting to operate on a 24-hour work schedule, especially in high-stress environments, this only accelerates burnout. Instead, leaders must enforce regular, consistent breaks where individuals can rest without distraction or concern. This might involve setting up multiple shifts for critical roles like guards or scouts, ensuring that some members are always resting while others are on duty.

In addition to sleep, recovery periods should include time for other restorative activities. This could involve light, non-strenuous duties, opportunities for social interaction, or even time spent alone if that helps certain individuals decompress. While these moments may seem insignificant in the face of larger survival concerns, they play an essential role in maintaining psychological health. Providing time to read, write, or simply talk to fellow members of the group helps to maintain a sense of normalcy and prevent individuals from becoming consumed by the pressures of their environment.

RECOGNIZING THE SIGNS OF PSYCHOLOGICAL FATIGUE

An important aspect of managing psychological fatigue is recognizing the early signs before it becomes a more serious issue. Leaders must be vigilant for signs of exhaustion, both physical and mental, among their group. These signs may include irritability, difficulty concentrating, memory lapses, increased anxiety, or visible signs of depression. If a member of the group begins to show these symptoms, immediate action should be taken to address their well-being.

One of the challenges in extreme environments is that individuals may be reluctant to admit they are struggling out of fear of appearing weak or letting down the group. Leaders must create an environment where members feel safe discussing their mental state and where asking for rest is seen as a responsible action, not a failure. A culture of open communication about mental health ensures that issues are caught early and addressed before they lead to more significant problems, such as total mental collapse or an inability to perform under pressure.

When psychological fatigue does begin to affect a member of the group, pulling them off high-stress duties and allowing for extended rest or lighter responsibilities can prevent the situation from escalating. It is crucial that these measures are seen not as punishments or failures but as necessary steps in maintaining the overall strength and health of the group.

THE ROLE OF LEADERSHIP IN PREVENTING BURNOUT

Leaders set the tone for the group when it comes to managing psychological fatigue. Leaders who demonstrate the importance of rest and who manage their own fatigue effectively inspire others to do the same. Conversely, leaders who push themselves to the point of burnout or who refuse to take rest can create a culture of overwork, where members of the group feel pressured to ignore their own limits.

Leading by example means modeling behaviors that promote mental and physical resilience. Taking scheduled breaks, delegating tasks, and seeking feedback from the group are all ways that leaders can show they value both their own well-being and that of their team. Encouraging open conversations about mental health, stress, and fatigue also demonstrates that these issues are a shared concern, not something to be dealt with in isolation.

Leaders should also focus on delegating responsibilities. One of the reasons leaders burn out is that they try to manage every aspect of the group themselves, believing that only they can handle the pressure. Delegating smaller tasks to trusted team members not only reduces the leader's workload but also empowers others, fostering a greater sense of responsibility and unity within the group.

CREATING OPPORTUNITIES FOR MENTAL DECOMPRESSION

Beyond rest, providing opportunities for mental decompression is essential for preventing the buildup of stress and fatigue. These opportunities can be as simple as allowing group members time to engage in activities that take their mind off immediate threats, such as conversation, entertainment, or even light exercise. In environments where resources are limited, these activities don't need to be elaborate—something as simple as sharing stories or making light of a difficult situation can have a powerful impact on morale.

Small rituals or routines that reinforce normalcy, such as eating meals together, discussing non-strategic matters, or creating moments of laughter, help balance out the intensity of survival. These moments remind the group that they are not just fighting for survival but living through an unprecedented time together. The bonds formed during these lighter moments help carry the group through more stressful periods, strengthening cohesion and morale.

In extreme conditions, maintaining a sense of purpose beyond survival can also help reduce the psychological toll. Individuals need to believe that they are working toward something meaningful, whether it's protecting their loved ones, securing a future for the group, or simply maintaining their dignity in a chaotic world. Leaders should reinforce this purpose regularly, ensuring that everyone understands how their individual actions contribute to the larger mission.

MANAGING GROUP DYNAMICS UNDER STRESS

Psychological fatigue doesn't just affect individuals; it can destabilize group dynamics if left unchecked. Exhaustion breeds irritability and short tempers, which can lead to conflicts within the group. Leaders must be proactive in managing these dynamics, recognizing when fatigue is driving conflict and addressing it before it escalates.

Rotating team members between different groups can prevent cliques or divisions from forming. Additionally, offering opportunities for team members to discuss their frustrations or air grievances in a controlled setting can prevent these issues from boiling over during high-stress situations. The goal is to maintain unity and trust within the group, ensuring that everyone is working toward the same goal despite the immense pressures they face.

Encouraging empathy and mutual support within the group also helps manage psychological fatigue. When members look out for each other—offering help, providing encouragement, or simply listening—it strengthens the bonds that keep the group resilient. Leaders should foster this sense of camaraderie, making sure that everyone feels supported by their fellow members, not isolated in their struggles.

In the unrelenting conditions of a collapsed society, managing psychological fatigue is as critical to survival as securing food, water, or shelter. The constant strain of defending against threats, securing resources, and navigating uncertainty wears down even the strongest individuals. Through careful rotations, structured rest periods, and open communication, leaders can ensure that their group remains physically and mentally resilient. By recognizing the signs of fatigue early and addressing them through proper rest, recovery, and mental decompression, the group can maintain its cohesion, morale, and effectiveness over the long term.

Ultimately, survival in a collapsed society requires more than just physical endurance. It demands mental toughness and the ability to sustain oneself and others through periods of intense stress and exhaustion. By prioritizing psychological health, managing group dynamics, and fostering a culture of empathy and resilience, leaders can ensure that their group remains strong, united, and ready to face whatever challenges come their way.

CHAPTER 10: DEFENSIVE STRATEGIES AGAINST LARGER FORCES

In a post-collapse environment, there will be times when small groups are forced to defend themselves against numerically superior forces. Larger enemy forces often have the advantage of more personnel, greater firepower, and better logistical support. However, numerical superiority does not guarantee victory. A well-organized, disciplined, and tactically sound defense can neutralize or mitigate the advantages of a larger force, exploiting weaknesses in their command, logistics, and mobility. The key to survival in these engagements is a clear, methodical approach that prioritizes strategic positioning, resourcefulness, and precise execution.

When defending against a larger force, the primary objective is not necessarily to achieve total victory but to survive, wear down the enemy, and retain control of vital assets or territory. Attrition, ambushes, deception, and the use of terrain are the tools that small groups must rely on to achieve these objectives. The following strategies are designed to maximize the defensive potential of smaller units, allowing them to resist and repel larger adversaries through superior planning and execution.

UTILIZING TERRAIN TO OFFSET NUMERICAL DISADVANTAGE

One of the most effective ways to defend against a larger force is to exploit the terrain to create natural advantages that mitigate the enemy's numerical superiority. Defensive positions should always be chosen with the terrain in mind, prioritizing areas that are difficult for large forces to maneuver in, such as narrow passes, dense forests, or urban environments with complex structures. Terrain features like high ground, cliffs, or ridgelines give defenders a vantage point for controlling the battlefield, enabling them to observe enemy movements and apply accurate fire from a position of relative safety.

In urban environments, buildings, alleyways, and streets can be turned into defensible positions that limit the mobility of a larger force. The use of barricades, traps, and choke points within cities or towns can slow the enemy's advance and force them into positions where they are vulnerable to ambushes and concentrated fire. Urban combat favors defenders because it neutralizes many of the advantages a larger force might have, such as the ability to mass troops effectively or use heavy vehicles.

In rural environments, natural cover like forests, rocky terrain, or marshes provides excellent opportunities for hit-and-run tactics and ambushes. Dense terrain prevents large formations from advancing quickly or maintaining cohesion, allowing smaller, more agile units to exploit gaps in the enemy's defenses. The goal is to force the enemy to overextend, divide their forces, and present smaller, more manageable targets.

ESTABLISHING LAYERED DEFENSES

A layered defense strategy is essential when facing a larger force. Rather than concentrating all defensive efforts in one location, a layered defense distributes defensive assets across multiple positions, creating a series of obstacles that the enemy must overcome. This approach not only slows the enemy's advance but also causes attrition by forcing them to engage in multiple smaller battles rather than a single decisive confrontation.

The outermost defensive layer should consist of early warning systems, including sentries, scouts, or surveillance equipment. These provide critical intelligence on the enemy's movements and allow defenders to prepare before direct contact is made. The next layer might include minefields, traps, or obstacles designed to disrupt enemy formations and channel them into more advantageous positions for the defenders.

Each subsequent layer of defense should be progressively stronger, with the final defensive position being the most fortified. This approach forces the enemy to exhaust resources and personnel as they push forward, while defenders can withdraw in a controlled manner to stronger positions, regroup, and continue the defense. Each defensive layer must be carefully planned, ensuring that retreat routes are clear and that defenders can fall back without being cut off.

MAXIMIZING FIREPOWER AND AMMUNITION EFFICIENCY

In a defensive posture, firepower must be deployed strategically. Small groups facing larger forces cannot afford to waste ammunition or engage in prolonged firefights where the enemy can bring their numerical advantage to bear. Precision and discipline are paramount. Each shot must count, and defenders must avoid being drawn into a battle of attrition where they are outgunned. Instead, fire should be concentrated at critical moments to disrupt enemy movements, eliminate high-value targets, and create confusion.

The use of well-placed **kill zones** is an essential tactic. These are areas where the enemy can be funneled or ambushed, and where the defenders can apply overwhelming firepower at a moment of vulnerability. Kill zones should be set up in areas where the terrain favors the defenders and limits the enemy's ability to maneuver. For example, a kill zone might be established at the end of a narrow pass, with heavy fire directed from concealed positions on either side. Once the enemy enters the kill zone, concentrated fire should be applied swiftly, with the goal of eliminating as many enemy forces as possible before they have a chance to react.

Ammunition conservation is critical in defensive engagements. Defenders must prioritize high-value targets such as officers, radio operators, or heavy weapons crews, aiming to disrupt the enemy's command structure and communications. Engaging large groups of enemy troops with suppressive fire should only be done when absolutely necessary, and only to buy time for maneuvering or repositioning.

AMBUSHES AND HIT-AND-RUN TACTICS

When facing a larger force, direct confrontation should be avoided unless the defender has a significant advantage in terrain or position. Ambushes and hit-and-run tactics are far more effective in wearing down a numerically superior enemy. These tactics rely on speed, surprise, and the ability to disengage before the enemy can bring their full strength to bear.

An ambush should be set up in an area where the enemy is most vulnerable, such as when moving through narrow terrain or during moments of logistical resupply. Ambush teams should be positioned in concealed locations with clear escape routes, allowing them to strike quickly and retreat without being pinned down. The goal is to inflict maximum damage in the shortest possible time, then withdraw before the enemy can respond effectively.

Hit-and-run tactics are particularly useful when the enemy is spread out over a large area or is overextended in their pursuit of the defenders. Small units can move quickly to strike at isolated elements of the enemy force, such as rear guards, supply convoys, or communications hubs, before retreating to safe ground. These tactics force the enemy to divert resources to protect their vulnerable assets, reducing the overall pressure on the main defensive force.

DECEPTION AND PSYCHOLOGICAL WARFARE

Deception is a critical tool for a smaller force defending against a larger enemy. The goal is to create confusion, uncertainty, and hesitation in the enemy's ranks, disrupting their plans and undermining their confidence. Deception can take many forms, from false radio communications to decoy positions or feigned retreats.

Setting up **dummy positions**—fake fortifications or empty defensive emplacements—can draw enemy fire and attention away from the real defensive positions. These decoys can be as simple as placing empty helmets on sticks or constructing false barricades in locations where the enemy is likely to advance. By misleading the enemy into wasting resources attacking decoy positions, the defenders gain valuable time and reduce the pressure on their actual defensive lines.

Feigning retreat is another powerful tactic, particularly when used in conjunction with ambushes or layered defenses. By pretending to withdraw from a position, defenders can lure the enemy into a more vulnerable area, where they can be ambushed or funneled into a kill zone. However, this tactic requires careful execution to avoid being overrun or outflanked during the retreat.

Psychological warfare can also be employed to weaken the enemy's resolve. Harassment tactics, such as night raids, constant ambushes, and sabotage of supply lines, create a sense of insecurity within the larger force. Over time, these tactics can lead to exhaustion and demoralization, reducing the enemy's effectiveness and making them more vulnerable to decisive strikes.

LOGISTICS AND RESUPPLY: KEEPING THE DEFENSIVE EFFORT SUSTAINABLE

Defending against a larger force is not just about tactical engagements; it's also about maintaining the logistical support needed to sustain the defense over time. Ammunition, food, water, and medical supplies must be managed carefully to avoid shortages during prolonged engagements. In a situation where resupply is difficult or impossible, conservation and resourcefulness are critical.

Supply caches should be established in secure, hidden locations along the defensive perimeter or within fallback positions. These caches ensure that defenders can access critical supplies even if their main base is compromised. Distributing supplies across multiple locations also reduces the risk of losing everything in a single raid or attack.

The defense force must also be prepared to conduct resupply operations under fire. This might involve sending small, fast-moving teams to scavenge or raid enemy supply lines, or it could mean foraging from the surrounding environment. In extreme cases, defenders may need to rely on captured enemy supplies to sustain their operations, making it imperative to exploit any opportunities for raiding or intercepting enemy logistics.

Defending against larger forces requires discipline, strategic foresight, and a thorough understanding of terrain and tactics. By leveraging superior positioning, utilizing deception, and applying precise, focused firepower, smaller forces can neutralize the advantages of a larger adversary. A defensive effort built on careful planning, resource management, and an unwavering commitment to executing these strategies without hesitation will enable a small group to resist, outlast, and repel even the most overwhelming force. Success in these engagements is achieved through methodical application of proven defensive principles, unwavering focus on the objectives, and the ability to adapt to the evolving situation on the ground.

Dealing with Paramilitary and Conventional Forces

When facing paramilitary and conventional forces in a collapsed society, the tactical challenges become more pronounced, and the stakes even higher. Unlike disorganized militias or bandit groups, paramilitary units and conventional military forces operate with greater discipline, better training, and superior resources. They often possess heavier weaponry, advanced communication systems, and structured command hierarchies, giving them a significant advantage in any engagement. However, these advantages also come with vulnerabilities that can be exploited by a smaller, more agile force using unconventional tactics.

The key to successfully defending against paramilitary or conventional forces lies in understanding their operating procedures and identifying where they are most susceptible. These forces often rely on predictable patterns, rigid command structures, and heavy logistical demands. A smaller, more flexible defense force can undermine their effectiveness through hit-and-run tactics, sabotage, deception, and the exploitation of terrain and urban environments. The objective is not to engage in prolonged, direct battles but to erode their operational capacity, morale, and supply lines, forcing them into a position of vulnerability.

UNDERSTANDING PARAMILITARY FORCES

Paramilitary forces occupy a gray area between conventional

military units and irregular militias. While they often lack the full range of resources and capabilities of formal military units, paramilitary groups are usually well-trained, equipped, and organized. They may operate with a degree of discipline and coordination that exceeds that of local militias or criminal gangs, and they are often tasked with maintaining control over specific areas, protecting key infrastructure, or supporting the operations of larger military forces.

The organizational structure of paramilitary units tends to be more flexible than that of conventional forces, allowing them to adapt quickly to changing circumstances. This adaptability makes them particularly dangerous in a post-collapse environment, where fluidity and rapid response are key to success. Paramilitary forces are often tasked with counterinsurgency operations, securing areas against resistance groups, or eliminating local threats.

However, their relatively small size and reliance on specific leaders or commanders make them vulnerable to disruption. Leadership decapitation—targeting key figures within the paramilitary hierarchy—can disorient these units and cause confusion. Additionally, paramilitary forces often depend on local knowledge or support, which can be exploited by defenders who understand the terrain better or have more significant support from the local population.

UNDERSTANDING CONVENTIONAL FORCES

Conventional forces, unlike paramilitary units, follow strict command structures and military doctrine. These forces are typically highly trained, with access to heavier equipment, armored vehicles, air support, and advanced technology such as drones and surveillance systems. While this makes them formidable opponents, it also makes them slower to adapt, especially when facing unconventional or guerrilla-style tactics. Their reliance on a rigid command hierarchy can be exploited, particularly in environments where rapid decision-making and flexibility are crucial.

Conventional military units often prioritize maintaining control of strategic locations—bridges, supply routes, communication hubs, and infrastructure. They operate with defined objectives and focus on overwhelming their adversaries through superior firepower and logistics. However, this focus on controlling specific locations means they are less adept at responding to small, mobile units that strike unexpectedly and withdraw before a coordinated response can be mounted.

Conventional forces are heavily reliant on supply lines to maintain their operations. Food, fuel, ammunition, and medical supplies must be continuously transported to the front lines or operational areas. Disrupting these supply lines —through ambushes, sabotage, or targeting logistical hubs— can severely hamper their ability to sustain operations, forcing them to retreat or abandon their objectives.

AVOIDING DIRECT CONFRONTATION

When dealing with paramilitary or conventional forces, the first and most important principle is to avoid direct confrontation unless it is absolutely necessary or unless there is a significant tactical advantage. Engaging in head-on combat with these forces will often lead to catastrophic losses for a smaller defense unit, as paramilitary and conventional forces are likely to have superior firepower, greater numbers, and better logistical support.

Instead, focus on employing guerrilla tactics that exploit the weaknesses of larger, more structured forces. Ambushes, sabotage, and harassment tactics allow a smaller group to inflict damage on these forces without exposing themselves to overwhelming retaliation. Striking at isolated elements, such as supply convoys, command posts, or lightly defended outposts, is far more effective than attempting to engage a well-fortified position.

When forced to engage, prioritize mobility and speed. Quick strikes followed by rapid withdrawal are essential to avoid being pinned down or encircled by a larger force. This requires careful planning, with escape routes mapped out in advance and fallback positions secured.

TARGETING VULNERABILITIES IN COMMAND AND CONTROL

Paramilitary and conventional forces rely heavily on effective command and control structures to coordinate their operations. Disrupting these structures is one of the most effective ways to weaken their operational capacity. By targeting communications systems, command vehicles, or key personnel, defenders can create confusion and delays in the enemy's response, reducing their effectiveness.

Paramilitary units, in particular, may be more dependent on charismatic or experienced leaders. Targeting these individuals—whether through direct engagement or sabotage—can demoralize the unit and lead to internal conflicts over succession or decision-making. Similarly, attacking the chain of command in a conventional military force, such as through the elimination of officers or the disruption of communication networks, can lead to disorganization and slower response times.

Electronic warfare can also be employed to disrupt enemy communications. Jamming radio frequencies, intercepting communications, or spreading disinformation can confuse paramilitary and conventional forces, leading them to make mistakes or delay their actions. While electronic warfare requires specific equipment, it can be highly effective in neutralizing the advantages of a technologically superior force.

SABOTAGING LOGISTICS AND SUPPLY LINES

Conventional and paramilitary forces are heavily reliant on their logistical infrastructure. Without regular resupply, these forces cannot sustain operations for long periods. Defenders should prioritize targeting supply lines, fuel depots, ammunition dumps, and other logistical assets to weaken the enemy's ability to maintain their presence in the area.

Ambushes on supply convoys are particularly effective, as they disrupt the flow of critical resources and force the enemy to divert manpower to protect their logistical routes. These convoys often move through predictable routes, which can be identified through reconnaissance and intelligence gathering. Once identified, supply convoys can be attacked using mines, improvised explosive devices (IEDs), or ambushes from concealed positions. The goal is not only to destroy the supplies but also to make it increasingly difficult and costly for the enemy to transport resources.

In addition to ambushing convoys, sabotage of key logistical infrastructure—such as bridges, fuel depots, or vehicle maintenance facilities—can create long-term disruption. Destroying fuel supplies or damaging vehicles reduces the enemy's mobility, forcing them to slow their operations or withdraw entirely.

EXPLOITING TERRAIN AND WEATHER CONDITIONS

Paramilitary and conventional forces often struggle in environments where the terrain is complex or where weather conditions limit their mobility and visibility. Defenders should use this to their advantage by choosing defensive positions that maximize the difficulties faced by the enemy.

In mountainous or forested terrain, large forces cannot move as quickly or maintain formation as easily, making them vulnerable to ambushes and harassment. Defenders can use natural features such as ridges, ravines, or dense forest to conceal their movements and launch attacks from elevated or hidden positions. Similarly, in urban environments, the dense network of buildings, alleyways, and underground passages offers numerous opportunities for guerrilla-style warfare. Urban terrain negates many of the advantages that larger forces possess, such as the use of armored vehicles or air support.

Weather conditions also play a significant role. Rain, fog, or snow can reduce the visibility and mobility of paramilitary and conventional forces, providing cover for smaller units to move undetected or launch surprise attacks. In harsh climates, these forces may also struggle with supply issues, as food, fuel, and medical supplies become harder to transport. Defenders should exploit these conditions by launching attacks during periods of poor visibility or extreme weather, where their smaller numbers and greater familiarity with the terrain give them an advantage.

SETTING TRAPS AND USING DECEPTION

When dealing with larger, more organized forces, deception and the use of traps can be highly effective in weakening the enemy before they can engage the defenders. Setting up ambushes with decoys—such as fake positions, false retreats, or misleading trails—can lure paramilitary or conventional forces into vulnerable positions where they can be attacked from concealed locations.

For example, defenders can use the terrain to create choke points where the enemy is forced to concentrate their forces. By appearing to retreat, defenders can lure the enemy into pursuing them through a narrow pass or a dense urban area, where pre-positioned ambush teams are waiting. Once the enemy is trapped, concentrated fire from multiple angles can inflict heavy casualties before the defenders withdraw to a secondary position.

Additionally, spreading misinformation—such as false radio

transmissions or planting misleading intelligence—can confuse the enemy about the defenders 'intentions, strength, or position. This can force the enemy to divert resources to areas where no threat exists, weakening their ability to launch coordinated attacks.

PSYCHOLOGICAL WARFARE AND ATTRITION

Paramilitary and conventional forces, despite their discipline and organization, are not immune to the psychological effects of warfare. Constant harassment, sabotage, and the unpredictability of guerrilla tactics can wear down the morale of these forces over time. The goal of psychological warfare is to create a sense of insecurity and frustration within the enemy ranks, leading them to question their leadership or the value of their mission.

Regular night raids, sniper attacks, or sabotage of key infrastructure create a constant sense of danger, forcing the enemy to remain on high alert at all times. This level of sustained pressure leads to exhaustion, reducing their effectiveness in combat. Additionally, targeting leadership figures or key personnel can demoralize the enemy, leading to confusion and a lack of direction.

The psychological impact of fighting an unseen, elusive enemy can be as devastating as physical losses. By maintaining pressure on the enemy through constant small-scale attacks, defenders can gradually erode their will to fight, forcing them to retreat or abandon their objectives.

Dealing with paramilitary and conventional forces requires a strategic, methodical approach that prioritizes mobility, deception, and the exploitation of vulnerabilities in the enemy's logistics and command structures. Direct engagement should be avoided unless it is heavily in the defenders 'favor. Instead, the focus should be on wearing down the enemy through a combination of guerrilla tactics, sabotage, and psychological warfare. By exploiting the terrain, disrupting supply lines, and creating confusion within the enemy's ranks, a smaller defense force can resist and weaken larger, more organized adversaries. Success against these forces comes not from brute strength but from precision, discipline, and superior tactical execution.

Tactics for Outnumbered and Outgunned Citizen Defenders

In situations where citizen defenders are both outnumbered and outgunned, the challenges become acute. The enemy has superior firepower, more personnel, and often better access to resources. Under these conditions, engaging in a direct firefight is not a viable option, as it would almost certainly result in defeat. Instead, the focus must shift to leveraging tactical ingenuity, superior knowledge of the terrain, mobility, and exploiting the weaknesses of the enemy's size and logistical needs. Outnumbered and outgunned defenders can still prevail by adopting unconventional methods designed to offset the advantages of a larger, better-armed force.

The essence of survival and success in such scenarios lies in adopting guerrilla warfare principles that prioritize mobility, deception, psychological warfare, and the strategic use of available resources. The objective is not to overpower the enemy but to undermine their ability to wage an effective campaign by increasing their costs, reducing their morale, and forcing them to fight on terms they are unprepared for. This chapter outlines the key tactics that outnumbered and outgunned defenders can use to resist and even overcome a superior force.

AVOIDING DIRECT ENGAGEMENT

When facing a force with superior numbers and firepower, direct engagement should be avoided unless there is a clear tactical advantage. Fighting head-on against an enemy that has more soldiers and heavier weapons will lead to unnecessary casualties and depletion of critical resources like ammunition and medical supplies. Instead, the goal should be to minimize contact while maximizing the damage inflicted on the enemy. This means using stealth, careful planning, and only striking when the conditions are favorable.

One of the primary ways to achieve this is through the use of ambushes, where the defenders can engage the enemy on their own terms. Ambushes allow defenders to choose the time and place of the engagement, using surprise and terrain to neutralize some of the enemy's advantages. In an ambush, a small, well-positioned force can inflict significant casualties on a much larger group before disengaging and retreating to safety. The key to a successful ambush is preparation—knowing the enemy's movements, understanding the terrain, and having a clear escape route for when the ambush is completed.

Urban environments offer particular advantages for avoiding direct engagement. Cities and towns provide countless opportunities for guerrilla warfare tactics, where small groups can attack and then disappear into the urban landscape. The complexity of urban terrain—buildings, alleyways, underground tunnels—allows defenders to strike from unexpected locations and disappear before the enemy can organize an effective counterattack. By keeping the engagement fluid and avoiding prolonged firefights, defenders can frustrate the enemy and reduce their numerical advantage.

MAXIMIZING TERRAIN ADVANTAGE

One of the most effective ways for outnumbered and outgunned defenders to neutralize an enemy's advantages is by using the terrain to their benefit. Knowledge of the local geography—whether it's a dense forest, mountainous region, or urban area—can provide defenders with opportunities to set traps, launch ambushes, and control the flow of the enemy's movement. Terrain becomes the great equalizer, allowing a smaller force to dictate the terms of engagement and making it difficult for a larger, more cumbersome enemy to bring their full force to bear.

In rural or forested areas, natural features like hills, valleys, and rivers can be used to channel enemy forces into vulnerable positions. Narrow mountain passes, dense forests, and marshy ground slow down large forces, making them vulnerable to hit-and-run tactics and ambushes. Defenders can position themselves in concealed locations, such as behind ridges or in elevated positions, allowing them to observe enemy movements and strike at opportune moments. The more difficult it is for the enemy to move their forces, the greater the advantage for the defenders.

In urban environments, buildings and infrastructure offer multiple layers of defense. Streets can be barricaded to control enemy movement, while rooftops and windows provide vantage points for snipers and lookouts. The confined spaces of cities make it difficult for large, heavily armed forces to maneuver, and defenders can exploit this by using small, mobile teams to strike at isolated enemy units. Additionally, the use of tunnels, sewers, and underground passages allows defenders to move undetected, setting up ambushes or escaping before the enemy can respond.

USING MOBILITY AND HIT-AND-RUN TACTICS

Mobility is the greatest asset for a smaller force facing a numerically superior enemy. Outnumbered defenders must stay light, fast, and adaptable, avoiding prolonged engagements that favor the enemy's superior firepower. Hit-and-run tactics—striking the enemy quickly and retreating before they can react—are central to this strategy. The goal is to harass and wear down the enemy over time, rather than attempting to defeat them in a single battle.

Hit-and-run tactics are most effective when combined with careful planning and reconnaissance. Defenders must know the enemy's movements and capabilities, allowing them to choose moments of vulnerability to strike. Supply convoys, isolated patrols, and rear guard units are prime targets for hit-and-run attacks. These engagements should be swift and decisive, with the defenders retreating to pre-designated safe zones as soon as the attack is completed. The key is not to overextend—strike hard, then disappear before the enemy can organize a counteroffensive.

Mobility also applies to how the defense force operates on a larger scale. Outnumbered defenders must constantly shift their base of operations, never staying in one location long enough for the enemy to mount a concerted attack. By keeping the enemy guessing about their location, defenders force the larger force to expend resources and energy chasing them, creating opportunities for ambushes and sabotage along the way. This "war of movement" disrupts the enemy's operational tempo, making it difficult for them to maintain control of the battlefield.

CONSERVING RESOURCES

In any conflict where a force is outnumbered and outgunned, resource management becomes critical. Ammunition, food, water, and medical supplies are finite and difficult to replenish, so every action must be weighed against the cost in resources. Defenders must learn to fight with precision and efficiency, ensuring that every bullet fired and every engagement undertaken serves a strategic purpose.

Fire discipline is essential. In prolonged engagements, the temptation to fire indiscriminately can quickly lead to the depletion of ammunition, leaving the defenders vulnerable. Instead, fire should be concentrated on high-value targets, such as officers, heavy weapons operators, or supply units. Every shot should be aimed with the intent of inflicting maximum damage on the enemy while using the least amount of ammunition possible. In ambushes, concentrated fire on key personnel or vehicles can disrupt the enemy's ability to fight effectively, creating chaos and confusion.

Medical supplies must be used judiciously, with priority given to those who are most likely to return to combat. In extreme situations, difficult decisions may need to be made about who receives treatment, based on the likelihood of survival and the strategic value of keeping that individual in the fight. In terms of food and water, stockpiling in hidden caches throughout the area of operations can help ensure that defenders have access to vital resources even if their main base is compromised.

PSYCHOLOGICAL WARFARE AND ATTRITION

In a conflict where the enemy has superior numbers and firepower, the psychological aspect of warfare becomes even more critical. Outnumbered defenders must use every opportunity to undermine the enemy's morale, creating a sense of insecurity and fear. Guerrilla tactics—night raids, constant ambushes, and sabotage—are designed not only to inflict physical damage but also to exhaust and demoralize the enemy over time.

Night raids, in particular, can have a powerful psychological effect. Striking the enemy under the cover of darkness creates a sense of vulnerability, as they are forced to remain on high alert at all times, never knowing when or where the next attack will come. These raids do not need to result in large numbers of casualties to be effective. The psychological toll of being under constant threat wears down the enemy, leading to fatigue, paranoia, and decreased effectiveness in combat.

Another critical element of psychological warfare is the use of deception. Defenders can use false trails, decoys, and misinformation to confuse and mislead the enemy, forcing them to waste time and resources pursuing phantom threats. For example, defenders might stage a false retreat to lure the enemy into an ambush or spread false intelligence about their numbers and location to make the enemy overestimate their strength.

Over time, the cumulative effect of these tactics can lead to a situation where the enemy, despite their superior numbers, becomes disorganized, demoralized, and less willing to continue the fight. The goal is to create an environment where every movement, every action, and every decision becomes a source of stress for the enemy, eroding their will to fight and leading to mistakes that can be exploited.

EXPLOITING LOGISTICAL VULNERABILITIES

One of the inherent weaknesses of a larger force is its dependence on logistics. Armies that are larger and better equipped require vast amounts of supplies—fuel, food, ammunition, and medical support—to maintain their operations. Outnumbered defenders can exploit this by targeting the enemy's logistical infrastructure, disrupting their supply lines, and forcing them to expend resources faster than they can replace them.

Ambushing supply convoys is one of the most effective ways to disrupt the enemy's logistical support. Convoys tend to follow predictable routes and often lack the same level of protection as frontline units. By targeting these convoys, defenders can cut off the enemy's access to essential supplies, forcing them to slow their advance or withdraw. Destroying fuel supplies, in particular, can cripple the enemy's mobility, making it difficult for them to redeploy forces or bring in reinforcements.

In addition to ambushes, sabotage of critical infrastructure —such as fuel depots, bridges, or communication lines—can further weaken the enemy's logistical network. Defenders can plant explosives on key routes, set fire to supply caches, or disable vehicles through mechanical sabotage. The objective is to create bottlenecks in the enemy's supply chain, making it more difficult for them to sustain their operations and increasing their vulnerability to further attacks.

LEVERAGING LOCAL KNOWLEDGE AND SUPPORT

In most cases, outnumbered defenders will have a better understanding of the local environment than the enemy. This knowledge of the terrain, weather patterns, and population dynamics can be used to offset the numerical and technological superiority of the enemy. Defenders should use this local knowledge to outmaneuver the enemy, setting traps, creating choke points, and using natural features to hide or escape when necessary.

In addition to terrain knowledge, local support from the population can provide a critical advantage. Civilians who are sympathetic to the defenders 'cause can offer shelter, food, intelligence, or medical assistance. Gaining and maintaining the trust of the local population is essential for long-term resistance. Defenders must cultivate relationships with local leaders, ensuring that their presence is seen as beneficial rather than burdensome.

Local knowledge also allows defenders to predict the enemy's movements and anticipate their actions. By understanding how the enemy will likely operate in unfamiliar terrain, defenders can prepare ambushes or traps in areas where the enemy is most vulnerable. For example, if the enemy is unfamiliar with the local climate or seasonal changes, defenders can exploit these conditions—such as sudden floods or extreme heat—to further disrupt their operations.

ADAPTING TO CHANGING CONDITIONS

One of the most important traits of outnumbered and outgunned defenders is adaptability. Conflict in a collapsed society is unpredictable, and conditions on the ground can change rapidly. Whether it's a sudden shift in enemy tactics, the arrival of reinforcements, or the depletion of critical supplies, defenders must be ready to adapt their strategies to meet new challenges.

This requires constant intelligence gathering and reassessment of the tactical situation. Defenders should be in regular communication with scouts, lookouts, and other intelligence sources to stay informed about the enemy's movements and intentions. Plans should be flexible enough to change quickly based on new information, and defenders must be ready to seize opportunities as they arise.

Flexibility also applies to the composition and structure of the defense force itself. If casualties occur, or if certain units are cut off, remaining forces must be able to reorganize and continue the fight without hesitation. This means training every member of the group in multiple roles and ensuring that command and control structures are decentralized enough to operate independently if necessary.

For outnumbered and outgunned defenders, survival hinges on a combination of tactical ingenuity, resourcefulness, and relentless pressure on the enemy. The use of mobility, terrain, and deception allows defenders to level the playing field, while strategic attacks on the enemy's logistical infrastructure and morale create opportunities to undermine their superior numbers and firepower. Success in these engagements is not about achieving total victory in a single battle but rather about wearing down the enemy over time, forcing them to fight on unfavorable terms, and eroding their capacity to wage an effective campaign.

By adhering to these principles and maintaining discipline, outnumbered defenders can transform their apparent disadvantages into strengths, proving that superior tactics, preparation, and execution can overcome even the most formidable adversaries.

How to Exploit Enemy Weaknesses and Overwhelm Superior Forces

When facing superior forces, exploiting enemy weaknesses is the only viable path to victory or survival. Outnumbered defenders cannot rely on traditional methods of engagement, as they lack the manpower and firepower to prevail in a head-to-head confrontation. Instead, they must focus on identifying and exploiting specific vulnerabilities within the enemy's structure, command, logistics, and morale. By pinpointing these weaknesses, smaller forces can turn the tide of battle, forcing the enemy to overextend, make mistakes, and lose effectiveness. The goal is to apply maximum pressure at key points, causing the enemy to falter and creating opportunities for the defender to gain the upper hand.

Superior forces often rely on their size, firepower, and perceived control of the battlefield, leading to a false sense of security. Defenders can use this overconfidence to their advantage, disrupting the enemy's cohesion and exploiting gaps in their strategy. The following section outlines key tactics for exploiting enemy weaknesses, designed to allow smaller forces to overwhelm larger, better-equipped opponents through precision, deception, and the targeted use of available resources.

TARGETING LOGISTICAL WEAKNESSES

Larger forces, particularly conventional military units, are heavily reliant on logistics to maintain their operational capability. Supplies of fuel, ammunition, food, and medical resources must constantly flow to sustain their fighting power. Without these essentials, even the most powerful force can be rendered ineffective. This is where smaller, more agile forces have the advantage—they can move quickly to disrupt these supply lines, striking at the heart of the enemy's logistical network.

One of the most effective ways to exploit logistical weaknesses is by targeting **supply convoys**. These convoys often move along predictable routes and may be less well-protected than frontline units. By identifying choke points along these routes—such as narrow roads, bridges, or terrain features that force the convoy to slow down—defenders can set ambushes that disable key supply vehicles, destroy fuel, or capture critical resources. Even a small-scale disruption of an enemy's supply lines can have a cascading effect, forcing the enemy to divert forces to protect these routes or slow their overall advance due to supply shortages.

In addition to ambushing convoys, defenders should consider sabotaging key infrastructure that the enemy relies on for logistics. **Bridges, fuel depots, rail lines, and communications hubs** are all critical to the enemy's ability to transport and resupply their forces. Destroying or disabling these assets will force the enemy to expend time and resources repairing or rerouting their logistical efforts, weakening their ability to fight effectively.

DISRUPTING COMMAND AND CONTROL

The larger and more complex a military force becomes, the more dependent it is on its command structure. Orders flow from the top down, and any disruption to this chain of command can create confusion, delays, and breakdowns in coordination. Smaller forces can exploit this vulnerability by targeting the enemy's communication systems, command vehicles, and leadership personnel.

Attacking the enemy's communication networks—whether through physical sabotage, electronic jamming, or intercepting transmissions—can cripple their ability to coordinate movements, issue orders, and respond to threats. Defenders should focus on disabling or capturing radio towers, cutting communication lines, or using electronic warfare to jam critical frequencies. Without reliable communication, the enemy will be forced to operate in a more disorganized manner, making them more vulnerable to ambushes and deception.

Leadership **decapitation** is another effective tactic for disrupting command and control. By identifying and targeting key officers or commanders, defenders can create a power vacuum that leads to disarray within the enemy's ranks. Leaders are often critical to maintaining discipline and morale, and their removal can lead to a collapse in cohesion. These high-value targets should be prioritized during engagements—whether through snipers, ambushes, or sabotage—allowing defenders to capitalize on the resulting chaos.

EXPLOITING GAPS IN MORALE AND DISCIPLINE

While superior forces may possess greater firepower, they are often more vulnerable to psychological warfare. Larger units, particularly those that are far from their supply bases or operating in unfamiliar territory, are prone to morale breakdowns if subjected to constant harassment, uncertainty, and fear. Smaller forces, by contrast, can remain cohesive and agile, especially when operating in familiar terrain or with strong local support.

Psychological warfare—such as night raids, sniper attacks, and the use of traps or decoys—creates a sense of unease among the enemy. Even the perception of constant threat can wear down morale, leading to exhaustion, paranoia, and loss of combat effectiveness. Night raids, in particular, are highly effective because they disrupt the enemy's sleep patterns and force them to remain on high alert at all times. The constant pressure of never knowing when or where the next attack will come can lead to mistakes, overreactions, and breakdowns in discipline.

Defenders should also seek to **sow dissent and confusion** within the enemy's ranks. This can be achieved through disinformation campaigns, spreading false intelligence about the defenders 'strength, location, or intentions. By feeding the enemy misleading information—whether through intercepted communications, captured prisoners, or planted informants—defenders can cause them to make strategic errors, such as overcommitting forces to the wrong location or failing to prepare for an ambush.

USING MOBILITY TO DIVIDE AND ISOLATE ENEMY UNITS

Large forces are often less mobile and more dependent on maintaining cohesion to bring their firepower to bear. This makes them vulnerable to tactics that divide and isolate portions of their forces, leaving them exposed to smaller, more mobile units. The defender's goal is to avoid fighting the enemy's entire force at once, instead breaking them into smaller, more manageable pieces that can be overwhelmed individually.

One effective method for achieving this is through **feigned retreats**. By appearing to withdraw from a position, defenders can lure a portion of the enemy force into a trap, where they are cut off from reinforcements and vulnerable to ambush. This tactic works especially well in terrain that restricts movement, such as narrow passes, dense forests, or urban environments. The enemy, believing they are pursuing a retreating force, may overextend and find themselves encircled or attacked from multiple directions.

Once isolated, smaller enemy units can be destroyed, demoralizing the remaining force and creating confusion about where the defenders will strike next. By keeping the enemy on the defensive, defenders can prevent them from consolidating their strength and maintaining the initiative.

DECEPTION AND THE USE OF DECOYS

Deception is a powerful tool in the hands of an outnumbered defender. Larger forces rely on accurate intelligence to make decisions, and by feeding them false information or misleading them about the defenders 'intentions, smaller forces can force the enemy to commit resources to the wrong objectives, weakening their overall effectiveness.

Decoy positions are one of the most straightforward forms of deception. By creating false defensive positions —such as empty fortifications, dummy gun emplacements, or abandoned vehicles—defenders can draw enemy fire and attention away from their real defenses. The enemy, believing they are attacking a fortified position, may waste time, ammunition, and personnel attacking an empty target. These decoy positions should be set up in areas that appear strategically important to the enemy but offer little actual value.

Another effective tactic is the use of **feigned offensives**. By launching small, inconsequential attacks at one location, defenders can give the impression that they are concentrating their forces there, causing the enemy to divert troops to defend it. Meanwhile, the real attack or ambush is prepared elsewhere, where the enemy's defenses have been weakened by their own overreaction.

EXPLOITING ENEMY FATIGUE

Superior forces, especially those engaged in prolonged campaigns far from their bases of operation, are susceptible to fatigue. Extended deployments, logistical strain, and constant threats wear down even the most disciplined forces over time. Defenders can exploit this by engaging in **warfare of attrition**, where the goal is not to defeat the enemy outright but to grind them down gradually through sustained pressure.

Small, regular attacks—whether through ambushes, sniper fire, or sabotage—force the enemy to remain on high alert, never allowing them to rest or regroup. Over time, this constant pressure depletes their physical and mental energy, making them more prone to mistakes and lowering their combat effectiveness. Defenders should aim to extend the duration of the conflict, knowing that superior forces are less able to sustain long-term operations without significant logistical support.

In addition to military pressure, defenders can **target the enemy's logistical tail**, cutting off their access to fresh supplies, reinforcements, and medical support. This forces the enemy to overextend themselves, reducing their ability to rest or resupply. Eventually, fatigue will lead to a breakdown in discipline, as soldiers become more concerned with self-preservation than following orders. At this point, smaller forces can begin to escalate their attacks, capitalizing on the enemy's weakened state.

SABOTAGE AND THE DESTRUCTION OF KEY ASSETS

When facing a superior force, outright destruction of enemy personnel may not be necessary to achieve victory. Instead, **sabotage of critical infrastructure**—such as fuel depots, bridges, or airfields—can cripple the enemy's ability to sustain their operations, forcing them to retreat or abandon their objectives. Sabotage is often more efficient than direct combat, as it allows defenders to achieve strategic results without engaging in costly firefights.

The key to successful sabotage is careful planning and execution. Defenders must identify key assets that are critical to the enemy's operational success, such as communication lines, fuel depots, or transportation hubs. These targets should be attacked swiftly and decisively, using minimal resources to achieve maximum disruption. Sabotage operations can be conducted by small, specialized teams that operate behind enemy lines, striking at night or during periods of low visibility to avoid detection.

The destruction of key assets not only weakens the enemy's immediate operational capability but also has a demoralizing effect. Soldiers who see their supplies destroyed or their communications cut off will lose confidence in their ability to fight effectively, making them more susceptible to further attacks or ambushes.

OVERLOADING ENEMY DEFENSES

Even superior forces have limits to their defensive capabilities. By **overloading the enemy's defensive perimeter** with multiple, simultaneous threats, defenders can force them to stretch their resources thin, creating gaps in their defenses that can be exploited. This tactic works particularly well when the enemy is defending a fixed position, such as a base or fortified location.

Defenders can use diversionary attacks to force the enemy to commit forces to one area, while the real attack occurs elsewhere. For example, a series of small skirmishes or false attacks on the enemy's flanks or rear can draw their attention and resources away from the main defensive line, creating an opening for a more concentrated assault on a critical point. The key is to keep the enemy guessing, never allowing them to focus their full strength on any single threat.

In addition to overloading their defenses with physical attacks, defenders can use **psychological overload** by keeping the enemy in a constant state of uncertainty. Misinformation, decoy operations, and feigned retreats all contribute to a sense of confusion and unpredictability within the enemy's ranks. The enemy, unsure of where or when the next attack will come, will find it increasingly difficult to maintain effective control over their forces.

Overwhelming superior forces is not about matching them in firepower or numbers—it's about exploiting their weaknesses, leveraging tactical ingenuity, and applying constant pressure until they falter. By targeting the enemy's logistics, disrupting their command and control, and exploiting psychological vulnerabilities, smaller forces can erode the enemy's operational effectiveness and force them to fight on unfavorable terms. Success in these engagements requires precision, patience, and the ability to adapt quickly to changing conditions. Through a combination of guerrilla tactics, sabotage, deception, and relentless pressure, outnumbered and outgunned defenders can achieve victory against even the most formidable adversaries.

CHAPTER 11: NAVIGATING ETHICAL DILEMMAS IN GUERRILLA WARFARE

The Moral Costs of Survival

In the brutal landscape of guerrilla warfare, where survival is often the primary objective, the lines between ethical conduct and ruthless necessity can blur. The absence of a centralized authority, the collapse of societal norms, and the urgency of defending one's group or territory lead to situations where difficult moral choices must be made. Guerrilla warfare, by its nature, often involves tactics that can challenge traditional ethical frameworks: deception, sabotage, assassination, and the targeting of enemy logistics can create ethical quandaries that may haunt those involved long after the conflict has ended.

While this book is designed to provide practical, no-nonsense strategies for survival, it is impossible to ignore the ethical dimension of guerrilla warfare. The moral costs of survival must be acknowledged, even if they are not the primary focus of the defender's tactical decisions. This chapter will not engage in moral debates, nor will it dwell on subjective reflections. Instead, it will outline the practical ethical dilemmas that arise in guerrilla warfare, providing clear, objective guidance on how to navigate them with the ultimate goal of survival and operational success. In the end, ethical decisions in a collapsed society become part of the broader strategic framework, impacting the long-term sustainability of a defense force and its relations with the local population and other factions.

USE OF DECEPTION AND MISINFORMATION

Deception is a cornerstone of guerrilla warfare. Smaller forces rely on deception to compensate for their lack of firepower, numbers, and resources. Ambushes, feigned retreats, false intelligence, and the use of decoys are all standard tactics employed by guerrilla forces to mislead and confuse the enemy. However, the ethical dilemma arises when deception crosses the line from tactical necessity to manipulation of non-combatants or allies.

Misinformation can have long-term consequences beyond the immediate tactical benefits. Spreading false information about the enemy or about the defender's capabilities may serve to destabilize the enemy or cause confusion, but it can also lead to collateral damage, particularly if civilians are caught in the crossfire or if local populations are misled about the nature of the conflict. In guerrilla warfare, the relationship with the local population is crucial to long-term survival. Deceiving civilians, even if it serves a short-term objective, can erode trust and support, leading to isolation or even betrayal by those who were once sympathetic to the cause.

Leaders must weigh the consequences of deception, not only in terms of its immediate tactical benefits but also its long-term impact on relationships with civilians, allies, and other resistance groups. Tactical deception should always be focused on misleading the enemy, not those whose support is critical to the survival of the defense force. In some cases, it may be necessary to withhold information from civilians to protect operational security, but outright deception of non-combatants should be avoided whenever possible.

TARGETING NON-MILITARY INFRASTRUCTURE

Another ethical dilemma that often arises in guerrilla warfare is the targeting of non-military infrastructure, such as roads, bridges, communication lines, and even medical facilities. Sabotaging these targets can have significant tactical benefits by disrupting enemy logistics, communications, and movement. However, such actions can also have severe consequences for civilians, cutting off their access to essential services and making life in a collapsed society even more precarious.

The ethics of targeting non-military infrastructure must be evaluated through a lens of necessity. If a bridge is used by the enemy to transport troops and supplies, its destruction can be justified as a legitimate military target. However, if that same bridge is also used by civilians for evacuation or access to food and medical supplies, its destruction creates an ethical quandary. The decision to destroy such infrastructure must be based on a clear assessment of its value to the enemy versus its importance to civilian survival.

When forced to make such decisions, leaders must remain focused on the larger objective of survival and operational success, but they should also consider the potential for long-term consequences. Destroying essential infrastructure may weaken the enemy, but it can also create resentment among the local population, leading to a loss of support or the creation of new enemies. In some cases, it may be more effective to sabotage or disable infrastructure temporarily, allowing it to be restored once the immediate threat has passed.

ETHICS OF ASSASSINATION AND TARGETED KILLINGS

In guerrilla warfare, assassination and targeted killings are often employed as a way to eliminate key enemy personnel, disrupt command structures, or demoralize the opposing force. These actions are seen as pragmatic, reducing the enemy's effectiveness while avoiding direct, large-scale confrontations that could lead to heavy losses for the defenders. However, targeted killings raise significant ethical questions, particularly when non-combatants or political leaders are involved.

The distinction between combatants and non-combatants becomes blurred in a collapsed society, where political, military, and paramilitary roles often overlap. Targeting a high-ranking military commander is a clear act of warfare, but assassinating a political figure who supports the enemy may not be as straightforward. Leaders must assess the strategic value of such actions against the potential fallout, both in terms of enemy retaliation and the erosion of ethical boundaries that could undermine the legitimacy of the defense force.

When deciding whether to carry out a targeted killing, the key question should be whether the target's elimination will directly contribute to the defense force's survival or operational success. If the target's death will create a power vacuum, disrupt enemy operations, or prevent further attacks on the defending group, it may be justified as a necessary action. However, leaders must also consider the potential consequences of such actions on the broader conflict. Targeted killings can escalate violence, leading to retaliatory actions that may harm civilians or erode support for the defense force.

The decision to carry out an assassination should never be taken lightly, and it should always be based on a clear, objective analysis of the target's strategic importance. The goal of survival must remain paramount, but leaders must also be mindful of the long-term consequences of such actions, both for the conflict and for the moral integrity of their group.

DEALING WITH CIVILIAN CASUALTIES AND COLLATERAL DAMAGE

One of the most difficult ethical dilemmas in guerrilla warfare is the inevitability of civilian casualties and collateral damage. In many cases, the enemy will use civilians as shields or will occupy civilian areas, making it difficult for defenders to engage without causing harm to non-combatants. While every effort should be made to minimize civilian casualties, the reality of guerrilla warfare is that such casualties are often unavoidable.

Leaders must develop clear guidelines for how to engage the enemy in areas where civilians are present. Avoiding civilian casualties should be a priority, but not at the expense of operational success or the survival of the defense force. In some cases, the decision may be made to delay an attack or change the method of engagement to reduce the risk to civilians. However, if the enemy is using civilian areas as cover or as a base of operations, the defenders may have no choice but to engage, even if it means causing collateral damage.

The key to navigating this dilemma is **proportionality**. Leaders must always weigh the potential harm to civilians against the tactical necessity of the attack. If the benefits of the attack outweigh the potential harm, it may be deemed acceptable within the framework of guerrilla warfare. However, if civilian casualties are likely to undermine the support of the local population or provoke retaliatory actions that will harm the defense force, alternative tactics should be considered.

In all cases, efforts should be made to **warn civilians** when possible, giving them an opportunity to evacuate or seek shelter before an attack is carried out. The use of precision weapons, sniper fire, or other targeted methods can help reduce the risk of collateral damage, but defenders must accept that some level of civilian harm is inevitable in any conflict where the enemy embeds itself within civilian areas.

ETHICS OF FORCED RECRUITMENT AND CONSCRIPTION

In a collapsed society, where manpower is limited and survival is uncertain, the temptation to engage in forced recruitment or conscription can arise. Guerrilla forces may find themselves short on personnel and may seek to recruit or conscript individuals from the local population, whether voluntarily or by force. This presents a significant ethical dilemma, as the use of forced labor or conscription can alienate the local population and create internal divisions within the defense force.

Forced recruitment, especially of non-combatants or unwilling participants, is a morally hazardous path that can lead to long-term instability within the group. Individuals who are coerced into fighting are unlikely to be effective soldiers, and their presence may weaken the cohesion of the defense force. Moreover, forced recruitment risks alienating the local population, who may see the defense force as no different from the enemy.

If recruitment becomes necessary, leaders should focus on **voluntary enlistment**, offering incentives or protection to those who join the fight. Efforts should be made to recruit individuals who are willing and capable of contributing to the defense effort, rather than resorting to coercion. In some cases, recruitment drives may focus on training civilians in self-defense or non-combat support roles, allowing them to contribute to the war effort without forcing them into direct combat.

Ultimately, the use of forced recruitment should be avoided whenever possible. The cohesion and morale of the defense force depend on the trust and loyalty of its members, and coercion undermines both. Leaders must remain focused on building a force that is united by a shared commitment to survival and defense, rather than one held together by fear or coercion.

NAVIGATING THE GREY AREAS OF SURVIVAL

Guerrilla warfare presents defenders with numerous grey areas, where the lines between right and wrong, necessity and excess, become difficult to define. In these situations, survival often takes precedence, and decisions must be made with the ultimate goal of ensuring the continued existence of the defense force. However, leaders must remain aware that the choices they make—whether tactical, logistical, or ethical—can have long-term consequences that extend beyond the immediate battlefield.

The goal of guerrilla warfare is not just to survive in the short term, but to sustain a viable defense force that can endure the conflict and emerge victorious. This requires a careful balancing act between the ruthless pragmatism needed to defeat a superior enemy and the moral integrity needed to maintain cohesion, support, and legitimacy. Ethical dilemmas will arise, and leaders must be prepared to navigate them with a clear, objective understanding of the costs and benefits of each decision.

In the end, the moral costs of survival are an inherent part of guerrilla warfare. Every decision—whether to deceive, assassinate, or engage in sabotage—must be made with the understanding that there are no easy answers. What matters most is that each choice serves the overarching goal of survival and operational success, while minimizing harm to civilians, maintaining the support of the local population, and preserving the integrity of the defense force.

By remaining focused on these core principles, leaders can navigate the ethical dilemmas of guerrilla warfare with clarity and purpose, ensuring that their decisions contribute to the long-term survival and success of the defense force, even in the most difficult and morally ambiguous situations.

Balancing Civilian Protections with Tactical Necessity

In the context of guerrilla warfare, where the line between combatants and civilians can often blur, one of the most pressing challenges is balancing civilian protections with the tactical necessity of ensuring the survival of the defense force. Civilian populations in conflict zones are both a source of potential support and a vulnerable group at risk of becoming collateral damage in the ongoing struggle. For guerrilla forces, maintaining the trust and goodwill of the civilian population is critical for long-term survival. However, the tactical realities of guerrilla warfare can often place civilians in harm's way, particularly when they are used as cover by the enemy, or when the defense force is forced to operate within or around civilian areas.

Navigating this balance is essential for guerrilla forces not only from an ethical standpoint but also from a strategic one. Civilians provide crucial support in terms of shelter, intelligence, food, and logistical help. Losing their support or, worse, alienating them through actions that harm their safety or livelihood can be catastrophic for a guerrilla campaign. On the other hand, failing to take necessary tactical actions because of the presence of civilians can lead to defeat, allowing a numerically or technologically superior enemy to exploit the guerrilla force's restraint.

This section addresses how defenders in a collapsed society can balance the need to protect civilians with the tactical necessities of guerrilla warfare. The goal is to provide a clear, practical framework that minimizes harm to non-combatants while ensuring that the defense force remains effective and capable of meeting its strategic objectives.

UNDERSTANDING THE ROLE OF CIVILIANS IN GUERRILLA WARFARE

In any conflict, civilians are both bystanders and key players. In guerrilla warfare, they often play a dual role—caught between opposing forces but also capable of influencing the course of the conflict. In collapsed societies, where the rule of law has broken down, civilians frequently find themselves in situations where they must choose between aligning with the guerrilla forces or the enemy. As such, they become targets for both sides, either as sources of potential support or as strategic vulnerabilities.

Civilians provide essential services to guerrilla forces, often acting as a hidden logistical network for food, medical supplies, and shelter. They also offer critical intelligence about enemy movements, morale, and vulnerabilities. Without civilian cooperation, guerrilla forces are isolated and exposed. Conversely, if civilians believe that the defense force is acting recklessly or is indifferent to their safety, they may turn to the enemy for protection or even actively work against the guerrilla fighters.

It is therefore essential that guerrilla forces recognize the strategic importance of protecting civilians. Not only is this a moral imperative, but it also ensures that the defense force retains the support it needs to continue its operations. This means that decisions made in the heat of battle—whether to launch an attack, retreat, or sabotage infrastructure—must be carefully considered with the civilian population in mind.

MINIMIZING CIVILIAN CASUALTIES DURING ENGAGEMENTS

One of the most difficult decisions for any guerrilla force is how to engage the enemy when civilians are present. In many cases, the enemy will intentionally occupy civilian areas, using them as cover to deter attacks. This creates a moral and tactical dilemma: should the defenders strike at the enemy and risk civilian casualties, or should they avoid conflict and allow the enemy to operate freely?

When civilian areas are involved, the first priority must be to minimize harm to non-combatants without sacrificing the defense force's overall strategic objectives. This can be achieved by employing more precise tactics and focusing on hit-and-run operations that reduce the risk of prolonged engagements where civilian casualties are more likely to occur. Defenders should always strive to avoid using heavy firepower or indiscriminate attacks in civilian areas. Sniper fire, small-unit raids, and ambushes that target specific enemy positions are more effective in minimizing collateral damage.

In addition to choosing the right tactics, defenders should aim to **warn civilians whenever possible**. If an attack is planned in a civilian area, efforts should be made to discreetly inform civilians so that they can evacuate or take cover before the engagement begins. This not only reduces casualties but also reinforces the perception that the defense force is committed to protecting the civilian population.

The use of **precision strikes** is another important factor in minimizing civilian harm. When possible, defenders should employ small arms fire or targeted explosives rather than relying on area-effect weapons like mortars or improvised explosive devices (IEDs) that could result in indiscriminate damage. By targeting enemy combatants directly and avoiding widespread destruction, guerrilla forces can effectively strike at the enemy while preserving the integrity of civilian areas.

CIVILIAN EVACUATIONS AND THE CREATION OF SAFE ZONES

In situations where prolonged conflict is likely to occur, guerrilla forces should consider facilitating civilian evacuations or the creation of **safe zones** where non-combatants can find shelter. Civilians caught in the middle of a conflict zone are vulnerable not only to direct attacks but also to deprivation, starvation, and disease. Ensuring their safety through evacuation or the establishment of protected areas helps prevent unnecessary casualties and maintains goodwill with the population.

Evacuating civilians from high-conflict areas requires careful coordination and planning. Guerrilla forces must first assess whether an evacuation is feasible and whether it can be carried out without compromising operational security. If possible, defenders should work with local civilian leaders to organize the evacuation, using non-combatants as guides to identify safe routes out of the conflict zone. Communication with civilians is critical during these operations, as they must be informed of the risks and guided to safety in an orderly manner.

Safe zones can be established in less contested areas where civilians can shelter without the immediate threat of combat. These zones should be positioned far from military targets to discourage enemy attacks, and guerrilla forces should ensure that basic needs—such as food, water, and medical care—are met. Although establishing and maintaining safe zones requires resources, the long-term benefits of securing civilian trust and support far outweigh the short-term logistical challenges.

One of the greatest advantages of creating safe zones is that it prevents civilians from being used as human shields by the enemy. If civilians are evacuated from contested areas, the enemy loses its ability to hide behind them, allowing guerrilla forces to engage more freely without worrying about civilian casualties.

DEALING WITH CIVILIAN INFORMANTS AND COLLABORATORS

While civilian cooperation is critical to the success of a guerrilla campaign, there will inevitably be individuals within the population who choose to collaborate with the enemy, either out of fear, necessity, or loyalty. Dealing with civilian informants or collaborators presents a difficult ethical dilemma for guerrilla forces. On one hand, collaborators pose a direct threat to the security of the defense force, as they can provide the enemy with intelligence about positions, movements, or weaknesses. On the other hand, targeting civilians suspected of collaboration can lead to a loss of legitimacy and trust, particularly if those civilians were coerced or misled by the enemy.

The decision to take action against civilian collaborators must be based on clear evidence of their involvement with the enemy and the degree of harm they pose to the defense force. If a civilian is providing critical intelligence to the enemy, guerrilla forces may have no choice but to neutralize the threat. However, these actions must be carefully controlled to avoid alienating the larger population. Arbitrary or unjustified attacks on civilians—especially those suspected without evidence—can quickly lead to distrust and opposition from the local population.

When possible, **non-lethal measures** should be considered as an alternative to direct retaliation against collaborators. Public shaming, isolation, or confiscation of resources can serve as a deterrent without resorting to violence. Additionally, guerrilla forces can work to **win back collaborators** by offering them protection from the enemy, addressing their grievances, or providing incentives to switch allegiances. This approach helps maintain moral authority while reducing the risk of further collaboration.

THE TACTICAL USE OF CIVILIAN RESOURCES

In many cases, guerrilla forces will rely on civilian resources —such as food, shelter, or transportation—to sustain their operations. This presents another ethical challenge, as the depletion of civilian supplies can leave non-combatants vulnerable to starvation, exposure, or economic hardship. While it may be necessary for the defense force to requisition supplies in times of extreme need, this must be done in a way that respects civilian property and ensures that their basic needs are still met.

When using civilian resources, guerrilla forces should prioritize **fair compensation** wherever possible, offering payment in kind or future promises of protection and support. If civilians are providing food or shelter voluntarily, every effort should be made to protect their property from enemy retaliation. Requisitions should always be conducted in an organized, respectful manner, and the defense force should ensure that civilians are left with enough resources to survive. If civilian resources are overused or taken by force, it creates resentment and can lead to the loss of critical support.

In some cases, guerrilla forces may need to **protect civilian resources** from being exploited by the enemy. If the enemy is requisitioning supplies or using civilian properties as staging grounds, guerrilla forces should consider launching targeted raids to recapture these resources or deny them to the enemy. This can be done without causing unnecessary damage to civilian infrastructure, preserving the ability of non-combatants to rebuild once the conflict subsides.

MAINTAINING MORAL AUTHORITY IN THE EYES OF THE POPULATION

One of the key strategic considerations for any guerrilla force is the need to maintain **moral authority** in the eyes of the civilian population. Civilians will not support a force they view as reckless, predatory, or indifferent to their suffering. Guerrilla leaders must always be conscious of how their actions are perceived by the population and should work to demonstrate that they are acting in the best interests of the community, even when forced to make difficult tactical decisions.

Maintaining moral authority does not mean avoiding hard decisions or compromising tactical necessity—it means ensuring that every action is justifiable within the broader context of survival and protection. When civilians see that guerrilla forces are committed to minimizing harm, protecting their interests, and fighting for their survival, they are more likely to offer support, even in the face of significant hardship.

Leaders must communicate clearly with the civilian population, explaining why certain actions—such as sabotage, requisitioning, or evacuations—are necessary and how they will ultimately contribute to the community's safety. Regular communication helps build trust and reassures civilians that the defense force is working in their interests, rather than simply exploiting them for military gain.

Balancing civilian protections with tactical necessity is one of the most difficult challenges facing guerrilla forces in a collapsed society. Civilians are both a critical source of support and a vulnerable group that must be protected. While the tactical realities of guerrilla warfare may occasionally force defenders to engage in actions that put civilians at risk, these decisions must always be made with careful consideration of the long-term consequences.

By minimizing harm, protecting civilian interests, and maintaining moral authority, guerrilla forces can preserve the trust and support of the population while continuing to wage an effective defense. Leaders must always be mindful of the strategic importance of civilian protections, ensuring that their actions contribute not only to immediate survival but also to the long-term success of the defense force. Through careful planning, clear communication, and a commitment to balancing tactical necessity with ethical conduct, guerrilla forces can navigate the complexities of civilian involvement in conflict and emerge stronger as a result.

Rebuilding Society After

the Collapse

Rebuilding society after a collapse presents one of the most daunting tasks imaginable. In the aftermath of civil unrest, societal breakdown, and widespread violence, the infrastructure, governance systems, and social order that once held a community or nation together are often in ruins. While survival is the immediate priority during the collapse itself, long-term stability and security depend on the ability to restore order, rebuild institutions, and create a sustainable framework for the future.

Reconstruction is not merely about restoring what was lost —it is about rethinking and redesigning the systems that led to collapse in the first place. This means addressing not only the physical damage but also the underlying social, economic, and political fractures that were exposed during the collapse. The task requires a methodical approach, focusing on the establishment of security, governance, economic recovery, and the rebuilding of trust within the community. While this book is primarily focused on survival tactics, no discussion of surviving a collapse would be complete without addressing what comes next: the rebuilding process.

This chapter outlines the key elements necessary for rebuilding society after the collapse. It focuses on the practical steps that must be taken to restore stability and lay the foundations for a sustainable future. While the process will differ depending on the specific circumstances of the collapse, certain core principles remain applicable across different contexts. The goal is to provide clear, actionable guidance for those tasked with leading or participating in the reconstruction process, ensuring that they approach the task with clarity, purpose, and long-term vision.

ESTABLISHING SECURITY AND RULE OF LAW

The first and most immediate priority in any post-collapse

scenario is the re-establishment of security. Without security, efforts to rebuild are doomed to fail. Armed groups, criminal organizations, or rogue factions that continue to operate after the collapse must be neutralized or brought under control, and lawlessness must be addressed swiftly and decisively. This is often the most challenging task, as it requires not only physical force but also the restoration of legitimacy and authority to the governing bodies responsible for maintaining order.

The re-establishment of **rule of law** is critical in this phase. While guerrilla warfare tactics may have been necessary for survival during the collapse, the post-collapse period requires a transition from irregular warfare to structured, lawful governance. Defenders who led the fight for survival must now shift their focus to enforcing laws, preventing retribution or vigilantism, and ensuring that justice is administered fairly and impartially. This can be achieved by reinstating a judicial system or creating a provisional legal framework that provides the basic structure for resolving disputes, prosecuting crimes, and maintaining public order.

Security forces must be restructured or reformed to ensure that they serve the community rather than acting as oppressive or corrupt forces. Whether this involves professionalizing former guerrilla fighters or retraining remnants of pre-collapse military or police forces, the goal should be to create a disciplined, accountable security apparatus that protects the population and enforces the law. In many cases, **local militias or defense group**s will need to be integrated into the new security structure, transitioning from irregular fighters to formal peacekeepers.

In parallel with the restoration of security, it is crucial to **disarm and demobilize** groups that were involved in the conflict. The continued presence of heavily armed factions in society undermines efforts to restore order and can lead to renewed violence. Demobilization programs should be carefully managed, ensuring that former combatants are provided with pathways to reintegrate into civilian life, whether through employment, education, or community service. Weapons collection initiatives can also help reduce the number of arms circulating in society, reducing the risk of future conflict.

RESTORING GOVERNANCE AND POLITICAL STABILITY

Once security has been re-established, the next priority is restoring or rebuilding governance systems that can provide effective leadership and management of public affairs. The collapse of a government or political system often leaves a power vacuum that can be exploited by opportunists or rival factions, leading to further instability. To prevent this, the restoration of governance must be approached with care, focusing on the creation of inclusive, transparent, and accountable institutions.

In some cases, it may be possible to **rebuild existing institutions**, especially if they retain a degree of legitimacy in the eyes of the population. However, in many post-collapse scenarios, the old political system is seen as corrupt or ineffective, requiring a complete overhaul. This may involve the creation of **transitional governance structures**, such as provisional councils or assemblies, that can provide leadership during the initial stages of reconstruction. These bodies should include representatives from various factions, communities, and interest groups to ensure broad-based support and to prevent any one group from monopolizing power.

The establishment of governance should also include the development of a **constitution or legal framework** that outlines the rights and responsibilities of citizens, as well as the structure of government. This framework should prioritize checks and balances, preventing the concentration of power in a single entity or individual. A transparent legal framework is essential for rebuilding trust and ensuring that governance is seen as legitimate and fair.

Rebuilding political stability also requires **fostering reconciliation** among different groups, particularly if the collapse was driven by civil conflict or ethnic, religious, or political divisions. Efforts to rebuild trust must be made through open dialogue, conflict resolution mechanisms, and the establishment of truth and reconciliation commissions if necessary. These processes help address the grievances that led to the collapse, paving the way for a more stable and inclusive political environment.

REVITALIZING THE ECONOMY

Rebuilding a collapsed economy is a monumental task, particularly in cases where infrastructure, markets, and supply chains have been severely disrupted. Economic recovery is essential not only for restoring livelihoods but also for ensuring long-term stability. Without economic opportunities, the risk of renewed conflict or widespread discontent grows, as people struggle to meet their basic needs.

The first step in revitalizing the economy is **restoring basic services and infrastructure**, including power, water, transportation, and communication networks. These services are essential for the functioning of both the public and private sectors, enabling businesses to operate, goods to be transported, and communication to take place. Infrastructure rebuilding efforts should be prioritized based on strategic importance, focusing first on areas that will have the greatest impact on economic recovery.

Next, attention must be given to **restoring markets and trade**, particularly local and regional trade networks. In many collapsed societies, informal markets often emerge to fill the void left by the collapse of formal economies. These markets, while crucial in the short term, can be prone to exploitation by criminal groups or warlords. To ensure sustainable economic recovery, formal trade systems must be re-established, and the rule of law must be enforced to prevent exploitation and corruption.

Agriculture is often a cornerstone of economic recovery, particularly in rural areas where industrial or service-based economies have collapsed. Providing **support to farmers**, such as seeds, tools, and access to markets, is essential for reviving food production and ensuring food security. In urban areas, efforts should focus on **reviving small businesses**, creating employment opportunities, and encouraging entrepreneurship through microfinance programs or government-backed initiatives.

Long-term economic stability requires the establishment of a **stable currency** and financial system. If the national currency has been rendered worthless by hyperinflation or collapse, efforts must be made to stabilize the economy through currency reform or the introduction of new, trusted financial systems. This may involve partnering with international organizations or neighboring countries to stabilize exchange rates, attract investment, and rebuild financial institutions.

REBUILDING SOCIAL COHESION AND TRUST

One of the most profound challenges after a societal collapse is the loss of trust and social cohesion. During the collapse, communities are often torn apart by violence, mistrust, and betrayal. Neighbors turn against neighbors, and entire regions or groups may become estranged from one another due to political, ethnic, or religious divisions. Rebuilding society after the collapse requires a concerted effort to heal these divisions and rebuild trust within and between communities.

Reconciliation efforts must be at the forefront of this process. This can be achieved through the creation of **community-**

based reconciliation initiatives that provide a platform for dialogue, mediation, and the resolution of grievances. Local leaders, religious figures, and respected members of the community should be involved in these efforts to ensure that they are seen as legitimate and impartial. In some cases, **truth and reconciliation commissions** may be necessary to address the wrongs committed during the collapse, allowing victims and perpetrators to come forward and seek justice or forgiveness.

Education plays a key role in rebuilding social cohesion, particularly for younger generations who may have grown up during the collapse without access to formal schooling. **Rebuilding schools and educational systems** should be a priority, with a focus on teaching values of tolerance, cooperation, and citizenship. Education not only provides individuals with the skills they need to participate in the economy but also fosters a sense of national identity and shared purpose, helping to heal the fractures created by the collapse.

The rebuilding process should also include efforts to **restore cultural and social institutions** that were lost or damaged during the collapse. These institutions—such as religious organizations, community centers, and cultural associations—play an important role in fostering social cohesion and providing a sense of belonging. Restoring these institutions helps create a sense of normalcy and stability, allowing people to reconnect with their heritage and with one another.

PREPARING FOR FUTURE RESILIENCE

As society rebuilds after the collapse, it is crucial to take steps to **prevent future breakdowns**. The collapse has exposed vulnerabilities in the old system, and the rebuilding process provides an opportunity to address these weaknesses and create a more resilient society. This requires a forward-thinking approach, focusing not only on immediate recovery but also on long-term sustainability and preparedness for future crises.

One key aspect of future resilience is the establishment of **early warning systems** that can detect and respond to potential threats, whether they are natural disasters, economic shocks, or political instability. These systems should include mechanisms for monitoring and assessing risks, as well as protocols for mobilizing resources and coordinating responses in the event of a crisis. Building a resilient society also requires **diversifying the economy**, ensuring that no single sector or resource is overly relied upon, making the society less vulnerable to economic downturns or external shocks.

In addition to structural reforms, efforts must be made to **strengthen civil society** and ensure that citizens are actively engaged in governance and decision-making. A strong, informed, and empowered civil society acts as a check on government excesses and provides a critical feedback loop that can help identify emerging issues before they escalate into full-blown crises. Encouraging civic participation through local councils, grassroots organizations, and community engagement initiatives helps build a culture of accountability and cooperation.

Finally, **educating and training future leaders** is essential for ensuring long-term stability. The next generation of political, business, and community leaders must be equipped with the skills and values necessary to guide society through future challenges. Leadership training programs, mentorship, and opportunities for young people to take on leadership roles in their communities will help create a pipeline of capable individuals who can continue the work of rebuilding and strengthening society long after the immediate crisis has passed.

Rebuilding society after a collapse is a complex and multifaceted process that requires careful planning, sustained effort, and a commitment to addressing the root causes of the collapse. While the challenges are immense, the collapse also provides an opportunity to rethink and redesign the systems that failed, creating a more resilient, inclusive, and just society. By focusing on security, governance, economic recovery, social cohesion, and future resilience, those tasked with leading the rebuilding process can lay the foundations for a better future, ensuring that the mistakes of the past are not repeated and that society is prepared for whatever challenges lie ahead.

CHAPTER 12: POST-CONFLICT RECOVERY AND STABILIZATION

Transitioning from Conflict to Reconstruction

The transition from conflict to reconstruction is one of the most difficult and complex phases in post-conflict recovery and stabilization. It marks the point where the immediate needs of survival and defense give way to longer-term efforts aimed at rebuilding society, restoring governance, and ensuring that peace and stability take root. This transition is fraught with challenges, as the scars of conflict—physical, psychological, and social—continue to linger. However, it is a necessary step toward the future, one that requires careful planning, leadership, and a clear vision of the society that is to be rebuilt.

Post-conflict recovery is not simply about returning to the status quo that existed before the collapse. In most cases, the pre-conflict system was riddled with flaws—political corruption, social inequality, and economic instability—that contributed to the breakdown in the first place. Reconstructing society after conflict involves addressing these underlying issues while simultaneously providing for the basic needs of the population, restoring infrastructure, and rebuilding institutions. The path to stabilization is long and difficult, requiring patience, perseverance, and a commitment to creating sustainable peace.

This chapter explores the critical elements of post-conflict recovery and stabilization, focusing on the practical steps that must be taken to transition from conflict to reconstruction. The goal is to provide a framework for those tasked with leading recovery efforts, whether they are former defenders, community leaders, or newly established governing authorities. The key to successful post-conflict recovery is recognizing that it is a process, not a single event, and that each step must be carefully planned and executed to ensure long-term stability.

REESTABLISHING GOVERNANCE AND LAW ENFORCEMENT

The foundation of any post-conflict recovery effort is the reestablishment of governance and the rule of law. Without effective governance, it is impossible to maintain order, provide basic services, or facilitate economic recovery. In the immediate aftermath of conflict, governance structures are often weak, fragmented, or completely destroyed. This power vacuum must be filled quickly and effectively to prevent chaos and lawlessness from taking hold.

The first step in reestablishing governance is the creation of a **transitional authority** that can provide leadership and direction during the recovery phase. This transitional authority may be composed of former defense leaders, local community leaders, or representatives from various factions involved in the conflict. The key is to ensure that the authority is inclusive, representative of the population, and capable of making decisions that will be accepted by the majority of the community. In many cases, transitional authorities will need to operate with limited resources and legitimacy, but their role is critical in laying the groundwork for longer-term governance structures.

In parallel with the establishment of governance, it is essential to rebuild **law enforcement and judicial systems**. Law enforcement agencies, including the police and local militias, must be reorganized and professionalized to ensure that they operate with discipline and accountability. This may involve retraining former combatants, recruiting new personnel, or creating new institutions entirely. The focus should be on restoring the rule of law, preventing vigilante justice, and ensuring that the rights of all citizens are protected.

The reestablishment of a **judicial system** is equally important. Courts, legal frameworks, and mechanisms for dispute resolution must be put in place to provide a sense of justice and fairness in the aftermath of conflict. In many cases, transitional justice mechanisms—such as truth and reconciliation commissions—may be necessary to address the crimes and abuses committed during the conflict. These processes are essential for healing divisions within society and restoring trust in the justice system.

RESTORING SECURITY AND DISARMAMENT

Security is the cornerstone of post-conflict recovery. Without security, efforts to rebuild infrastructure, restart the economy, and restore governance are likely to fail. The immediate priority in post-conflict stabilization is to **restore public safety** by ensuring that armed groups, criminal organizations, and rogue factions are neutralized or integrated into legitimate security forces. This requires a comprehensive approach that includes disarmament, demobilization, and reintegration (DDR) of former combatants.

Disarmament is the first step in the DDR process. All combatants, whether they fought for the defense force, militias, or other factions, must be required to hand over their weapons. This is a delicate process, as many individuals will be reluctant to disarm due to fears of retaliation or the possibility of renewed conflict. However, disarmament is essential for reducing the overall level of violence and preventing the re-emergence of armed groups. Weapons collection programs should be conducted in a manner that ensures the safety and dignity of those involved, providing incentives for compliance when possible.

Following disarmament, the focus shifts to **demobilization**, the process of disbanding armed groups and transitioning former combatants back into civilian life. Demobilization programs should provide combatants with clear paths to reintegrate into society, whether through vocational training, education, or employment opportunities. Reintegration is the final and most critical phase, ensuring that former combatants become productive members of society rather than turning to crime or forming new armed groups. Successful reintegration requires a comprehensive support system, including psychological counseling, economic assistance, and community-based programs that foster reconciliation and social cohesion.

REBUILDING INFRASTRUCTURE AND ESSENTIAL SERVICES

The physical destruction caused by conflict can leave communities without access to basic services such as water, electricity, healthcare, and transportation. Rebuilding infrastructure is one of the most visible and immediate needs in post-conflict recovery, as it directly impacts the well-being of the population and the ability to restart economic activity. However, rebuilding infrastructure is also one of the most resource-intensive tasks, requiring significant investment and careful planning.

The first priority in infrastructure rebuilding is to **restore essential services**, such as water and electricity, which are critical for public health and safety. In many cases, this will involve repairing damaged infrastructure, such as water treatment plants, power stations, and distribution networks.

In some areas, it may be necessary to create temporary solutions—such as portable water purification systems or generators—while longer-term repairs are made.

Healthcare is another critical area of focus. Conflict often leaves healthcare systems in disarray, with hospitals destroyed, medical personnel displaced, and supplies depleted. Efforts to rebuild the healthcare system should prioritize **emergency care and public health**, addressing immediate needs such as the treatment of injuries, prevention of disease outbreaks, and the provision of basic medical services. In the long term, the healthcare system must be rebuilt to provide comprehensive services, including mental health care for those traumatized by the conflict.

Transportation networks—such as roads, bridges, and railways—are also essential for both economic recovery and the delivery of humanitarian aid. Rebuilding these networks should be prioritized based on strategic importance, with a focus on reconnecting communities and facilitating the movement of goods and services. In some cases, **international aid and investment** may be necessary to finance large-scale infrastructure projects, particularly in areas where local resources have been depleted by the conflict.

REBUILDING THE ECONOMY

Economic recovery is a key component of post-conflict stabilization, as it provides the foundation for long-term peace and stability. A thriving economy creates jobs, reduces poverty, and provides the resources needed to rebuild infrastructure, fund governance, and maintain security. In the immediate aftermath of conflict, the economy is often in a state of collapse, with markets destroyed, industries disrupted, and livelihoods lost. Rebuilding the economy requires a multifaceted approach that addresses both short-term recovery and long-term growth.

The first step in economic recovery is to **restart local markets and trade**, particularly in essential goods such as food, water, and medical supplies. In many cases, informal markets will have emerged during the conflict, and these can serve as the foundation for rebuilding the formal economy. Efforts should be made to provide support to local businesses, farmers, and traders, ensuring that they have access to the resources and capital they need to resume operations. Microfinance programs, loans, and grants can be used to stimulate economic activity at the local level.

Agriculture is often the backbone of the post-conflict economy, particularly in rural areas. Providing support to **farmers and agricultural communities** is essential for ensuring food security and creating livelihoods. This support can include the provision of seeds, tools, and livestock, as well as access to markets and training in modern agricultural techniques. In urban areas, efforts should focus on **revitalizing small businesses** and creating employment opportunities in sectors such as construction, manufacturing, and services.

In the long term, economic recovery requires the creation of a **stable financial system** that facilitates investment, trade, and the flow of capital. This may involve the introduction of a new currency, the stabilization of exchange rates, and the rebuilding of financial institutions such as banks and credit unions. Attracting international investment is also critical for large-scale infrastructure projects and the development of key industries, such as energy, mining, or manufacturing. Governments should work to create a business-friendly environment that encourages both domestic and foreign investment.

SOCIAL RECONCILIATION AND PSYCHOLOGICAL RECOVERY

The social wounds left by conflict are often as deep as the

physical destruction, and they can take years or even decades to heal. Communities that have been torn apart by violence, mistrust, and division must find ways to reconcile and rebuild relationships. This process of **social reconciliation** is essential for long-term peace and stability, as unresolved grievances can lead to renewed conflict or ongoing cycles of violence.

One of the key challenges in social reconciliation is **addressing the legacy of violence**. This may involve creating truth and reconciliation commissions, war crimes tribunals, or other mechanisms for addressing the abuses and atrocities committed during the conflict. These processes provide a platform for victims to tell their stories, seek justice, and begin the process of healing. At the same time, efforts should be made to **foster dialogue and understanding** between different factions, communities, or ethnic groups that were involved in the conflict.

Psychological recovery is also a critical component of social reconciliation. The trauma of conflict can have long-lasting effects on individuals, families, and communities, leading to mental health issues such as depression, anxiety, and post-traumatic stress disorder (PTSD). **Mental health services** must be an integral part of the recovery process, providing support to those who have been directly affected by the violence. Community-based programs, counseling services, and support groups can help individuals and families cope with the psychological impact of the conflict and begin the process of rebuilding their lives.

Education plays a key role in both social reconciliation and psychological recovery. **Rebuilding schools** and educational systems should be a priority, with a focus not only on providing basic education but also on promoting values of tolerance, cooperation, and citizenship. Education helps to restore a sense of normalcy and stability, while also providing young people with the skills they need to participate in the rebuilding process.

INTERNATIONAL ASSISTANCE AND COOPERATION

In many post-conflict scenarios, local resources and capacities are insufficient to meet the enormous challenges of recovery and stabilization. **International assistance and cooperation** play a critical role in providing the financial, technical, and humanitarian support needed to rebuild societies after conflict. This assistance can take many forms, from direct humanitarian aid and peacekeeping missions to long-term development programs and financial investment.

Humanitarian aid is often the first response to post-conflict needs, providing food, water, medical care, and shelter to those affected by the conflict. International organizations such as the United Nations, the Red Cross, and non-governmental organizations (NGOs) are often at the forefront of these efforts, working alongside local authorities to provide immediate relief. However, humanitarian aid is only the first step in the recovery process. Long-term stabilization requires a shift from emergency aid to **development assistance**, which focuses on rebuilding infrastructure, restoring governance, and promoting economic growth.

International organizations and donor countries can provide critical support for large-scale reconstruction projects, such as rebuilding roads, schools, hospitals, and power plants. They can also provide technical assistance and expertise in areas such as governance reform, economic development, and security sector reform. In many cases, **peacekeeping missions** may be deployed to help maintain security and prevent renewed violence, allowing local authorities to focus on rebuilding.

International assistance should be coordinated with local efforts to ensure that it meets the needs of the population and supports the long-term goals of recovery and stabilization. It is essential that local leaders and communities are actively involved in the planning and implementation of recovery programs, ensuring that they are tailored to the specific needs and circumstances of the post-conflict society.

Transitioning from conflict to reconstruction is a complex and difficult process, but it is also an opportunity to rebuild a more resilient and just society. Post-conflict recovery and stabilization require careful planning, strong leadership, and the active involvement of the entire community. By focusing on security, governance, economic recovery, social reconciliation, and psychological healing, those tasked with leading the recovery can ensure that the foundations are laid for a peaceful and stable future. International cooperation and assistance can provide critical support, but ultimately, the success of the recovery process depends on the commitment and determination of the people themselves to rebuild their society after the collapse.

Establishing Alliances and Local Governance

In the wake of societal collapse and conflict, establishing alliances and reconstituting local governance structures are crucial to the long-term stability of the region. The immediate post-conflict period is a time of vulnerability, where competing factions may still hold considerable power, and loyalties can shift rapidly. Establishing alliances and building local governance structures is not just about regaining control or consolidating power; it is about creating a sustainable framework that fosters cooperation, trust, and long-term development.

Alliances—whether between different factions, communities, or external entities—help stabilize a region by bringing together diverse groups with shared interests. These alliances create the political, economic, and social foundations necessary for rebuilding society. Similarly, establishing or rebuilding local governance is essential for maintaining law and order, managing resources, and addressing the needs of the population. Without functioning local governance, efforts to stabilize and rebuild society are likely to be undermined by ongoing violence, power struggles, or social unrest.

This section will explore the strategies for forming strategic alliances in a post-collapse context and provide practical guidance on how to establish or rebuild local governance. The focus is on creating inclusive, flexible, and resilient structures that can adapt to the needs of the community while ensuring the sustainability of peace and order. In this process, the balance between power-sharing and governance becomes a delicate but essential component for long-term stability.

ROLE OF ALLIANCES IN POST-CONFLICT STABILIZATION

Alliances are often a necessary feature of post-conflict stabilization efforts, as no single group or faction is likely to have the power or resources to govern effectively on its own. In fact, the very nature of conflict often fractures society into multiple factions or power centers, each of which may represent different ethnic, religious, political, or regional interests. In this fractured landscape, forming alliances is critical to uniting disparate groups around a shared vision for the future and ensuring that power is distributed in a way that prevents renewed violence.

When considering alliances, it is important to identify potential partners who have complementary goals and whose interests align with the long-term stability of the region. **Mutual benefit** should be the foundation of any alliance. Groups that were once in opposition during the conflict may find common ground in the post-conflict environment, where the need for peace, stability, and economic recovery outweighs the previous enmities. The key to successful alliance-building is to frame the new political landscape as one in which cooperation is more beneficial than continued rivalry.

One of the first steps in establishing alliances is to initiate **dialogue between former enemies** or competing factions. These dialogues should be facilitated by neutral intermediaries when possible, and the goal should be to identify shared interests—such as restoring security, rebuilding infrastructure, or improving access to resources—that can serve as the basis for cooperation. Trust-building measures are crucial at this stage, as deep-seated mistrust may remain from the conflict. These dialogues may need to begin with small, low-risk agreements (such as joint efforts to restore essential services) before evolving into broader political or military alliances.

Strategic alliances are not limited to domestic actors. In many post-conflict scenarios, **international alliances** are just as important, particularly when it comes to securing financial aid, humanitarian assistance, or peacekeeping forces. Neighboring countries, international organizations, and donor states can provide essential support in rebuilding efforts. However, such alliances must be carefully managed to avoid creating dependency or ceding too much influence to external actors. The key is to ensure that any international alliances are aligned with the goals of local governance and sovereignty, and that external assistance is used to support, rather than supplant, domestic efforts.

TYPES OF ALLIANCES

In a post-conflict setting, alliances can take various forms depending on the immediate and long-term needs of the parties involved. The three most common types of alliances are **political, military, and economic**.

Political alliances focus on power-sharing agreements and the creation of inclusive governance structures. In these alliances, former warring factions agree to share control over political institutions, often through a coalition government or transitional council. These alliances are essential in preventing one group from monopolizing power, which could lead to renewed conflict. Political alliances may also involve constitutional reforms, devolution of powers to regional governments, or agreements on how to manage key issues such as ethnic representation, resource distribution, and electoral systems.

Military alliances are often formed to ensure security during the transition to peace. These alliances may involve joint operations to disarm rogue factions, patrol contested areas, or protect civilians. In some cases, formerly hostile military forces may be integrated into a single national defense force, with former combatants from various factions given positions in the military or police. The success of military alliances depends on the ability to create a unified command structure that is seen as legitimate by all parties.

Economic alliances focus on rebuilding the economy and improving the livelihoods of the population. These alliances may involve joint efforts to rebuild infrastructure, restart trade, or develop natural resources. In some cases, former combatants or factions may agree to pool resources for mutual benefit, particularly if they control different parts of the economy (such as agriculture, manufacturing, or mining). Economic alliances can be a powerful tool for fostering cooperation and reducing tensions, as they create tangible benefits for all parties involved.

ESTABLISHING LOCAL GOVERNANCE

Local governance is the backbone of post-conflict recovery, providing the day-to-day leadership and administrative capacity needed to rebuild communities and restore order. In many cases, national governments may be too weak or disconnected from the realities on the ground to effectively manage local affairs. This is where local governance comes in, offering a more immediate and responsive form of leadership that is capable of addressing the specific needs of individual communities.

Establishing or rebuilding local governance structures requires a **bottom-up approach**, focusing first on the immediate needs of the population and then gradually expanding to include more complex forms of governance. In the early stages, local governance may be informal, relying on community leaders, former defense commanders, or traditional authorities to provide leadership. Over time, these informal structures can be formalized into local councils or assemblies, with clear rules and responsibilities.

The success of local governance depends on its **legitimacy and inclusiveness**. Governance structures must represent the interests of the entire community, not just the dominant group or faction. This requires mechanisms for **power-sharing** and **decision-making** that allow all voices to be heard, whether through elected representatives, consultative bodies, or participatory decision-making processes. Power-sharing arrangements at the local level help prevent marginalization and ensure that governance is viewed as fair and accountable.

Transparency and accountability are also essential. Local governance must operate with a clear set of rules and procedures that are understood and accepted by the population. This includes mechanisms for resolving disputes, managing resources, and addressing grievances. In many post-conflict settings, **traditional leaders**—such as tribal chiefs or elders—play a key role in dispute resolution and governance, particularly in rural areas where formal institutions may not yet be operational. Incorporating these traditional leaders into the local governance structure can provide a sense of continuity and stability.

KEY FUNCTIONS OF LOCAL GOVERNANCE

Local governance structures serve several key functions that are critical to post-conflict recovery. These include **security, public services, resource management, and dispute resolution**.

In terms of **security**, local governance plays a crucial role in maintaining order and preventing violence. Local councils or assemblies may work in coordination with national security forces or peacekeeping missions to patrol neighborhoods, monitor potential threats, and ensure that rogue elements do not destabilize the community. In some cases, local defense forces or militias may continue to operate under the authority of local governance structures, although these forces should be integrated into a broader security framework to ensure discipline and accountability.

Providing **public services**—such as water, sanitation, healthcare, and education—is one of the most visible and immediate functions of local governance. Communities that have experienced the breakdown of public services during the conflict are often desperate for the restoration of basic services, and the ability of local governance structures to meet these needs is critical to their legitimacy. In the early stages, service delivery may rely on humanitarian aid or international assistance, but over time, local governments must develop the capacity to provide these services independently.

Resource management is another key function of local governance, particularly in regions that rely on natural resources such as agriculture, mining, or forestry. Local councils must establish clear rules for the use and distribution of resources, ensuring that they are managed sustainably and that the benefits are shared equitably among the population. Resource management also involves protecting the environment, regulating land use, and preventing over-exploitation of natural assets.

Finally, local governance is responsible for **dispute resolution**, providing a framework for addressing conflicts over land, property, or political representation. In post-conflict settings, disputes are often rooted in deep-seated grievances, and local governance must have the capacity to mediate these disputes in a way that prevents further violence. This may involve creating local courts, mediation bodies, or truth and reconciliation commissions to address the legacies of the conflict.

CHALLENGES AND OPPORTUNITIES IN LOCAL GOVERNANCE

While establishing local governance is essential for post-conflict recovery, it is not without challenges. One of the main challenges is the potential for **power struggles** between different factions or interest groups. In the absence of strong national oversight, local governance structures may be vulnerable to capture by warlords, criminal organizations, or corrupt officials who seek to use them for personal gain. To prevent this, local governance must be anchored in the principles of transparency, accountability, and inclusiveness.

Another challenge is the **lack of resources and capacity** at the local level. Many post-conflict communities are impoverished and lack the financial or technical resources to provide basic services or manage complex governance functions. This is where alliances with international organizations, NGOs, and donor states can play a critical role. External support can provide the funding, training, and infrastructure needed to help local governments function effectively. However, it is important that international assistance is provided in a way that builds local capacity rather than creating dependency.

Despite these challenges, local governance also presents significant opportunities for **community empowerment and resilience**. By giving communities a direct role in managing their own affairs, local governance fosters a sense of ownership and responsibility for the future. It creates a space for dialogue and cooperation between different groups, helping to rebuild social cohesion and trust. Moreover, local governance is often more responsive to the specific needs of the population than national-level institutions, making it a critical driver of long-term recovery and development.

Establishing alliances and rebuilding local governance are essential components of post-conflict recovery and stabilization. Alliances—whether political, military, or economic—help unite disparate groups around shared goals and create the foundations for peace and cooperation. Local governance structures provide the leadership, administrative capacity, and public services needed to restore order and meet the needs of the population.

The success of these efforts depends on their inclusiveness, transparency, and accountability. Alliances must be built on mutual benefit, and local governance must represent the interests of all segments of the community. By fostering cooperation, sharing power, and providing effective leadership, alliances and local governance can help prevent the recurrence of conflict and lay the groundwork for a more resilient, peaceful, and prosperous society.

Role of the Citizen Defender in Rebuilding Order

In the aftermath of a societal collapse or conflict, the role of the citizen defender—those who took up arms or organized in defense of their communities—extends beyond mere survival. Once the immediate threat has been neutralized and the focus shifts toward rebuilding, the citizen defender assumes a new, critical role in restoring order, governance, and stability. Their experience, leadership, and local knowledge, forged in the crucible of conflict, are invaluable assets in the challenging task of post-collapse reconstruction.

The transition from conflict to rebuilding is not always a straightforward one. The skills necessary for survival in a collapsed society are not always the same as those required for governance and social reconstruction. However, the citizen defender often occupies a unique position of trust and influence within the community, having proven their commitment to protecting their neighbors and the broader social fabric. Their leadership is essential not only for maintaining security but also for guiding the community toward a sustainable future. In this role, citizen defenders must adapt their tactics from military engagement to civic leadership, from focusing on defense to ensuring long-term peace, security, and governance.

This section explores the evolving role of the citizen defender in rebuilding order, emphasizing how they can leverage their influence and leadership to restore stability, promote governance, and foster social cohesion. It offers practical guidance on how citizen defenders can transition from their wartime roles to peacetime leadership, with a focus on ensuring that the principles of justice, accountability, and transparency guide their efforts.

FROM DEFENSE TO CIVIC LEADERSHIP

In the immediate aftermath of societal collapse, the primary responsibility of the citizen defender was to ensure the survival and safety of their community. This often meant organizing armed resistance, defending against external threats, and maintaining a degree of law and order when formal governance structures had disintegrated. As society begins to stabilize, the role of the citizen defender must evolve from purely defensive operations to one of civic leadership and governance.

The skills that made citizen defenders effective in conflict

—strategic thinking, organization, and decisive action—are also critical in the process of rebuilding. However, leadership in a post-conflict society requires a broader range of skills, including diplomacy, negotiation, and the ability to manage resources and personnel effectively. Citizen defenders, particularly those who led small defense units or community militias, are often well-positioned to take on leadership roles within local governance structures, where their experience and credibility give them a natural authority.

One of the key challenges for citizen defenders is making the transition from combat to governance. This involves shifting their focus from security and conflict to long-term stability and prosperity. In many cases, citizen defenders may find themselves asked to lead local councils, assist in the formation of law enforcement, or manage reconstruction efforts. While these responsibilities may be outside the traditional scope of military leadership, the underlying principles of discipline, strategic planning, and decision-making remain essential.

MAINTAINING SECURITY AND RULE OF LAW

One of the most immediate tasks for citizen defenders in the post-conflict phase is maintaining security and restoring the rule of law. While formal police and military structures may eventually be reestablished, in the early stages of recovery, it is often the citizen defenders who continue to provide the primary security force in the community. This role is critical in preventing looting, retaliatory violence, and the resurgence of criminal or rogue elements that could destabilize the fragile peace.

The citizen defender's role in maintaining security should evolve from armed defense to enforcing the law. This means working to transition from a combat mindset to one of **law enforcement and justice**, ensuring that their actions are governed by principles of accountability and fairness. In this context, citizen defenders must avoid the temptation to take justice into their own hands, as vigilantism undermines the rule of law and can lead to further cycles of violence. Instead, they should work to create or support local judicial systems, ensuring that disputes are resolved through established legal channels.

In some cases, citizen defenders may be called upon to **organize local militias or defense forces** into a formal security apparatus. This involves training, disciplining, and professionalizing the force to ensure that it operates according to the rule of law and serves the interests of the entire community. The goal should be to create a security structure that is transparent, accountable, and responsive to the needs of the population. As part of this process, citizen defenders must work to ensure that the security force is inclusive, representing all segments of society and preventing any one group or faction from monopolizing power.

FOSTERING SOCIAL COHESION AND RECONCILIATION

In the post-conflict period, one of the most important roles of the citizen defender is fostering **social cohesion and reconciliation**. Conflict often leaves deep divisions within communities, whether along ethnic, religious, political, or ideological lines. These divisions, if left unaddressed, can lead to further instability or renewed conflict. Citizen defenders, who have often earned the trust of their communities through their actions during the collapse, are in a unique position to bridge these divides and promote unity.

Reconciliation is a delicate and long-term process, but it is essential for rebuilding a stable and peaceful society. Citizen defenders can facilitate this process by serving as **mediators** between different groups, encouraging dialogue and understanding. Their influence can help de-escalate tensions and prevent retaliatory violence, which is often a major risk in the immediate post-conflict period.

In addition to mediation, citizen defenders can promote reconciliation by supporting initiatives that bring communities together. This might include organizing joint reconstruction projects, fostering dialogue between former adversaries, or supporting **truth and reconciliation commissions** that provide a platform for addressing grievances and promoting healing. By leading or participating in these efforts, citizen defenders can help rebuild the social fabric of their communities, ensuring that trust and cooperation replace suspicion and division.

REBUILDING LOCAL GOVERNANCE AND INSTITUTIONS

The collapse of formal governance structures during a conflict often leaves a power vacuum that must be filled quickly to ensure stability. In the absence of national government leadership, **local governance** becomes critical, and the citizen defender plays a key role in establishing or rebuilding these institutions. Their familiarity with the community, combined with their leadership skills, positions them to contribute to or lead efforts to create local councils, assemblies, or governance bodies that can manage public affairs in the post-conflict period.

The goal of rebuilding local governance is to create **inclusive, accountable, and transparent institutions** that represent the interests of the entire population. Citizen defenders should advocate for the establishment of democratic mechanisms—whether through elections, local councils, or representative assemblies—that allow all members of the community to have a voice in decision-making. In this role, citizen defenders must transition from being military leaders to **civilian leaders**, focusing on public administration, service delivery, and dispute resolution.

One of the challenges citizen defenders may face in this role is ensuring that governance structures are not dominated by any single faction, including their own. It is essential that power is distributed equitably and that governance is seen as fair and impartial. This requires a commitment to **transparency** and **accountability**, with clear mechanisms for overseeing the actions of public officials and ensuring that decisions are made in the public interest.

Citizen defenders can also support the **restoration of essential services**—such as water, healthcare, and education—which are critical to the long-term stability of the community. In many cases, this will require partnerships with international organizations, NGOs, or other external actors who can provide the resources and technical expertise needed to rebuild infrastructure and restore public services. Citizen defenders can play a key role in coordinating these efforts, ensuring that they align with the needs and priorities of the local population.

ECONOMIC RECONSTRUCTION AND RESOURCE MANAGEMENT

Another critical role for the citizen defender in rebuilding order is contributing to the **economic recovery** of the community. The collapse of society often leads to the destruction of livelihoods, markets, and industries, leaving the population without access to basic goods or opportunities for employment. Economic instability, if left unaddressed, can lead to social unrest and further conflict.

Citizen defenders, with their local knowledge and leadership skills, can play an important role in organizing economic recovery efforts. This might involve supporting **agriculture, small businesses, and local trade**, which are often the backbone of post-conflict economies. By organizing labor, securing resources, and facilitating trade, citizen defenders can help stimulate economic activity and provide opportunities for their communities to rebuild their livelihoods.

One of the key challenges in economic reconstruction is **resource management**, particularly in areas where valuable resources—such as land, minerals, or timber—are at stake. Citizen defenders must ensure that these resources are managed equitably and sustainably, preventing exploitation by powerful factions or external actors. This requires the establishment of clear rules and regulations for resource use, as well as mechanisms for ensuring that the benefits of resource extraction or agriculture are shared fairly among the population.

PREVENTING THE RETURN OF CONFLICT

As the community transitions from conflict to reconstruction, one of the most important tasks of the citizen defender is preventing the return of violence. Post-conflict societies are often fragile, with unresolved grievances, power struggles, and economic hardship creating the conditions for renewed conflict. Citizen defenders, as trusted leaders, must work proactively to address these risks and ensure that peace and stability are maintained.

Preventing the return of conflict requires a combination of **security measures**, **governance reforms**, and **social reconciliation efforts**. Citizen defenders must remain vigilant against threats to security, such as criminal elements, rogue factions, or external actors who seek to destabilize the region. At the same time, they must ensure that governance structures are responsive to the needs of the population and that grievances are addressed through legal and political channels rather than violence.

In this role, citizen defenders must continue to engage with the community, building trust and ensuring that the population feels that their voices are heard and their concerns are being addressed. This may involve creating forums for public dialogue, supporting local dispute resolution mechanisms, and promoting **inclusive governance** that allows all segments of society to participate in the rebuilding process.

The role of the citizen defender in rebuilding order after a collapse is critical to the long-term success of post-conflict recovery. Their leadership, trust, and experience in protecting their communities during the conflict position them as key figures in the reconstruction process. However, the transition from defender to civic leader requires a shift in focus, from military defense to governance, reconciliation, and economic recovery.

Citizen defenders must embrace their new responsibilities, working to restore security, rebuild governance structures, foster social cohesion, and promote economic recovery. By doing so, they can ensure that the sacrifices made during the conflict were not in vain and that their communities emerge from the collapse stronger, more resilient, and better prepared for the future. Their role is not just about surviving the collapse but about leading the way toward a more stable and prosperous society.

CONCLUSION: THRIVING IN THE MIDST OF COLLAPSE

The idea of thriving in the midst of collapse may seem paradoxical at first. A society in collapse is typically marked by widespread instability, violence, the breakdown of governance, and the erosion of the social fabric. Yet, history has shown that human beings are remarkably resilient, capable not only of surviving but of rebuilding and adapting, even in the most challenging circumstances. Thriving during a collapse is not about the luxury or prosperity that one might associate with times of peace and order. Instead, it is about finding ways to flourish amidst chaos, ensuring not only survival but also the preservation of values, community, and a vision for the future.

In the context of this book, thriving during collapse goes beyond simply enduring the hardships of a fractured society. It is about making strategic decisions, harnessing individual and collective strengths, and adopting a mindset that embraces adaptability and resourcefulness. For the citizen defender and the communities they protect, thriving is defined by maintaining security, fostering resilience, and taking proactive steps to rebuild the structures that ensure long-term stability. It is about turning the collapse into an opportunity—not to return to the status quo but to create something better, more resilient, and more just.

The journey from surviving to thriving in a collapsed society is a difficult one. It demands a combination of mental toughness, tactical ingenuity, and an unwavering commitment to long-term goals, even in the face of immediate chaos. This conclusion will outline the key principles and strategies that define what it means to thrive in the midst of collapse, providing a framework for navigating the challenges of a post-collapse world while maintaining a focus on future success.

One of the greatest challenges in any collapse scenario is balancing the immediate need for survival with the long-term goal of rebuilding. The urgency of securing food, water, shelter, and safety often overwhelms the ability to plan for the future. However, those who thrive during collapse are those who recognize that long-term vision must guide even short-term decisions. While survival is the immediate priority, every action taken in the present should be evaluated for how it contributes to the broader goals of recovery and stabilization.

This long-term vision must begin with a clear understanding of what kind of society is being rebuilt. Is it one that simply mimics the flawed system that led to the collapse? Or is it a new, more resilient society that addresses the underlying causes of instability? For the citizen defender, this means thinking beyond the immediate threat and considering the kind of governance, social structures, and economic systems that will ensure the future well-being of the community. Thriving during collapse requires moving from a reactive mindset—focused solely on survival—to a proactive mindset that plans for recovery and growth.

While it may seem that long-term planning is a luxury reserved for more stable times, the reality is that some of the most important decisions about the future are made in the midst of crisis. For example, the alliances formed, the leadership established, and the values upheld during the collapse will shape the trajectory of the post-collapse society. Those who maintain a focus on long-term goals, even while navigating immediate dangers, are best positioned to emerge from the collapse not just as survivors but as leaders in the rebuilding process.

At the heart of thriving in a collapsed society is the concept of resilience. Resilience is the ability to absorb shocks, adapt to changing circumstances, and continue functioning in the face of adversity. In a societal collapse, resilience is not just a personal trait but a collective one. Communities, institutions, and networks that can bend without breaking are the ones that thrive. Building resilience is therefore a critical part of surviving collapse and laying the foundation for long-term success.

Resilience is built in several ways. At the individual level, it requires a mindset that embraces adaptability and remains focused on problem-solving, even when the situation seems overwhelming. The ability to manage stress, maintain mental clarity, and make rational decisions under pressure is essential for personal resilience. For the citizen defender, this means staying focused on the mission—whether that is ensuring the safety of the community, maintaining order, or rebuilding governance structures—while remaining flexible enough to adapt to the constantly shifting realities of a collapsed society.

At the community level, resilience is built through strong social networks and the ability to cooperate in the face of crisis. Communities that can organize quickly, share resources, and support one another are far more likely to thrive than those that remain fragmented and isolated. For this reason, the citizen defender must focus on fostering unity and cohesion within the community, bringing together different factions or groups to work toward common goals. Thriving in the midst of collapse is a collective endeavor, and no individual or small group can succeed alone. Strong alliances, mutual support, and shared leadership are the pillars of a resilient community.

Resilience also applies to the physical infrastructure of society. In many cases, the collapse may have damaged or destroyed key infrastructure, such as transportation networks, communication systems, or power grids. Thriving in such an environment means finding ways to rebuild or repurpose these systems to ensure that they serve the needs of the community. This may involve innovative, low-tech solutions, such as local food production, water conservation systems, or decentralized energy sources, all of which reduce dependence on fragile, large-scale infrastructure and create more resilient local systems.

Surviving a societal collapse requires more than just physical toughness or tactical skill—it demands an extraordinary level of psychological fortitude and mental discipline. Thriving in the midst of collapse involves maintaining a clear and steady mindset, even when faced with fear, uncertainty, and loss. The psychological toll of living in a collapsed society can be immense, as individuals are often separated from loved ones, deprived of basic comforts, and exposed to constant danger. Yet, those who thrive are those who can master their emotions, focus their energy on productive action, and maintain a sense of purpose.

For the citizen defender, psychological fortitude is not just about individual mental health—it is about maintaining morale and cohesion within the broader community. The defender's role as a leader means that they must project confidence and stability, even in the most uncertain times. By modeling mental discipline and emotional control, citizen defenders can inspire those around them to remain calm and focused, preventing panic or despair from undermining the collective effort to rebuild.

One of the most important aspects of psychological resilience is the ability to **compartmentalize immediate stresses** while keeping the broader mission in mind. Citizen defenders must be able to focus on the task at hand—whether that is organizing a defense, negotiating with other factions, or managing a supply line—without becoming overwhelmed by the larger challenges of the collapse. This ability to maintain focus and clarity in the face of chaos is what allows defenders to lead effectively and make decisions that contribute to long-term recovery.

At the same time, thriving requires acknowledging the psychological impact of the collapse and taking steps to mitigate it. This may involve providing mental health support to the community, creating spaces for individuals to express their fears and concerns, or developing rituals and routines that bring a sense of normalcy and stability to daily life. Thriving is not about denying the reality of hardship—it is about facing it head-on, while also recognizing the need for emotional and psychological healing.

Thriving in a collapsed society often requires a level of innovation and adaptability that goes beyond traditional thinking. In a post-collapse world, many of the old systems and structures will no longer function, and survival may depend on the ability to think creatively and develop new solutions to emerging problems. This is particularly true in areas such as resource management, infrastructure rebuilding, and governance.

One of the hallmarks of those who thrive in collapse is their ability to **innovate under pressure**. Whether it is finding new ways to produce food in a resource-scarce environment, developing alternative methods of communication in the absence of functioning networks, or creating makeshift medical facilities to treat the injured, innovation is key to overcoming the challenges of a post-collapse world. The ability to adapt quickly to new circumstances, experiment with different approaches, and learn from failure is what sets apart those who merely survive from those who truly thrive.

For the citizen defender, fostering a culture of innovation within the community is essential. This means encouraging creative problem-solving, empowering individuals to take initiative, and being open to unconventional ideas. Thriving communities are those that can adapt to changing circumstances, seize opportunities in the midst of crisis, and remain flexible in the face of uncertainty. By promoting a spirit of innovation and adaptability, the citizen defender can help the community navigate the complexities of rebuilding and create systems that are more resilient and sustainable than those that existed before the collapse.

In many cases, the societal collapse that the citizen defender and their community face is the result of deep systemic failures—whether political, economic, or social—that undermined the integrity of the pre-collapse order. As the community begins to rebuild, there is an opportunity to create a new social and moral framework that addresses these failures and provides a stronger foundation for the future.

Thriving in a collapsed society means not only restoring order but also **rethinking the principles and values** that will guide the new order. The citizen defender has a critical role to play in shaping this framework, ensuring that the lessons learned from the collapse are integrated into the rebuilding process. This may involve promoting greater equity and inclusion in governance, developing more transparent and accountable systems of leadership, or fostering a stronger sense of social responsibility and mutual support within the community.

At the heart of this new framework is the recognition that the collapse was not simply a natural disaster or an inevitable event—it was the result of human choices and systemic weaknesses. Thriving in the aftermath requires a commitment to addressing these weaknesses and building a society that is more just, resilient, and adaptable. This may involve creating new institutions that reflect the needs and aspirations of the post-collapse community, as well as redefining the relationship between individuals and the state, between communities and the environment, and between different factions or groups within society.

Ultimately, thriving in the midst of collapse is not a solitary endeavor—it is a collective effort that depends on the strength and resilience of the entire community. While the citizen defender plays a crucial leadership role, the process of rebuilding and thriving requires the participation of everyone. It requires a shared commitment to the long-term vision of recovery, a collective willingness to adapt and innovate, and a deep sense of responsibility for the well-being of others.

In a post-collapse world, thriving is defined not by the accumulation of wealth or power but by the ability to rebuild a society that is more resilient, more just, and more capable of withstanding future challenges. It is about creating a new social order that reflects the lessons learned from the collapse, while also embracing the opportunities for growth and transformation that emerge from crisis.

For the citizen defender, thriving means more than just surviving the collapse—it means leading the way toward a brighter future. By maintaining a focus on long-term goals, fostering resilience and innovation, and promoting a new social and moral framework, the citizen defender can ensure that their community not only survives but thrives in the aftermath of collapse. It is a difficult and demanding path, but it is one that ultimately leads to a stronger, more united, and more resilient society.

Hope Amid Destruction: Building a New Normal

Amid the ruins of a collapsed society, where destruction and chaos have taken root, the prospect of building something new can seem distant and almost impossible. The devastation—both physical and emotional—leaves deep scars on individuals and communities. The familiar structures of governance, law, and social order crumble, leaving behind uncertainty and fear. Yet, within this environment of destruction, the seeds of hope persist. For those who have survived, the task is not just to rebuild but to create a new normal, one that learns from the past and envisions a future that is more resilient and just.

Hope is not a passive feeling in these moments. It is an active force, born from the belief that something better can emerge from the wreckage. For those who take on the responsibility of rebuilding—whether they are citizen defenders, community leaders, or ordinary people striving to protect their families—hope becomes the foundation upon which the new normal is built. It drives the decisions, actions, and sacrifices that will ultimately determine the shape of the future. In a society that has been torn apart by conflict or collapse, the path forward is neither clear nor easy. But it is this very uncertainty that opens the door for innovation, growth, and transformation.

As the immediate threats subside and the process of reconstruction begins, the first step toward a new normal is the establishment of stability. In the absence of centralized authority, local communities often become the building blocks of this new reality. The citizen defender, who may have taken up arms to protect their neighbors during the collapse, now finds themselves in a position of leadership, guiding the efforts to restore order and security. This transition from defense to governance is one of the most critical phases of post-collapse recovery. It is not enough to merely survive the collapse—there must be a vision for what comes next, and it is the citizen defenders who are often tasked with articulating and implementing that vision.

Stability, however, is not simply about the absence of violence or conflict. It is about creating an environment where people can begin to rebuild their lives with a sense of security and predictability. The establishment of basic governance structures—whether through local councils, informal leadership, or newly formed institutions—provides the framework within which this stability can grow. But governance must be inclusive and responsive, shaped by the needs and aspirations of the community. This is where the role of the citizen defender evolves further, from a protector to a steward of the community's future. Their leadership must reflect the values of fairness, transparency, and justice, ensuring that all voices are heard and that power is not concentrated in the hands of a few.

The process of rebuilding a new normal is not just about restoring physical infrastructure or establishing law and order. It is also about healing the social fabric that was torn apart during the collapse. Communities that were once cohesive may have been fractured by violence, distrust, or competing loyalties. The task of rebuilding these relationships is as important as rebuilding roads, schools, or hospitals. Reconciliation, trust, and cooperation are the pillars upon which the new normal rests, and these cannot be imposed from the top down. They must be nurtured through dialogue, mutual respect, and shared goals. The citizen defender, having earned the trust of the community through their actions during the collapse, plays a crucial role in fostering this social healing. They must encourage reconciliation, mediate conflicts, and promote unity where division once reigned.

Reconciliation does not happen overnight, and it requires

patience, commitment, and often forgiveness. In many cases, individuals and groups within the community may have committed acts during the collapse that cannot be easily forgotten or forgiven. The process of reconciliation, then, is not about erasing the past but about finding a way to move forward despite it. This is where truth-telling mechanisms, such as local reconciliation councils or informal truth commissions, can help address grievances and create a space for healing. The new normal that emerges must be one where old wounds are acknowledged and addressed, but not allowed to define the future.

Alongside the rebuilding of relationships, the physical rebuilding of society must also take place. The destruction of infrastructure, homes, and essential services during the collapse leaves a void that must be filled. The new normal will be shaped by how communities approach this reconstruction. In many cases, the collapse provides an opportunity to rethink and redesign the systems that failed. Rather than simply restoring what was lost, there is a chance to create something better—more resilient, more inclusive, and more sustainable. This applies to everything from local economies to healthcare systems, from education to governance structures.

Innovation becomes a key component of the new normal. In a post-collapse world, many of the old systems no longer function, and the resources available for rebuilding may be limited. This scarcity forces communities to think creatively about how to rebuild in ways that maximize efficiency and sustainability. Whether it's developing local food production systems, implementing decentralized energy solutions, or creating alternative means of communication and transport, innovation is not just a tool for survival but a foundation for thriving in the new normal. Those who can harness the power of innovation, while keeping the needs of the community at the forefront, will be the ones who lead the way toward a more sustainable future.

Yet, even with innovation, the path to the new normal is fraught with challenges. The psychological impact of the collapse—the trauma, fear, and loss experienced by individuals and communities—cannot be ignored. Thriving in the new normal requires addressing the mental and emotional well-being of the population, particularly those who were directly affected by violence or displacement. Mental health support must be an integral part of the rebuilding process, providing individuals with the tools they need to cope with their experiences and move forward. This may take the form of community-based counseling, support groups, or simply creating spaces where people feel safe to share their stories and emotions. Healing the psychological wounds of the collapse is just as important as healing the physical and social wounds, and it is essential for creating a society that is capable of thriving in the long term.

For the citizen defender, their role in building the new normal extends beyond leadership in governance or security. They are also symbols of resilience, embodying the hope that something better can emerge from destruction. Their actions, both during the collapse and in the rebuilding process, serve as an example to others that it is possible to rise above adversity and create a future that is stronger and more just than what came before. In this way, they are not only defenders of their communities but also architects of the new normal.

Ultimately, thriving in the new normal is about creating a society that is resilient to future challenges—whether those challenges come in the form of economic shocks, political instability, or environmental disasters. It is about building systems and structures that can withstand pressure, adapt to change, and continue to function even in the face of adversity. But it is also about more than just systems and structures. It is about building a sense of community, shared responsibility, and collective purpose that allows individuals and groups to work together toward common goals.

The new normal will not be perfect, nor will it be without its difficulties. The scars of the collapse will remain, and the process of rebuilding will take time. But it is the possibility of something better—the hope that out of destruction can come renewal—that drives the efforts of those who take on the task of rebuilding. For the citizen defender and the communities they protect, this hope is not abstract; it is the guiding force that turns the chaos of collapse into an opportunity for transformation.

In the end, hope amid destruction is not a passive sentiment. It is a deliberate choice, made each day, to build a future that is stronger, more just, and more resilient. It is the belief that, even in the darkest moments of collapse, the foundations for a better society can be laid. The new normal may look different from what came before, but it is shaped by the experiences, sacrifices, and hard-won lessons of those who survived the collapse and chose to rebuild. For those who embrace this challenge, thriving in the midst of collapse is not only possible —it is the ultimate testament to human resilience and the enduring power of hope.

REFERENCES

1. **US Army Resistance Manual**
U.S. Department of the Army, FM 3-05.130, "Army Special Operations Forces Unconventional Warfare"
A fundamental resource on unconventional warfare, providing in-depth strategies for resistance movements, subversion, and guerrilla tactics. This manual is key for understanding the principles behind organizing and executing resistance operations when conventional warfare is not an option.

2. **Guerrilla Warfare and Special Forces Operations**
U.S. Army, FM 31-21
This field manual covers the essential tactics of guerrilla warfare and special operations, offering detailed information on small unit tactics, hit-and-run strategies, and asymmetrical warfare. It's an invaluable resource for citizen defenders adopting irregular tactics in the absence of structured military forces.

3. **The Art of War**
Sun Tzu, translated by Samuel B. Griffith
A timeless text on strategy and warfare, Sun Tzu's work outlines principles of conflict, deception, and leadership that are as relevant in modern guerrilla warfare as they were in ancient times. Understanding the psychological and strategic elements of war is critical for any defender navigating societal collapse.

4. **Counterinsurgency Field Manual**

U.S. Army, FM 3-24

This manual provides a comprehensive framework for counterinsurgency operations, a key focus for post-collapse scenarios where maintaining order and suppressing emerging threats is critical. It offers insight into both the practical and psychological dimensions of controlling insurgent movements.

5. **Small Wars Manual**

United States Marine Corps

This manual offers a detailed examination of small-scale conflicts, irregular warfare, and operations in complex environments, providing relevant lessons for those facing paramilitary or guerrilla forces in a collapsed society.

6. **Total Resistance: Swiss Army Guide to Guerrilla Warfare and Underground Operations**

Major Hans von Dach

Written for Swiss citizens during the Cold War, this guide covers guerrilla warfare and resistance movements in extreme conditions. It is an important reference for organizing civilian defense units and understanding the logistics of resistance in a hostile environment.

7. **The SAS Survival Handbook**

John 'Lofty' Wiseman

An essential survival manual covering everything from wilderness survival to urban disaster preparedness. This book provides practical advice on navigating and surviving in environments where basic services have broken down, making it an indispensable resource for survival in the aftermath of societal collapse.

8. **On Guerrilla Warfare**

Mao Zedong, translated by Samuel B. Griffith

A critical analysis of guerrilla tactics, Mao's work outlines the theory and execution of guerrilla warfare, with a focus on flexibility, mobility, and the strategic importance of civilian support. It provides a philosophical and tactical underpinning for much of modern insurgent warfare.

9. **Psychological Operations: Principles and Case Studies**
U.S. Army, FM 3-05.301

This manual provides a detailed analysis of the principles of psychological warfare, perception management, and influence operations. It is a critical resource for those looking to use information and psychological tactics to gain an advantage in post-collapse environments.

10. **Rogue State: A Guide to the World's Only Superpower**
William Blum

A thought-provoking examination of the use of force and subversion by nation-states. Blum's work offers context for understanding how powers and insurgents may operate during or after a collapse, helping defenders prepare for the geopolitical consequences of instability.

11. **The Collapse of Complex Societies**
Joseph Tainter

Tainter's work analyzes historical collapses of complex societies and offers key insights into why large systems fail. This reference is crucial for understanding the patterns of societal collapse and the lessons that can be applied to prevent or mitigate such outcomes in the future.

12. **Civil War in Spain, 1936-1939**
Hugh Thomas

A comprehensive historical account of one of the most complex and brutal civil wars in modern history. The Spanish Civil War offers valuable lessons in guerrilla tactics, urban defense, and the political dynamics that unfold during the collapse of a state.

13. **The Ethics of War and Peace**
Paul Christopher

While this book focuses on the moral implications of warfare, it provides a critical understanding of the ethical challenges faced during both conflict and reconstruction. For those leading citizen defense forces, it is important to understand the delicate balance between tactical necessity and moral responsibility.

14. **War of the Flea: The Classic Study of Guerrilla Warfare**
Robert Taber
Taber's analysis of guerrilla warfare highlights the asymmetric nature of modern conflicts and provides key strategies for outnumbered and outgunned defenders. His work is particularly relevant to those navigating irregular warfare in post-collapse environments.

15. **Humanitarian Charter and Minimum Standards in Humanitarian Response (Sphere Handbook)**
Sphere Project
An essential guide for post-conflict recovery, the Sphere Handbook outlines standards for humanitarian aid and rebuilding efforts. It offers crucial insight into the best practices for providing food, water, sanitation, shelter, and medical aid in post-collapse environments.

14. **Controlling the Narrative: The Definitive Guide to Psychological Operations, Perception Management, and Information Warfare**
Josh Luberisse
An essential resource designed for military professionals, strategists, policymakers, and scholars engaged in the intricate fields of psychological warfare and strategic communications. This comprehensive guide equips readers with the knowledge necessary to effectively execute operations that influence perceptions, decisions, and behaviors on the global stage. It covers a broad spectrum of topics, from the basic concepts of propaganda and media manipulation to sophisticated strategies involving cyber

warfare, artificial intelligence, and data analytics.

BOOKS IN THIS SERIES

Military Strategy

Controlling The Narrative: The Definitive Guide To Psychological Operations, Perception Management, And Information Warfare

Controlling the Narrative: The Definitive Guide to Psychological Operations, Perception Management, and Information Warfare is an essential resource designed for military professionals, strategists, policymakers, and scholars engaged in the intricate fields of psychological warfare and strategic communications. This comprehensive guide delves into the multifaceted aspects of psychological operations (PSYOP), perception management and information warfare, exploring the theories, practices, and tools that shape today's information battle-spaces.

Structured to provide a deep understanding of the historical evolution, strategic considerations, and modern applications of PSYOP, this book equips readers with the knowledge necessary to effectively execute operations that influence perceptions, decisions, and behaviors on the global stage. It covers a broad spectrum of topics, from the basic concepts of propaganda and media manipulation to sophisticated strategies involving cyber warfare, artificial intelligence, and data analytics.

Each chapter in this guide is meticulously crafted to offer detailed insights and practical advice, enriched with case studies that highlight both successful and cautionary tales from past and present operations. The book emphasizes the importance of adhering to ethical and legal standards, providing readers with a clear framework for conducting operations that respect human rights and international laws.

Controlling the Narrative also addresses the strategic imperatives for military and governmental organizations, including the need for ongoing adaptation to emerging technologies and the shifting geopolitical landscape. With its rigorous analysis and comprehensive coverage, the guide serves as an indispensable resource for those tasked with safeguarding national security and advancing military objectives through the strategic use of psychological and influence operations.

This book is not only a manual but also a call to action, urging enhanced inter-agency collaboration, investment in research and development, and the cultivation of public-private partnerships to maintain a competitive edge in the evolving arena of global information warfare. It aims to inspire a new generation of strategic thinkers who are prepared to leverage the power of information in the pursuit of security, peace, and stability.

Cognitive Warfare In The Age Of Unpeace: Strategies, Defenses, And The New Battlefield Of The Mind

Cognitive Warfare in the Age of Unpeace: Strategies, Defenses, and the New Battlefield of the Mind is a definitive examination of the emergent arena of cognitive warfare—a battlefield where consciousness and cognition are under siege. Rooted in the historical lineage of warfare, this seminal tome charts a course from the stratagems of yesteryear's influence operations to the digital subversions that define our current epoch.

The book is structured to provide a layered understanding of the subject. Part I lays the foundation, explaining how the age of unpeace has given rise to a new form of warfare that exists between peace and war, where the battle for influence is paramount. Part II describes the modern tools at the disposal of state and non-state actors, including AI and neurotechnological advancements, and the ways in which these tools can manipulate and coerce on a mass scale.

Through real-world case studies, Part III illustrates the practical application of cognitive strategies and the impact of such warfare on democracies, highlighting the need for robust countermeasures. In Part IV, the focus shifts to strategic insights, examining both offensive strategies for influence and subversion and the defensive strategies necessary to maintain cognitive sovereignty.

The latter sections, Parts V and VI, provide a forward-looking perspective on building societal and governmental defenses against cognitive attacks. These include fostering societal resilience through public education, developing policy and governance frameworks, and addressing the ethical dimensions of cognitive defense.

The final chapters speculate on the future trajectory of cognitive warfare, emphasizing the importance of international cooperation and the establishment of 'cognitive peace'. With its conclusion and appendices providing a roadmap and additional resources, this book stands as an essential guide for policymakers, security experts, academics and citizens alike in understanding and countering the sophisticated threat of cognitive warfare in our increasingly interconnected world.

Waging Just Wars: The Ethical And Legal Principles Of Modern Warfare

"Waging Just Wars: The Ethical and Legal Principles of Modern Warfare" provides a comprehensive examination of the moral and legal dimensions of contemporary conflict. Authored by an expert in military ethics and international law, this book delves into the foundational principles of Just War Theory, including jus ad bellum, jus in bello, and jus post bellum.

The book explores historical precedents and modern applications, offering a detailed analysis of self-defense, humanitarian interventions, and the prevention of atrocities. It critically examines the impact of technological advancements, such as AI and autonomous weapons, on the conduct of war. Through rigorous ethical analysis and case studies, the author addresses the complexities of applying Just War principles in today's geopolitical landscape.

"Waging Just Wars" also highlights the importance of legitimate authority, right intention, and proportionality in the decision to go to war. The book discusses the ethical challenges of ensuring that military actions align with these principles and the necessity of exhausting all non-violent options before resorting to force.

Additionally, the book provides insights into the treatment of prisoners of war, the use of prohibited weapons, and the ethical considerations of modern warfare tactics. The analysis extends to post-war responsibilities, emphasizing the need for fair treatment of former enemies, reconstruction efforts, and accountability for war crimes.

This scholarly work is essential reading for national security researchers, scholars, policymakers, and ethicists. It offers a nuanced understanding of how ethical and legal standards can guide the conduct of warfare, ensuring that the use of force is both morally justified and legally compliant. With its thorough examination of Just War Theory and its application to contemporary conflicts, "Waging Just Wars" is a vital resource for anyone seeking to navigate the moral complexities of modern warfare.

Eyes In The Sky: A Global Perspective On The Role Of Uavs In Intelligence, Surveillance, Reconnaissance, And Security

From the simple plaything of hobbyists to the high-tech guardians of national security, the story of Unmanned Aerial Vehicles (UAVs) is a thrilling flight into the frontier of technological innovation. "Eyes in the Sky" charts this breathtaking ascent, offering readers an inside look at the machines and systems shaping the modern world, both in the air and on the ground.

Embark on a journey that spans continents, delving deep into the extraordinary uses of UAVs across military, civilian, and commercial sectors. Learn how these devices gather intelligence, conduct surveillance, and even wage war. Explore how, far from the battlefield, they monitor traffic, patrol borders, and aid humanitarian efforts.

But, like Icarus soaring too close to the sun, the story of UAVs isn't without its darker shades. In an age of cyber threats and geopolitical tension, the skies aren't always friendly. Witness how these mechanical marvels are used by criminals, terrorists, and cyber pirates, exploiting their strengths for nefarious purposes.

This comprehensive examination of UAVs wouldn't be complete without an exploration of what's being done to keep us safe. Through countermeasures and cybersecurity, witness the ongoing struggle between those who exploit technology and those who safeguard it.

From cutting-edge counter-drone technologies to the ethical hackers combating these airborne threats, this narrative unravels the complex world of UAVs, their implications for global security, and the measures in place to maintain the balance.

"Eyes in the Sky" is not just a tale of technology—it's a chronicle of change, detailing how we've reshaped the heavens to serve our needs. With unparalleled access to the latest trends and greatest minds in the field, this book is a must-read for technophiles, security enthusiasts, and anyone curious about our rapidly evolving world.

Fasten your seatbelts, dear readers. It's time to take off into a sky full of drones!

A Boydian Approach To Mastering Unconventional Warfare

A Boydian Approach to Mastering Unconventional Warfare" is a seminal work that delves deeply into the strategic principles of John Boyd, a legendary military strategist, and applies them to the complex realm of unconventional warfare. This book presents a comprehensive analysis of Boyd's key concepts, most notably the OODA Loop (Observe, Orient, Decide, Act), and explores their application in the context of irregular and asymmetric conflicts that dominate the modern geopolitical landscape.

The author meticulously explores how Boyd's principles of adaptability, speed, and fluidity in decision-making can be applied to unconventional warfare tactics such as guerrilla warfare, insurgency, counterinsurgency, and cyber warfare. The book emphasizes the importance of understanding the psychological and moral dimensions of warfare, in addition to the physical aspect, a concept Boyd championed and which remains highly relevant in today's conflict scenarios.

Through a blend of historical analysis, case studies, and contemporary examples, "A Boydian Approach to Mastering Unconventional Warfare" offers insightful strategies for dealing with non-traditional threats in a rapidly evolving global context. It addresses the challenges of combating non-state actors, the use of technology in irregular warfare, and the need for innovative and adaptive strategies in response to the unpredictable nature of modern conflicts.

This book is not only a tribute to Boyd's groundbreaking work but also an essential guide for military strategists, policymakers, and security professionals who are grappling with the complexities of contemporary warfare. It provides a nuanced understanding of how unconventional warfare strategies can be developed and executed effectively, making it a crucial addition to the field of military strategy and national security studies.

Machinery Of War: A Comprehensive Study Of The Post-9/11 Global Arms Trade

In "Machinery of War: A Comprehensive Study of the Post-9/11 Global Arms Trade," Josh offers an exhaustive exploration into the intricate world of global armaments in the aftermath of the tragic events of September 11, 2001. This seminal work probes the depths of the modern arms trade, revealing its multi-faceted nature, its key players, and its profound impact on the geopolitical landscape.

Josh delves into the roles of state actors, private military companies, and non-state entities, underlining their intertwined relationships and the ensuing effects on global security dynamics. With a balanced, objective lens, he navigates through the complexities of cyber warfare, drone technology, and the emergence of autonomous weapons systems, as well as the rise of private military and security companies.

Further, he scrutinizes the arms race in different regions, including the Middle East, Asia, Africa, and Latin America, offering a nuanced understanding of their unique circumstances and their roles in the broader arms trade. The author also addresses the significant role of regulatory efforts in the global arms trade, investigating the successes and failures of arms embargoes and international regulations. Lastly, he gazes into the future, offering predictions and identifying trends that may shape the global arms trade in years to come.

"Machinery of War" is an indispensable resource for policymakers, researchers, scholars, and anyone interested in understanding the complexities of the global arms trade in the 21st century. This in-depth study invites readers to ponder the geopolitical, ethical, and humanitarian implications of the arms trade, highlighting the urgent need for control and regulation in an increasingly interconnected world.

Private Armies, Public Wars: The Brave New World Of Private Military Companies

Private Armies, Public Wars: The Brave New World of Private Military Companies is a groundbreaking exploration of the contemporary landscape of warfare, examining the rise and impact of private military companies (PMCs) on the global stage. Written by an esteemed geopolitics expert and military history researcher, this book provides a comprehensive and thought-provoking examination of the multifaceted world of private military operations.

Drawing upon historical perspectives, legal frameworks, economic dynamics, and case studies from around the world, this book offers a nuanced and in-depth analysis of the complex relationship between states, armed conflicts, and the private entities that operate within them. It delves into the motivations, challenges, and implications of the growing presence of PMCs, shedding light on both the opportunities they present and the ethical dilemmas they raise.

Private Armies, Public Wars presents a balanced and objective assessment of the forces driving the expansion of the PMC industry. It explores the historical roots of mercenaries and traces their evolution into modern-day private military companies. The book examines the economic appeal of outsourcing military capabilities and the potential implications for state sovereignty and the monopoly on the use of force.

Through vivid case studies, the author uncovers the diverse roles that PMCs play in conflicts worldwide, from providing security and logistical support to participating in active combat. The author explores the impact of PMCs on local populations, human rights concerns, and the challenges of regulating an industry that operates beyond traditional legal frameworks.

Moreover, the book delves into emerging trends and challenges in the PMC industry, including the integration of advanced technologies such as artificial intelligence and machine learning, the use of biometric and identity verification technologies. It analyzes the potential benefits and risks associated with these technological advancements, providing valuable insights into the changing nature of warfare in the 21st century. It also addresses the growing importance of communication technologies, the role of private intelligence agencies in modern warfare and the implications of hybrid warfare and disinformation campaigns.

Private Armies, Public Wars is a critical examination of the complex interplay between states, private entities, and the pursuit of military objectives. It challenges conventional notions of warfare and offers a fresh perspective on the evolving dynamics of global conflicts. The author provides a comprehensive and well-researched analysis, drawing on a wide range of sources and expertise to present a comprehensive overview of the PMC industry.

This book is essential reading for scholars, policymakers, military professionals, and anyone interested in understanding the contemporary landscape of warfare and the evolving role of private military companies. It serves as a call to action, urging readers to engage in meaningful discussions and debates about the ethical, legal, and strategic implications of the growing influence of private actors in the world's conflicts.

Algorithmic Warfare: The Rise Of Autonomous Weapons

Autonomous weapons are changing the face of modern warfare, and their potential impact is both awe-inspiring and unsettling. "Algorithmic Warfare: The Rise of Autonomous

Weapons" is a comprehensive analysis of the development, deployment, and ethical considerations of autonomous weapons systems in modern warfare.

By speaking with leading experts in emerging weapons technologies, the author was able to draw in on their firsthand experience and proven expertise to examine the ethical, legal, and strategic implications of these next-generation weapons. From loitering munitions to homing missiles, this book explore how Autonomous Weapons are revolutionizing the battlefield and the way we fight wars.

Through analysis of work written by defense experts, ethicists, and military leaders, this book analyzes the movement to ban autonomous weapons and the legal and ethical issues surrounding their use and spotlights the latest advancements in artificial intelligence in military technology and how they are being used to develop these autonomous systems.

This book also examines the role of national and international regulations and the potential benefits and risks of Autonomous Weapons. With at least 30 countries already developing defensive autonomous weapons that operate under human supervision, it is clear that the ethical questions surrounding this topic grow more pressing each day.

At the forefront of this game-changing debate, "Autonomous Weapons: The Future of Algorithmic Warfare" engages with military history, global policy, and cutting-edge science to argue that we must embrace technology where it can make war more precise and humane, but without surrendering human judgment. When the choice is life or death, there is no replacement for the human heart.

This book is aimed at anyone interested in the future

of warfare, from military personnel to policy-makers and concerned citizens alike. From the history of the DOD's Third Offset Strategy to the development of CBRN capable autonomous weapon systems, readers will gain a deep understanding of the current landscape of algorithmic warfare and the challenges and opportunities that lie ahead. It is a must-read for those who want to gain a better understanding of the complex and ever-changing landscape of autonomous weapons and the impact they will have on our world.

From Roman Speculatores To The Nsa: Evolution Of Espionage And Its Impact On Statecraft And Civil Liberties

"From Roman Speculatores to the NSA: Evolution of Espionage and Its Impact on Statecraft and Civil Liberties" is a thrilling journey from the shadows of ancient espionage to the high-tech spy networks of today. It's a must-read for anyone captivated by the enigmatic world of spies, as depicted in iconic fiction like James Bond and John le Carré, but eager to peel back the curtain on the real-life drama of intelligence work.

Dive into the clandestine operations that shaped history, from the cunning Speculatores of Rome to the cutting-edge surveillance of the NSA. This book doesn't just recount tales of daring exploits and shadowy figures; it delves deep into the moral and ethical mazes navigated by spies throughout history. As you traverse through time, you'll discover the intricate dance of espionage and statecraft, and how it has continuously morphed to adapt to technological advancements and shifting geopolitical landscapes.

"From Roman Speculatores to the NSA" doesn't shy away from

the dark side of espionage. It confronts the ethical quagmires, the personal sacrifices of those living double lives, and the impact of clandestine operations on individual freedoms. It's a thought-provoking exploration of how intelligence work, often glamorized in popular culture, grapples with issues like torture, privacy invasion, and the thin line between security and liberty.

Perfect for fans of spy fiction seeking to understand the real-life complexities behind the glamour and action, this book is a fascinating guide through the evolution of espionage. It's an eye-opening read that reveals the high stakes and hard choices inherent in a world where knowledge is power, and secrecy is a necessary shield in the game of nations. Prepare to have your perceptions challenged and your understanding of the spy world transformed.

The narrative is enriched with case studies and real-world examples, making it a valuable resource for understanding the complexities and challenges of modern intelligence work. The book also addresses the legal frameworks and oversight mechanisms that govern espionage activities, providing a comprehensive overview of the contemporary intelligence landscape.

For professionals and scholars in the fields of international relations, security studies, political science, and history, "From Roman Speculatores to the NSA" offers a scholarly yet accessible analysis. It invites readers to critically engage with the strategic, ethical, and legal aspects of espionage and consider its future trajectory in an increasingly interconnected and digital world. This book is a thought-provoking contribution to the discourse on espionage and national security, offering a well-researched and balanced perspective on a subject that continues to be relevant in the field of international affairs

Silent Wars: Espionage, Sabotage, And The Covert Battles In Cyberspace

Silent Wars: Espionage, Sabotage, and the Covert Battles in Cyberspace delves into the shadowy world of covert cyber conflict, that unfold beyond the public eye. Scrutinizing the intricate balance between espionage and assault, the author, Josh, disentangles the convoluted web of digital warfare, where the line between intelligence-gathering and outright attack blurs.

Silent Wars navigates the intricate landscape of covert cyber operations, examining a multitude of cases that shed light on the diverse tactics and strategies employed by nations in this modern arena of intangible warfare. Through a meticulous analysis of case studies, military doctrines, and technical underpinnings, Josh unveils the striking reality that contemporary cyber operations, while seemingly groundbreaking, still embody the age-old essence of conflict waged through non-physical domains such as information space and the electromagnetic spectrum.

Silent Wars breaks down the multifaceted nature of offensive cyber operations, emphasizing the stark contrasts between various forms of cyberattacks. From the painstakingly slow and calculated infiltrations that demand unwavering discipline and patience, to the fleeting strikes designed to momentarily disrupt the adversary's tactics, Silent Wars scrutinizes the full spectrum of digital offensives.

Venturing into the clandestine strategies of prominent state actors such as the United States, Russia, China, and Iran, Josh's examination of their distinct approaches, strengths, and challenges reveals the complexities of leveraging cyber operations for strategic advantage. Silent Wars unravels the veiled intricacies of this evolving domain, exposing the concealed dynamics that shape the future of covert cyber warfare.

BOOKS BY THIS AUTHOR

Countdown To Extinction: Navigating The Existential Threats That Could End Humanity

Countdown to Extinction: Navigating the Existential Threats That Could End Humanity is a comprehensive and thought-provoking exploration of the critical risks that could define—or end—the future of human civilization. In a world increasingly shaped by rapid technological advancements, environmental degradation, and global interconnectedness, this book takes a deep dive into the most pressing existential threats of our time and examines how we can navigate them to secure a thriving future for all.

Spanning a wide range of topics, Countdown to Extinction begins by laying the groundwork with an introduction to the fragility of human civilization and the concept of existential risks. The book then systematically explores specific threats, including the transformative power and peril of Artificial General Intelligence (AGI), the revolutionary potential and catastrophic risks of nanotechnology, and the unseen dangers posed by high-energy particle collisions.

The narrative continues by examining the ever-present dangers of pandemics—both natural and engineered—and the ongoing threat of nuclear warfare, juxtaposed against the slow-burning crisis of climate change. It delves into cosmic hazards like asteroid impacts and supervolcanoes, the potential collapse of global ecosystems due to resource depletion, and the nightmarish scenarios involving rogue AI and cybersecurity failures.

The book also addresses emerging risks associated with synthetic biology, economic collapse, and societal breakdown, while considering the unpredictable nature of "unknown unknowns." Each chapter is meticulously researched, combining scientific analysis with ethical considerations, historical case studies, and expert insights to paint a vivid picture of the potential futures we may face.

Yet, Countdown to Extinction is not just about outlining dangers; it is equally a guide to mitigation and hope. The book offers a thorough discussion on global strategies for mitigating these risks, emphasizing technological safeguards, international cooperation, and the necessity of building societal resilience. It calls for the creation of a culture of awareness and preparedness, urging governments, businesses, and individuals to take responsibility and act decisively.

The book concludes with a powerful call to action, reflecting on the imperative of addressing these risks and the role of human ingenuity and adaptation in creating a secure and sustainable future. Through detailed analysis and an engaging narrative, Countdown to Extinction challenges readers to reconsider their assumptions, recognize the gravity of the challenges ahead, and embrace the opportunities for transformative change.

This is not just a book about survival; it is a manifesto for safeguarding humanity's future. It reminds us that while the risks are formidable, so too is our capacity to overcome them through collective action, innovation, and a deep commitment to the values that unite us all. The choices we make today will shape the course of history, and together, we can create a world that is secure, just, and sustainable for generations to come.

The Ethical Hacker's Handbook: A Comprehensive Guide To Cybersecurity Assessment

Get ready to venture into the world of ethical hacking with your trusty guide, Josh, in this comprehensive and enlightening book, "The Ethical Hacker's Handbook: A Comprehensive Guide to Cybersecurity Assessment". Josh isn't just your typical cybersecurity guru; he's the charismatic and experienced CEO of a successful penetration testing company, and he's here to make your journey into the fascinating realm of cybersecurity as engaging as it is educational.

Dive into the deep end of ethical hacking as Josh de-mystifies complex concepts and navigates you through the murky waters of cyber threats. He'll show you how the pros get things done, equipping you with the skills to understand and test the security of networks, systems, and applications - all without drowning in unnecessary jargon.

Whether you're a complete novice or a seasoned professional, this book is filled with sage advice, practical exercises, and genuine insider knowledge that will propel you on your journey. From breaking down the complexities of Kali Linux, to mastering the art of the spear-phishing technique, to getting intimate with the OWASP Top Ten, Josh is with you every step of the way.

Don't expect a dull textbook read, though! Josh keeps things light with witty anecdotes and real-world examples that keep the pages turning. You'll not only learn the ropes of ethical hacking, you'll understand why each knot is tied the way it is.

By the time you turn the last page of this guide, you'll be prepared to tackle the ever-evolving landscape of cybersecurity. You might not have started this journey as an ethical hacker, but with "The Ethical Hacker's Handbook: A Comprehensive Guide to Cybersecurity Assessment", you'll definitely finish as one. So, ready to dive in and surf the cyber waves with Josh? Your journey to becoming an ethical hacking pro awaits!

Hacker Mindset: Psychological Tactics And Strategies For Mastering Social Engineering

"Hacker Mindset: Psychological Tactics and Strategies for Mastering Social Engineering" is an authoritative and comprehensive guide that delves deep into the psychology of cyber attackers and equips cybersecurity professionals with the knowledge and tools to defend against social engineering attacks. This essential resource offers a unique blend of psychological insights and practical cybersecurity strategies, making it an invaluable asset for red teamers, ethical hackers, and security professionals seeking to enhance their skills and protect critical systems and assets. With a focus on understanding the hacker mindset, this book provides a thorough exploration of the techniques and methodologies used by social engineers to exploit human vulnerabilities.

Gain a deep understanding of the psychological principles behind social engineering, including authority, scarcity, social proof, reciprocity, consistency, and emotional manipulation. Learn how attackers leverage these principles to deceive and manipulate their targets. Discover the latest tools and techniques for conducting advanced reconnaissance, vulnerability scanning, and exploitation, covering essential frameworks and software, such as Metasploit, Cobalt Strike, and OSINT tools like Maltego and Shodan. Explore the unique social engineering threats faced by various sectors, including healthcare, finance, government, and military, and learn how to implement targeted defenses and countermeasures to mitigate these risks effectively.

Understand how AI, machine learning, and other advanced technologies are transforming the field of cybersecurity and how to integrate these technologies into your defensive strategies to enhance threat detection, analysis, and response. Discover the importance of realistic training scenarios and continuous education in preparing cybersecurity professionals for real-world threats. Learn how to design and conduct effective red team/blue team exercises and capture-the-flag competitions. Navigate the complex legal and ethical landscape of offensive cybersecurity operations with guidance on adhering to international laws, military ethics, and best practices to ensure your actions are justified, lawful, and morally sound. Benefit from detailed case studies and real-world examples that illustrate the practical application of social engineering tactics and defensive strategies, providing valuable lessons and highlighting best practices for safeguarding against cyber threats.

"Hacker Mindset: Psychological Tactics and Strategies for Mastering Social Engineering" is designed to not only enhance your technical skills but also to foster a deeper understanding of the human element in cybersecurity. Whether you are a seasoned cybersecurity professional or new to the field, this book provides the essential knowledge and strategies needed to effectively defend against the growing threat of social engineering attacks. Equip yourself with the insights and tools necessary to stay one step ahead of cyber adversaries and protect your organization's critical assets.

Leave No Trace: A Red Teamer's Guide To Zero-Click Exploits

Buckle up and prepare to dive into the thrilling world of Zero-Click Exploits. This isn't your average cybersecurity guide - it's a wild ride through the dark underbelly of the digital world, where zero-click exploits reign supreme.

Join Josh, a seasoned cybersecurity professional and the mastermind behind Greyhat Intelligence & Investigative Solutions, as he spills the beans on these sneaky attacks that can compromise systems without a single click. From Fortune 500 companies to the most guarded government agencies, no one is safe from the lurking dangers of zero-click exploits.

In this witty and engaging book, Josh takes you on a journey that will make your head spin. You'll uncover the secrets behind these stealthy attacks, learning the ins and outs of their mechanics, and unraveling the vulnerabilities they exploit. With real-world examples, he'll keep you on the edge of your seat as you discover the attack vectors, attack surfaces, and the art of social engineering.

But fear not! Josh won't leave you defenseless. He arms you with an arsenal of prevention, mitigation, and defense strategies to fortify your systems against these relentless zero-click invaders. You'll learn how to harden your systems, develop incident response protocols, and become a master of patch management.

But this book isn't all serious business. Josh infuses it with his signature wit and humor, making the complex world of zero-click exploits accessible to anyone with a curious mind and a passion for cybersecurity. So get ready to laugh, learn, and level up your red teaming skills as you navigate this thrilling rollercoaster of a read.

Whether you're a seasoned cybersecurity pro or just starting your journey, "Leave No Trace" is the ultimate guide to understanding, defending against, and maybe even outsmarting the relentless zero-click exploits. It's time to take the fight to the attackers and show them who's boss!

So fasten your seatbelt, grab your favorite energy drink, and get ready to unlock the secrets of zero-click exploits. Your mission, should you choose to accept it, starts now!

The Art Of Exploit Development: A Practical Guide To Writing Custom Exploits For Red Teamers

In an era where cyber threats loom large, understanding the art of exploit development is essential for any cybersecurity professional. This book is an invaluable guide for those looking to gain a deep understanding of this critical aspect of cybersecurity.

"The Art of Exploit Development: A Practical Guide to Writing Custom Exploits for Red Teamers" delivers an exhaustive, hands-on tour through the entire exploit development process. Crafted by an experienced cybersecurity professional, this resource is not just a theoretical exploration, but a practical guide rooted in real-world applications. It balances technical depth with accessible language, ensuring it's equally beneficial for newcomers and seasoned professionals.

The book begins with a comprehensive exploration of vulnerability discovery, guiding readers through the various types of vulnerabilities, the tools and techniques for discovering them, and the strategies for testing and validating potential vulnerabilities. From there, it dives deep into the core principles of exploit development, including an exploration of memory management, stack and heap overflows, format string vulnerabilities, and more.

But this guide doesn't stop at the fundamentals. It extends into more advanced areas, discussing how to write shellcode for different platforms and architectures, obfuscate and encode shellcode, bypass modern defensive measures, and exploit vulnerabilities on various platforms. It also provides a thorough look at the use of exploit development tools and frameworks, along with a structured approach to exploit development.

"The Art of Exploit Development" also recognizes the importance of responsible cybersecurity practices. It delves into the ethical considerations of exploit development, outlines secure coding practices, runtime exploit prevention techniques, and discusses effective security testing and penetration testing.

Complete with an extensive glossary and appendices that include reference material, case studies, and further learning resources, this book is a complete package, providing a comprehensive understanding of exploit development.

With "The Art of Exploit Development," you're not just reading a book—you're enhancing your toolkit, advancing your skillset, and evolving your understanding of one of the most vital aspects of cybersecurity today.

Silent Wars: Espionage, Sabotage, And The Covert Battles In Cyberspac

Silent Wars: Espionage, Sabotage, and the Covert Battles in Cyberspace delves into the shadowy world of covert cyber conflict, that unfold beyond the public eye. Scrutinizing the intricate balance between espionage and assault, the author, Josh, disentangles the convoluted web of digital warfare, where the line between intelligence-gathering and outright attack blurs.

Silent Wars navigates the intricate landscape of covert cyber operations, examining a multitude of cases that shed light on the diverse tactics and strategies employed by nations in this modern arena of intangible warfare. Through a meticulous analysis of case studies, military doctrines, and technical underpinnings, Josh unveils the striking reality that contemporary cyber operations, while seemingly groundbreaking, still embody the age-old essence of conflict waged through non-physical domains such as information space and the electromagnetic spectrum.

Silent Wars breaks down the multifaceted nature of offensive cyber operations, emphasizing the stark contrasts between various forms of cyberattacks. From the painstakingly slow and calculated infiltrations that demand unwavering discipline and patience, to the fleeting strikes designed to momentarily disrupt the adversary's tactics, Silent Wars scrutinizes the full spectrum of digital offensives.

Venturing into the clandestine strategies of prominent state actors such as the United States, Russia, China, and Iran, Josh's examination of their distinct approaches, strengths, and challenges reveals the complexities of leveraging cyber operations for strategic advantage. Silent Wars unravels the veiled intricacies of this evolving domain, exposing the concealed dynamics that shape the future of covert cyber warfare.

Cracking The Fortress: Bypassing Modern Authentication Mechanism

"Cracking the Fortress: Bypassing Modern Authentication Mechanism" is an essential guide for cybersecurity professionals navigating the intricate landscape of modern authentication. Written by industry expert, Josh, founder of Greyhat Intelligence & Investigative Solutions, this book delves deep into the mechanisms that protect our digital identities, from traditional passwords to cutting-edge biometrics.

Dive into the evolution of authentication, understanding the shift from rudimentary passwords to sophisticated multi-factor authentication (MFA) and biometric systems. Explore real-world case studies of major password breaches, and gain insights into the vulnerabilities that even the most advanced systems can harbor. With a special focus on red team operations and penetration testing, readers are provided with practical demonstrations, code snippets, and technical breakdowns of bypass methods.

Key features:
- Comprehensive exploration of 2FA, MFA, biometrics, and single sign-on (SSO) solutions.
- Detailed case studies of notable security breaches and their implications.
- Hands-on demonstrations and practical examples for bypassing modern authentication.
- In-depth analysis of potential flaws, vulnerabilities, and countermeasures in authentication systems.
- Future trends in authentication, including the impact of quantum computing and AI-powered mechanisms.

Perfect for cybersecurity professionals, red team operators, and penetration testers, "Cracking the Fortress" offers a blend of theoretical knowledge and practical expertise. Whether you're looking to fortify your organization's defenses or understand the attacker's perspective, this book is a must-have resource for staying ahead in the ever-evolving world of cybersecurity.

Hack The Airwaves: Advanced Ble Exploitation Techniques

In "Hack the Airwaves," Josh, a seasoned cybersecurity expert, delves deep into the intricate world of Bluetooth Low Energy (BLE) security. As BLE devices become increasingly integrated into our daily lives, the potential for vulnerabilities and threats grows exponentially. This comprehensive guide is designed for hackers, red team operators, pentesters, and other cybersecurity practitioners who seek both a foundational understanding and advanced knowledge of BLE's potential risks and defenses.

Drawing from hands-on experiences, real-world case studies, and practical demonstrations, Josh offers readers a unique blend of theoretical insights and actionable techniques. From understanding the core protocols of BLE to crafting custom payloads and defending against sophisticated attacks, "Hack the Airwaves" covers the full spectrum of BLE security.

Key features include:
- A deep dive into the BLE protocol stack, including GATT, GAP, and other core protocols.
- Techniques for signal interception, manipulation, and exploitation.
- Practical guides on setting up labs, crafting malicious payloads, and executing advanced Man-in-the-Middle attacks.
- Strategies for defending against BLE exploits, ensuring robust security for devices and systems.
- Ethical considerations and best practices for responsible and collaborative BLE hacking.

With a forward-thinking approach, Josh also explores the future landscape of BLE security, offering predictions and strategies for staying ahead of emerging threats. Whether you're a seasoned professional or new to the world of BLE hacking, "Hack the Airwaves" is an essential addition to your cybersecurity library.

The Survival Guide To Maintaining Access And Evading Detection Post-Exploitation

In the intricate dance of cyber warfare, the act of gaining unauthorized access is merely the first step. The real artistry lies in staying undetected, maintaining that access, and achieving objectives without raising alarms. "The Survival Guide to Maintaining Access and Evading Detection Post-Exploitation" delves deep into this complex and ever-evolving realm of post-exploitation in cybersecurity.

From the renowned experts at Greyhat Intelligence & Investigative Solutions, this comprehensive guide reveals the hidden nuances of post-exploitation activities. Learn how threat actors secure their foothold, escalate privileges, and maneuver through networks undetected. Discover the tactics, techniques, and procedures (TTPs) that distinguish an amateur attacker from a seasoned professional.

Each chapter of the guide offers a meticulously researched look into distinct aspects of post-exploitation:

- Grasp the importance of maintaining access within compromised systems and the myriad methods employed to persist through reboots, updates, and other adversities.

- Delve into the art of evading detection, a critical skill in a world where enterprises are investing heavily in fortifying their cyber defenses.

- Explore the "live off the land" philosophy, leveraging legitimate tools and native system features for clandestine operations, sidestepping the common detection avenues.

- Navigate through advanced realms of cyber-attacks, such as tunneling, pivoting, and memory-resident malware, and understand the counter-forensic measures that elite hackers employ.

- Equip yourself with the latest strategies to defend against these surreptitious techniques. Learn how to harden systems, enhance detection capabilities, and respond effectively when breaches occur.

- Reflect on the ethical dimensions of post-exploitation and the evolving global legal landscape that shapes this domain. Plus, anticipate the future challenges and opportunities that emerging technologies bring to the post-exploitation scene.

Bolstered by real-world case studies, detailed toolkits, and a glossary of terms, this book is an essential resource for cybersecurity professionals, digital forensics experts, and IT personnel. Whether you're looking to safeguard your organization's digital assets, enhance your penetration testing skills, or understand the adversary's playbook, "The Survival Guide to Maintaining Access and Evading Detection Post-Exploitation" is the definitive compendium you need in your arsenal.

From Roman Speculatores To The Nsa: Evolution Of Espionage And Its Impact On Statecraft And Civil Liberties

"From Roman Speculatores to the NSA: Evolution of Espionage and Its Impact on Statecraft and Civil Liberties" is a thrilling journey from the shadows of ancient espionage to the high-tech spy networks of today. It's a must-read for anyone captivated by the enigmatic world of spies, as depicted in iconic fiction like James Bond and John le Carré, but eager to peel back the curtain on the real-life drama of intelligence work.

Dive into the clandestine operations that shaped history, from the cunning Speculatores of Rome to the cutting-edge surveillance of the NSA. This book doesn't just recount tales of daring exploits and shadowy figures; it delves deep into the moral and ethical mazes navigated by spies throughout history. As you traverse through time, you'll discover the intricate dance of espionage and statecraft, and how it has continuously morphed to adapt to technological advancements and shifting geopolitical landscapes.

"From Roman Speculatores to the NSA" doesn't shy away from the dark side of espionage. It confronts the ethical quagmires, the personal sacrifices of those living double lives, and the impact of clandestine operations on individual freedoms. It's a thought-provoking exploration of how intelligence work, often glamorized in popular culture, grapples with issues like torture, privacy invasion, and the thin line between security and liberty.

Perfect for fans of spy fiction seeking to understand the real-life complexities behind the glamour and action, this book is a fascinating guide through the evolution of espionage. It's an eye-opening read that reveals the high stakes and hard choices inherent in a world where knowledge is power, and secrecy is a necessary shield in the game of nations. Prepare to have your perceptions challenged and your understanding of the spy world transformed.

The narrative is enriched with case studies and real-world

examples, making it a valuable resource for understanding the complexities and challenges of modern intelligence work. The book also addresses the legal frameworks and oversight mechanisms that govern espionage activities, providing a comprehensive overview of the contemporary intelligence landscape.

For professionals and scholars in the fields of international relations, security studies, political science, and history, "From Roman Speculatores to the NSA" offers a scholarly yet accessible analysis. It invites readers to critically engage with the strategic, ethical, and legal aspects of espionage and consider its future trajectory in an increasingly interconnected and digital world. This book is a thought-provoking contribution to the discourse on espionage and national security, offering a well-researched and balanced perspective on a subject that continues to be relevant in the field of international affairs.

A Comprehensive Framework For Adapting National Intelligence For Domestic Law Enforcement

"A Comprehensive Framework for Adapting National Intelligence for Domestic Law Enforcement" is a groundbreaking book that delves into the intricate process of integrating sophisticated national intelligence methodologies into domestic law enforcement practices. Authored by a seasoned expert in the field of private intelligence, this book emerges as a critical resource for military leaders, policymakers, members of the intelligence community, and law enforcement personnel.

This insightful work begins by exploring the historical evolution of intelligence sharing, offering a thorough analysis of past and present strategies. It then seamlessly transitions into discussing the current challenges and opportunities faced in integrating national intelligence into domestic law enforcement. The book provides an in-depth examination of legal and ethical frameworks, ensuring that the proposed methods adhere to the highest standards of civil liberties and legal compliance.

Central to the book is the development of a comprehensive framework that bridges the gap between national intelligence operations and local law enforcement requirements. This framework not only addresses operational aspects but also focuses on the technological advancements, such as AI and big data analytics, reshaping intelligence gathering and analysis.

The author brings to light the importance of cross-sector collaboration, suggesting innovative ways to enhance cooperation between various sectors – government, private, and non-profit – in intelligence activities. Case studies of successful intelligence collaboration, both domestic and international, are meticulously analyzed, offering practical insights and lessons learned.

Moreover, the book addresses the training and skill development necessary for effectively adapting national intelligence practices in a domestic context. It emphasizes the need for continuous professional development and the cultivation of a learning culture within law enforcement agencies.

"A Comprehensive Framework for Adapting National Intelligence for Domestic Law Enforcement" concludes with strategic recommendations for policy and practice, advocating for a progressive approach towards intelligence integration. This book is an invaluable asset for anyone involved in or interested in the intersection of national security, intelligence, and domestic law enforcement, providing a comprehensive guide to navigating this complex and evolving landscape.

Beyond The Wall: Border Security In The Age Of Ai And Facial Recognition Technology

In an ever-shrinking global landscape, "Beyond the Wall" dives deep into the future of border security, bridging the historical fortifications of the past with the digital guardians of tomorrow. With each page, readers are transported across time, from the towering walls of ancient civilizations to the cutting-edge surveillance technologies of the 21st century.

As nations grapple with questions of security, sovereignty, and the preservation of individual freedoms, the roles of Artificial Intelligence (AI) and Facial Recognition Technology emerge as pivotal players in the theater of international relations. These technologies, once the realm of science fiction, are now at the forefront, redefining what it means to protect a nation's boundaries.

Through meticulously researched case studies, "Beyond the Wall" showcases global efforts to integrate traditional and tech-driven border security measures. The book delves into the successes and pitfalls of these integrations, presenting a balanced analysis that is both technically sound and geopolitically insightful.

For tech enthusiasts, the detailed explorations of AI algorithms and the intricacies of facial recognition systems will provide a thorough understanding of the mechanics behind these revolutionary tools. Those keen on security and international relations will gain insights into how these technologies are reshaping global politics, alliances, and the very concept of national sovereignty.

"Beyond the Wall" isn't just a book; it's an invitation to envision a world where technology and humanity coalesce, forging a path for a more secure, intelligent, and interconnected global community.

The Future Of Money: How Central Bank Digital Currencies Will Reshape The Global Financial System

The global financial landscape is on the brink of a monumental shift. Central Bank Digital Currencies (CBDCs) promise to revolutionize the way we think about money, transactions, and economic policy. But what does this mean for the future of finance, and how will it affect you?

Authored by a leading expert in finance and technology, 'The Future of Money: How Central Bank Digital Currencies Will Reshape The Global Financial System' provides an in-depth exploration of CBDCs and their potential to transform the global economy. Drawing on extensive research and expert analysis, this book delves into the mechanics of CBDCs, their implementation by central banks, and the profound impacts they will have on international trade, financial inclusion, and monetary policy.

CBDCs aren't just a new form of money; they are a total overhaul of our financial infrastructure, promising to make transactions faster, cheaper, and more accessible for people everywhere—from bustling urban centers to remote rural communities. But how will these digital currencies affect global trade, privacy, or even the sovereignty of nations? And what can we do to prepare for this imminent financial transformation?

"The Future of Money" breaks down complex financial and technical concepts into clear, engaging language, making it accessible to both finance professionals and casual readers interested in the future of technology and money. Drawing on comprehensive research, expert interviews, and case studies, the book explores the potential of CBDCs to democratize financial services and outlines the challenges and opportunities that lie ahead.

Whether you're a policy maker, an investor, or simply curious about the future of digital currencies, this book provides everything you need to know about the upcoming shifts in global finance. Prepare to discover:

How CBDCs work, and their potential impact on global economic dynamics.
The technological infrastructure behind digital currencies.
The potential risks and rewards of a digitally dominated financial future.
The benefits and challenges of integrating CBDCs into existing financial systems
Strategic insights for businesses, governments, and individuals to navigate the new financial landscape.

With a focus on both the opportunities and challenges presented by CBDCs, "The Future of Money" is an essential resource for financial professionals, policymakers, and anyone interested in the future of finance. Luberisse's authoritative and accessible style makes complex concepts understandable, providing readers with the knowledge they need to navigate the digital transformation of global finance.

Prepare to be enlightened and empowered as you explore the cutting-edge of digital finance. Discover how CBDCs could democratize financial services, enhance efficiency, and ensure stability in the global financial system. Whether you're a seasoned finance expert or simply curious about the future of money, this book offers a comprehensive blueprint for understanding and embracing the financial revolution ahead.

The Quant Trader's Handbook: A Complete Guide To Algorithmic Trading Strategies And Techniques

In "The Quant Trader's Handbook," Josh masterfully navigates the intricate world of algorithmic trading, shedding light on its various complexities and revealing the secrets that drive the success of some of the most prominent quantitative hedge funds and traders. Through a blend of captivating storytelling and rigorous analysis, this guide offers readers an unparalleled opportunity to delve into the mechanics of quantitative trading, exploring the strategies, technologies, and practices that have transformed the financial landscape.

As modern markets continue to be shaped by the silent precision of algorithms, it becomes essential for traders and investors to understand the underlying mechanics that drive these systems. This book promises to immerse its readers in the rich tapestry of the algorithmic trading realm, stretching from its nascent beginnings in the 1970s to the AI-integrated strategies of the 21st century.

Inside, you'll embark on a chronological journey starting with the pioneering days of electronic stock markets and culminating in the sophisticated high-frequency trading systems of today. Alongside this, Josh takes you through the ins and outs of popular quantitative trading strategies, illustrated with intuitive pseudocode examples, like the Moving Average Crossover and the Pair Trading Strategy, ensuring even those new to the domain can grasp the nuances.

But this isn't just a book about code and numbers. The Quant Trader's Handbook paints the bigger picture. With detailed network diagrams, you'll gain insights into the architectural complexity and beauty of modern trading systems, understanding how various components seamlessly intertwine to make real-time decisions in the blink of an eye.

As you embark on this journey with Josh, you'll discover the foundational concepts of algorithmic trading, unravel the mysteries of quantitative analysis and modeling, and gain valuable insights into the inner workings of execution and order management. From the depths of data mining techniques to the heights of infrastructure and technology, each chapter is meticulously crafted to provide a thorough understanding of the various aspects that contribute to a successful algorithmic trading business.

In addition to its wealth of practical knowledge, "The Quant Trader's Handbook" also delves into the regulatory and compliance considerations that are essential for navigating today's financial markets. With a keen eye for detail and a remarkable ability to contextualize even the most technical topics, Josh brings to life the fascinating stories of industry giants like Renaissance Technologies, DE Shaw, and Two Sigma, painting a vivid picture of the rise of quantitative finance.

Whether you're an aspiring quant looking to make your mark in the world of finance, an investor trying to demystify the black box of algorithmic trading, or merely a curious soul eager to understand how bits and bytes are silently shaping the financial world, "The Quant Trader's Handbook" is an indispensable resource that will captivate, inform, and inspire you. Join Josh as he unravels the secrets of the world's most successful traders and embark on a journey that may just change the way you see the markets forever.

Sun Tzu In The Boardroom: Strategic Thinking In Economics And Management

In "Sun Tzu in the Boardroom," Josh, an esteemed entrepreneur and the innovative mind behind VC capital firm Other People's Capital and defense military contractor Fac Bellum Industries, casts a refreshing and enlightening gaze into the myriad ways ancient military strategies carve pathways to triumph in today's dynamic business terrains. Drawing from a well of timeless wisdom, the book molds the unyielding philosophies of Sun Tzu into a pragmatic guide tailored for the contemporary leader, entrepreneur, and strategist embedded in the enthralling world of economics and management.

Josh's unique vantage point, sculpted by his ventures that intertwine the worlds of venture capital and defense, beckons readers into a compelling journey through the seamless integration of military sagacity and business acumen. Inspired significantly by the entrepreneurial journeys and philosophies of Palmer Luckey, founder of Anduril Industries, and Peter Thiel of Palantir Technologies, Josh elucidates the inextricable ties binding strategic thought in ancient battlefields to decision-making amid the volatility of modern markets.

"Sun Tzu in the Boardroom" takes you on an exploratory odyssey, amalgamating profound ancient Chinese military strategies with the robust, high-stakes world of contemporary business. Through rich, expansive content that spans topics from leadership, competitive advantage, and ethical considerations to organizational culture and beyond, Josh deciphers and applies Sun Tzu's doctrines, delivering them through a lens focused sharply on the economic and managerial landscapes of today.

Whether diving into the subtle art of negotiation, peeling back layers on the ethical dimensions of strategic decisions, or meandering through the strategic corridors of marketing warfare, "Sun Tzu in the Boardroom" assures a compendium of wisdom that is as pragmatic as it is reflective, offering not just a lens to view the world of business, but a compass to navigate its multifaceted terrains.

This tome is not merely a guide; it is an invitation. An invitation to comprehend, to reflect, and to deploy the ageless wisdom of Sun Tzu into the boardrooms, marketplaces, and beyond. Here, Josh weaves a narrative that is both timeless and urgently contemporary, an invaluable asset for anyone looking to harness the strategic sagacity of the past to navigate, conquer, and thrive amid the complex challenges of the modern business world.

Embark on a journey through time, strategy, and business, and discover how the ancient can inform the present, shaping strategies, decisions, and pathways to success amid the ever-shifting sands of the economic and business environment.

The Ultimate Guide To Us Financial Regulations: A Primer For Lawyers And Business Professionals

Over the past several decades, the financial landscape and its regulation have experienced unprecedented growth and transformation. This era has seen significant advancements in financial markets, along with cyclical periods of regulatory reform, often in response to crisis situations. The recent financial crisis has generated immense interest in financial regulation from policymakers, economists, legal practitioners, and academics alike, sparking comprehensive regulatory reforms.

The Ultimate Guide to US Financial Regulations: A Primer for Lawyers and Business Professionals delivers an authoritative, up-to-date, and in-depth examination of the intricacies of financial regulation. With insights on banking, securities, derivatives, insurance, consumer financial protection, anti-money laundering, and international financial regulations, this comprehensive guide employs a contextual and comparative approach to explore academic, policy, and regulatory requirements.

The initial sections of the guide delve into the foundational themes that underpin financial regulation: financial systems and their regulation; the structure of financial system regulation; the evolution of Financial Regulation; the role of regulatory agencies as well as their various enforcement mechanisms; as well as insurance, banking and securities regulations. The latter sections focus on the core objectives of financial regulation, and explore key topics such as deposit insurance, consumer protection regulations, safety and soundness requirements, insider trading, securities fraud, and investment advisor regulations.

The Ultimate Guide to US Financial Regulations offers an indispensable resource for understanding and navigating the complex world of financial regulation, making it an essential read for professionals across the legal and business spectrum.

Acing Your Sie Exam: An In-Depth Guide To Securities Industry Essentials

Master the world of securities and set yourself up for success in the financial industry with 'Acing Your SIE Exam: An In-Depth Guide to the Securities Industry Essentials' This in-depth guide is designed to equip aspiring securities professionals with the knowledge and strategies they need to pass the SIE exam, an essential stepping stone towards a rewarding career in the securities industry.

Carefully aligned with the content of the SIE exam, this guide covers a wide array of topics: from understanding the intricacies of market structure and the functions of regulatory agencies, to detailed insights into equity and debt securities, options, investment companies, and more. It provides thorough explanations of trading procedures, customer account management, and important legislation that shapes the industry.

Beyond the raw information, this guide also aids in mastering the art of exam-taking. It offers invaluable advice on how to study effectively, manage your time, and develop successful test-taking strategies. The book's clear, easy-to-understand language makes complex concepts approachable, irrespective of your background in finance.

To enhance your understanding, each chapter is coupled with practical examples and key takeaways. Also included is a comprehensive glossary that provides clear definitions of the key terms you'll encounter on the exam.

"Acing Your SIE Exam: An In-Depth Guide to the Securities Industry Essentials" is more than just a study guide. It's a resource designed to launch your securities career. With this guide in your hands, you are well on your way to acing the SIE exam and establishing a strong foundation for your future in the financial industry.

The Insider's Guide To Securities Law: Navigating The Intricacies Of Public And Private Offerings

Navigate the intricate world of private equity and venture

capital with "The Insider's Guide to Securities Law: Navigating the Intricacies of Public and Private Offerings." This comprehensive guidebook illuminates the complexities of the industry, serving as an essential resource for legal practitioners, investment professionals, and entrepreneurs alike.

Venture into the fascinating domain of fund formation, understand the roles of limited and general partners, and uncover the strategic aspects of tax structuring. Get acquainted with the key regulatory authorities overseeing the industry, including the Securities and Exchange Commission (SEC), the Financial Industry Regulatory Authority (FINRA), and the Commodity Futures Trading Commission (CFTC).

Delve deeper into the regulatory landscape, exploring crucial compliance requirements, the essentialities of fiduciary duty, and the impact of the JOBS Act and other significant laws. Grasp the essentials of Anti-Money Laundering (AML) and Know Your Customer (KYC) compliance, and learn how to navigate through the processes of sourcing and closing deals, conducting due diligence, and managing and exiting investments effectively.

"The Insider's Guide to Securities Law" offers practical insights, actionable strategies, and a detailed glossary of key terms, making the labyrinth of private equity and venture capital law accessible to both seasoned professionals and newcomers. Embark on a journey through the dynamic landscape of global finance with confidence and insight with this indispensable guide.

From Calamity To Stability: Harnessing The Wisdom Of Past Financial Crises To Build A Stable And Resilient Global Financial System

In 'From Calamity to Stability: Harnessing the Wisdom of Past Financial Crises to Build a Stable and Resilient Global Financial System', author Josh delves deep into the history of financial crises, examining the causes, impacts, and lessons learned from each event. With a keen analytical approach, Josh expertly navigates the complex landscape of financial regulation, supervision, and policy that has evolved in response to these crises.

Drawing on a wealth of research and firsthand experience, the book presents a comprehensive overview of the regulatory frameworks that have emerged over time, from the Glass-Steagall Act to the Dodd-Frank Wall Street Reform and Consumer Protection Act, as well as the development of international standards such as the Basel Accords. By analyzing the interplay between innovation and stability, Josh identifies key areas where further action is necessary to maintain a resilient financial system capable of supporting sustainable economic growth.

Through a careful examination of the role of international cooperation, transparency, and trust in fostering financial stability, 'From Calamity to Stability' offers valuable insights into the challenges and opportunities facing policymakers, financial institutions, and society at large. The book not only underscores the importance of learning from past financial crises but also highlights the need for a flexible, forward-looking regulatory framework that can adapt to emerging trends and challenges.

'From Calamity to Stability' is an essential resource for anyone seeking to understand the complex dynamics of the global financial system and the ongoing efforts to ensure its stability and resilience. With its balanced and informed perspective, this book provides a compelling roadmap for navigating the uncertain global economic landscape and building a more secure financial future for all.

The Scalability Matrix: Expanding Your Business In The Digital Age

In the age of digital disruption and boundless opportunities, "The Scalability Matrix: Expanding Your Business in the Digital Age" emerges as a seminal guide for businesses eager to navigate the complex waters of growth in an increasingly digital world. Harnessing his vast expertise and diverse experience, author Josh presents a comprehensive roadmap for understanding and mastering the dynamics of scalability, a critical factor that often differentiates fleeting success from enduring impact.

Grounded in real-world examples and enlivened with insights from Josh's multifaceted career—from notable stints at financial powerhouses like Brown Brothers Harriman, Bank of America and Morgan Stanley to the establishment of groundbreaking startups such as Neuromorph Systems and OptimalOrbit—this book provides an exhaustive exploration of scalability. It delves into the nuances that influence scalable growth, from technical challenges and resource management to risk mitigation and the integration of cutting-edge technologies.

The text illuminates the strategies employed by e-commerce giants and dissects the pivotal role of AI in healthcare scalability. By offering both a historical perspective and a forward-looking analysis replete with predictions and projections, the book ensures that readers gain a 360-degree understanding of scalability in the present digital era.

But more than just theory and analysis, "The Scalability Matrix" is infused with actionable insights and pragmatic advice, catering to a spectrum of readers—from startups grappling with the initial challenges of growth to established enterprises seeking to rejuvenate their expansion strategies. With dedicated chapters on success stories, lessons from scalability mishaps, and a keen look at the future trends poised to shape the scalability discourse, the book is both a repository of knowledge and a catalyst for action.

In "The Scalability Matrix," Josh doesn't just share a concept; he hands you a compass—equipping businesses and leaders with the tools, strategies, and mindset to journey confidently into the vast expanse of scalable growth in the digital age. Whether you're an entrepreneur at the helm of a burgeoning startup, a leader in a mid-sized enterprise, or a strategist in a global conglomerate, this book promises to be an invaluable companion in your quest to scale new heights.

ABOUT THE AUTHOR

Josh Luberisse

Josh is a multifaceted entrepreneur and renowned author who has carved a niche for himself in the spheres of artificial intelligence, geopolitics, finance, and cybersecurity. With a myriad of authoritative books to his credit on these subjects, he is undeniably a luminary in the domain. Not just an author, Josh is also the charismatic host of "Disrupting Defense," a groundbreaking podcast that explores the intersection of technology and national security. Each episode unravel the intricacies of how cutting-edge innovations from Silicon Valley are not just enhancing military capabilities but are also transforming them. By tuning in you can stay at the forefront of defense innovation and discover how technology is not just supporting but leading the charge in modern military operations.

Josh's expertise and passion have made him a sought-after speaker and consultant, and his contributions have been widely recognized and appreciated. Whether through his books, his work with clients, or his field assignments, Josh continues to inspire and educate others in the hope of making a lasting impact on the world. If you're looking for practical and actionable insights be sure to check out Josh's other manuscripts and join his community of readers and followers.